Interpreting Cultural Symbols

Interpreting Cultural Symbols

Saint Anne

in Late Medieval Society

EDITED BY

Kathleen Ashley and Pamela Sheingorn

The University of Georgia Press

ATHENS AND LONDON

© 1990 by the University of Georgia Press
Athens, Georgia 30602
All rights reserved
Designed by Kathi L. Dailey
Set in Bembo and Goudy Medieval by
Tseng Information Systems, Inc.
Printed and bound by Thomson-Shore, Inc.
The paper in this book meets the guidelines for
permanence and durability of the Committee on
Production Guidelines for Book Longevity of the
Council on Library Resources.

Printed in the United States of America

94 93 92 91 90   5 4 3 2 1

Library of Congress Cataloging in Publication Data

Interpreting cultural symbols : Saint Anne in late medieval
society / edited by Kathleen Ashley and Pamela Sheingorn.
   p. cm.
Includes bibliographical references. ISBN 0-8203-1262-2 (alk.
paper). — ISBN 0-8203-1263-0 (pbk. : alk. paper)
1. Anne (Mother of the Virgin Mary), Saint—Cult. 2. Europe
—Religious life and customs. 3. Europe—Church history—
Middle Ages, 600–1500. 4. Women—Religious life—History.
I. Ashley, Kathleen M., 1944– . II. Sheingorn, Pamela.
BT685.I57 1990
232.9'33—dc20
            90-34737
            CIP

British Library Cataloging in Publication Data available

Sections 1.1–8.1 of "The Book of James" are reprinted
from *New Testament Apocrypha:* Volume 1: *Gospels and
Related Writings,* by Edgar Hennecke; edited by Wilhelm
Schneemelcher; English translation edited by R. McL.
Wilson. Copyright © 1959 J. C. B. Mohr (Paul
Siebeck), Tubingen; English translation © 1963
Lutterworth Press. Reprinted and used by permission
of Westminster/John Knox Press.

Title-page illustration is a detail from *Relics of Saint
Anne* by Lucas Cranach the Edler, 1509.

For our grandchildren

Contents

ix
Preface

I
Introduction
KATHLEEN ASHLEY AND PAMELA SHEINGORN

69
Saint Anne in Folk Tradition: Late Medieval France
FRANCESCA SAUTMAN

95
Saint Anne and the Religion of Childbed: Some East Anglian
Texts and Talismans
GAIL MCMURRAY GIBSON

III
Image and Ideology: Saint Anne in Late Medieval
Drama and Narrative
KATHLEEN ASHLEY

131
In the Defense of Florentine Republicanism: Saint Anne
and Florentine Art, 1343–1575
ROGER J. CRUM AND DAVID G. WILKINS

169
Appropriating the Holy Kinship: Gender and Family History
PAMELA SHEINGORN

199
"Madame Sainte Anne": The Holy Kinship, the
Royal Trinity, and Louise of Savoy
MYRA D. ORTH

229
Notes on Contributors

231
Index

Preface

The idea of collaborating on Saint Anne arose during a fortuitous conversation in which we discovered that both of us had been intrigued with the apocryphal figure from the first time we saw her represented in art. For Kathleen Ashley, it was magnificent Holy Kinship paintings in Munich and Cologne that demanded interpretation; for Pamela Sheingorn, the recognition of an English alabaster as a representation of the Holy Kinship stimulated interest in this complex subject.

We decided to organize two sessions on Saint Anne at the 1988 Kalamazoo Medieval Conference, to lure other secret Anne students out of hiding. The sessions were so well attended and the papers of such high quality that the next step of putting together a collection of essays proved irresistible.

Collaborative projects are notorious for their difficulty, but this one has been charmed. The research, writing, and editorial process have gone quickly and smoothly; participants have been cooperative; and all who have heard about the project have expressed enthusiasm for its outcome. Stimulating discussions with Carol Weisbrod of the University of Connecticut School of Law helped us to relate our work to current scholarship in a range of fields. The Hagiography Group of New York offered helpful responses to an early draft of part 2 of the Introduction. We would especially like to thank Ellen Schiferl of the art department at the University of Southern Maine, whose rigorous reading of the Introduction improved both its style and its logic. Comments by the two readers for the University of Georgia Press were also helpful in guiding revisions of the manuscript. Finally, the generous patronage of Clifford S. Reuter—in honor of his wife, Ann, and in recognition of his own extended kinship group—made possible the splendid color reproduction on the cover of the paperback edition of our book.

Interpreting Cultural Symbols

Introduction

KATHLEEN ASHLEY AND
PAMELA SHEINGORN

Locating Saint Anne in
Cultural and Gender Studies

O ur study of the figure of Saint Anne, mother of the Virgin
Mary and grandmother of Jesus, brings together a number
of disciplines, including art history, folklore, literary studies,
and social history. Most notably, our topic stands at the intersection of
popular culture, popular piety, and women's studies. At this intersection, many medievalists are now investigating phenomena that were
marginal to traditional art or literary or political or religious histories. The choice of Saint Anne as the focus of a collection of essays
thus transcends conventional disciplinary boundaries and signals the
formation of a new and inherently interdisciplinary methodology.

A major effort of scholars of women's studies over the past fifteen
years has been the recuperation of women's experiences and achieve-
ments and the rewriting of histories to incorporate them. For example, in history, *Medieval Women,* edited by Derek Baker, *Women of
the Medieval World,* edited by Julius Kirshner and Suzanne Wemple, *Becoming Visible: Women in European History,* edited by Renate Bridenthal,
Claudia Koonz, and Susan Stuard, and *A History of Their Own: Women
in Europe from Prehistory to the Present,* by Bonnie Anderson and Judith
Zinsser, all bring women as subjects into the writing of history. For
literature, *Medieval Women Writers,* edited by Katharina M. Wilson, and
Medieval Women's Visionary Literature, edited by Elizabeth A. Petroff, are
notable contributions; in art, Linda Nochlin and Ann Sutherland Har-

ris's *Women Artists, 1550–1950* and Eleanor Tufts's *Our Hidden Heritage: Five Centuries of Women Artists* come to mind.

In these essays on Saint Anne we have built on the work of scholars of women's studies in combination with two theoretical approaches, both of which encourage interdisciplinary inquiry: cultural studies and gender studies. Cultural studies have enabled us to explore the many contexts in which Saint Anne functioned as a symbol and to accept complexity and contradiction rather than striving for synthesis.[1] Conway, Bourque, and Scott tell us that "in studying gender systems we learn that they represent not the functional assignment of biologically prescribed social roles but a means of cultural conceptualization and social organization."[2] While this approach has enabled us to study Anne's many roles in late medieval culture, it has also motivated us to consider the possibility that some of her roles were not necessarily gendered. We are therefore working with two somewhat overlapping theoretical approaches.[3]

In accordance with gender theory, our exploration of the cult of Saint Anne bridges divisions between women's studies and traditional disciplinary inquiry,[4] and, following the lead of cultural studies, it also bridges divisions between popular and elite cultures, between sacred and secular concerns, between politics and religion, and between folklore and theology. Our essays show that the figure of Saint Anne functioned symbolically for a wide range of social groups in their cultural practices. She represented the cult of the family to gentry and aristocracy. She was called on by individual women as a sympathetic intercessor in childbearing. She bore a metaphorical relation to a number of crafts, such as woodworking, and was therefore their appropriate patron. She exemplified affective behaviors to nuns in a convent.

The appropriation of Saint Anne for so many purposes within late medieval and early modern culture thus encourages us to reexamine assumptions currently undergirding study of this culture.

The first of these assumptions, which has been challenged by feminist theory, is that women's concerns and experiences are always marginal to the dominant (male) culture. Within the dichotomy of private and public domains or domestic and political spheres, the female is assumed to occupy private, domestic space.[5] When male and female concerns come into contact with one another, the female exercises

a power that is subordinate to the male's. Since conventional histories focused primarily on public or political events, women's activities
in the private or domestic arena were neglected, and those women
who did perform public actions were treated as interesting anomalies.
Although we agree with Joan Gadol Kelly's hypothesis, as formulated
by Kristin B. Neuschel, that "the nature of the boundaries drawn
between public and private domains in a society [is] crucial in deter-
mining women's status in that society,"[6] our study of Anne suggests
that the public/private dichotomy is too limiting as a construct to describe the varied roles this female saint played in the lives of both men
and women.

The essays assembled here illustrate a variety of ways in which the
cult and imagery of Saint Anne were central to important aspects of
medieval culture, even though her frequent association with female
experience and concerns might suggest her existence at the margin.
We obviously need to refine our theoretical tools for apprehending
the cultural construction of gender in medieval society, and we might
begin by historicizing the dichotomy between public/male and do-
mestic/female. If we look at a typical image of the Holy Kinship group
(for example, fig. 2 in Sheingorn's essay), we see Anne and her three
daughters sitting in an enclosed garden surrounded by their young
children. Anne is certainly embedded within a world of female domes-
ticity, but at the same time the image presents her, not her husband,
Joachim, as the founding parent of the historical Christian community. From Anne and her daughters come not only Christ but most of
the apostles. Our own familiarity with the post-Renaissance public/
male *versus* domestic/female dichotomy, which has been linked with
a dominant bourgeois ideology, may have led scholars to universalize
aspects of gender roles that should instead be historicized.[7]

A second assumption of much recent feminist criticism is that where
women do find their voices or achieve public authority, they must
be using strategies for overcoming their marginality, whose terms are
defined by the dominant culture. For example, the influential feminist literary critic Elaine Showalter calls women's writing a "double-
voiced discourse." Drawing on the theories of anthropologists Shirley
Ardener and Edwin Ardener, she says, "Both muted and dominant
groups [in society] generate beliefs or ordering ideas of social reality
at the unconscious level, but dominant groups control the forms or

structures in which consciousness can be articulated. Thus, muted groups must mediate their beliefs through the allowable forms of dominant structures."[8] Although many feminists theorize a "wild zone" or "female space" outside the cultural dominant as the place from which women articulate their own reality, Showalter argues that this is still a utopian fantasy. Women's writings contain both a "dominant" and a "muted" story, and they pose for feminist criticism what she calls an "object/field problem" of keeping "two alternative oscillating texts simultaneously in view." Much ingenuity has gone into deciphering these "muted" stories within texts written in the cultural dominant by men as well as women. One might look, for example, at the collection entitled *Women in the Middle Ages and the Renaissance,* which announces that it will be "concerned with the effects of patriarchal sexual ideology on women's lives" and will examine "specific problems in self-definition which women faced in asserting themselves in a literary culture dominated by men."[9] In *Rewriting the Renaissance: The Discourses of Sexual Difference in Early Modern Europe,* feminists also join with other theorists, including Marxists and psychoanalytic and deconstructive interpreters, who seek to "analyze that which is suppressed or consigned to the margin by dominant ideological discourses of a particular society."[10]

But is an ideological "dominant" so easily identified? Although some feminist critics emphasize the dominance of official ideologies, seeing them as monological, other critics, most notably those influenced by the new history, may not see any dominant ideology at all, but rather multiple and contradictory voices. And feminists such as Elizabeth V. Spelman have begun to suggest that the male/female dichotomy is only one variable in a complex picture. She asks that we instead construct a map of differences in which class, race, and ethnicity assume as much significance as does gender.[11]

From our essays we can certainly conclude that many voices competed in the shaping of Anne's multifaceted image. The story of Saint Anne's growing up in the wilderness as a "wild child," retrieved by folklore study from medieval oral culture, certainly contrasts to the more orthodox legends of her life as exemplary *materfamilias.* Further, the canonicity of even orthodox Saint Anne materials was a perennial issue to theologians. As an apocryphal, nonbiblical figure, Anne's marital history could be written and rewritten to provide ammunition for theological controversies such as the Immaculate Conception. The narrative of Saint Anne becomes a locus for contesting interpretations within the learned culture. There is no one "culturally dominant" text but a variety of contesting and authoritative readings of Anne. In different periods, different readings assume cultural dominance, and what is suppressed or muted at one time may be voiced at another.

Perhaps most relevant to our study of Saint Anne is the assumption that dominant cultural symbols imply fixed meanings. That women might have access to such symbols for their own purposes or that a gendered image might also have a nongendered function is usually overlooked. Saint Anne is a good example of a medieval image associated with "female" experiences but also available to males. She could represent women's desires for motherhood, but at the same time she could express the dynastic impulses of royalty or symbolize the civic liberties of Florence, both of which are not obviously gendered functions. Our essays show that Anne can represent a genealogical mother, but also the genderless idea of lineage and dynasty. She can function as an image of the generative female, but she is not restricted to that representation. She is a "polysemic" symbol, in Victor Turner's terminology.[12]

One of the reasons that women's studies have assumed that if a symbol was used by women it was important only to women is the tendency to essentialize—to assume that symbols have an intrinsic and permanent meaning. Margaret Miles, for example, argues that medieval images of the Virgin offered women a vision of virginity as a powerful alternative to motherhood; women were able to read works of art as offering empowering models, rather than the constraining models intended by their male producers. The image is gendered, she implies, when it has a female subject and a female viewer.[13] We would resist such biological essentialism as applied to both image and receiver. The image of the Virgin obviously empowered males as well as females, and virginity could be a gendered or a genderless issue in medieval culture. An image that comes into being to solve a theological crux may also be appropriated for quite different purposes, as the essays in this volume show.

Although one can criticize Miles for ahistoricism in the way she interprets symbols and audiences, she does offer valuable methods to cultural history. She shows how to move beyond named artists and writers and toward studies of reception. Susan Groag Bell's "Medieval Women Book Owners: Arbiters of Lay Piety and Ambassadors of Culture" is another effective example of this approach to medieval texts and images. Both demonstrate the importance of often-neglected visual materials to cultural history and suggest methodologies for studying patronage. The meaning of patronage needs to be broadened to include not only elite patrons but also such patrons as convents and guilds (since so many cultural artifacts were produced for corporate groups during the Middle Ages). Historically locating images within an interpretive context will combat essentialist readings. The figure of Anne must be seen as part of ideological constellations employed in specific institutional contexts at specific historical times.

Development of the *Vita* and Cult of Saint Anne

Early Christian and Byzantine

Saint Anne receives no mention either in primary sources of the late antique period or in the New Testament.[14] As Pierre Delooz observes, she is a "constructed" saint: "Nothing is known about her, except that somebody must have existed who filled the role of mother to Mary, the mother of Jesus. The *real* saint is Jesus' anonymous maternal grandmother. Everything else has been constructed. But what a gigantic construction!"[15]

The construction began by devising for Jesus' maternal grandmother a life history that followed the paradigm in the Hebrew Bible for the mothers of children singled out by God, such as Isaac and Samuel. According to this paradigm, long years of barrenness followed by divine intervention result in the birth of a child whose life is pledged to God. Anne's life especially resembles that of Hannah, the mother of Samuel (see 1 Sam. 1–2:11), suggesting that the model of Hannah (the name means "grace" in Hebrew) was quite deliberately chosen by a Christian writer in order to create a typological fulfillment of the story in the Hebrew Bible. In the earliest source, the names are in fact identical—Hannah in Greek became Anna in Latin, suggesting either that the typological shaping of Anne's life was motivated by the shared names or that the anonymous woman who was Mary's mother was given the name Anne to reinforce the typological relationship.

The document in which Anne's story first appears is the apocryphal but very influential *Protevangelium of James* of about A.D. 150.[16] Written in Greek and by a writer probably from Syria or Egypt, the *Protevangelium* enjoyed wide circulation and great influence throughout the early Christian world. The *Protevangelium* shares with other apocryphal texts in circulation in the early Christian period the role of supplying information omitted from what would become the canonical Gospels —specifically, information regarding the early lives of Mary and of Jesus. The source of the irrepressible popularity of the *Protevangelium* lies in this quality. Anne is neither the heroine nor the main character of the tale, for that role always belongs to the Virgin, but she is an important member of the supporting cast. A much later Byzantine icon (fig. 1) shows how thoroughly the stories of Anne and Mary were seen as one continuous narrative and how closely that narrative followed the *Protevangelium*.[17] Centering on the Hodegētria, an image of the Madonna and Child, the icon presents a sequence of scenes beginning in the upper left-hand corner with the Meeting of Joachim and Anne at the Golden Gate (4.4), the Birth of Mary (5.2), and the Presentation of Mary in the Temple with her subsequent feeding by an angel (7.2–3 and 8.1). Below this last scene is a representation of Mary given into the care of Joseph (9.2), and below the Meeting at the Golden Gate is the Annunciation (11), followed by the Visitation (12). Opposite the Visitation is the Trial by Water (15–16). The scenes in the lower register, which read from left to right, go beyond the time frame of the *Protevangelium* and complete the *vita* of Mary with the Presentation of Jesus in the Temple, the Annunciation of Mary's Death, and Mary's Death with Christ Receiving Her Soul.

The *Protevangelium* lies at the root of the late medieval cult of Anne. It also touches on two problems whose various solutions were to be crucial in shaping medieval theologians' views of Anne. The first is the nature of Anne's conception of Mary. Although the oldest manuscript of the *Protevangelium*, Papyrus Bodmer V, reports that the angel said to Joachim, "Behold, your wife Anne has conceived in her womb," the majority of manuscripts use the future tense, "will conceive." Behind the difference in tense lies the fundamental issue: whether or not

Fig. 1. *Hodegetria with Life of Mary,* right wing of a limestone diptych. Berlin
(Dahlem). Staatliche Museen Preussischer Kulturbesitz, Frühchristlich-
Byzantinische Sammlung. Fourteenth or fifteenth century.
Photo: Staatliche Museen Preussischer Kulturbesitz.

Anne's conception of Mary was miraculous. This problem was not resolved by the Roman Catholic church until the nineteenth century, when it adopted the doctrine of the Immaculate Conception, or the belief that the conception of Mary in the womb of Anne was without sin. By contrast, the problem did not trouble the Greek fathers, and language supporting the Immaculate Conception appears in the Eastern liturgy for the Feast of the Conception, called in the East the Conception of Anne.[18] The second problem originates in the conflict between the perpetual virginity of Mary and the several references in the New Testament to brothers of Jesus. If Mary's perpetual virginity were to be defended, no other children could be attributed to her, and it was necessary to find other, convincing parentage for them. The *Protevangelium* handles this simply enough by turning to Jesus' other parent, Joseph, and assigning to him children by an earlier marriage.

Some of the Western fathers mention Anne, and their source is most likely to have been the *Protevangelium*. But Jerome, in a treatise defending the perpetual virginity of Mary, attacked the authority of a number of infancy gospels and singled out the *Protevangelium* for its treatment of the issue of Jesus' brothers: "Certain of the Apocrypha, following absurdities, suppose that the brothers of the Lord standing outside the door (Matt. 12:47) were the sons of Joseph by some woman; but we ought to understand 'the brothers of the Lord' here as the equivalent of 'the sons of mother's sisters.'"[19] Not only did Jerome succeed in establishing the church's belief in the perpetual virginity of Mary, but he further brought about the condemnation of a list of infancy gospels by Popes Damasus, Innocent I, and Gelasius.[20]

The attempted suppression of the main source of information about Anne apparently precluded early development of her cult in the West but had little impact on the Eastern church. Procopius reports that Justinian dedicated a church to Anne in Constantinople in about 550. The feast of Anne, celebrated on July 25, may celebrate the day of the dedication of this church. The Eastern liturgy also developed three Marian feasts with which Anne was intimately connected: the feast of the Nativity of Mary, which seems to have been celebrated by the early seventh century,[21] the Presentation of Mary in the Temple, possibly originating in as early as the fifth century in Jerusalem and known in Constantinople by the end of the seventh century,[22] and, by the eighth century, the feast of the Conception of Anne.[23] The three scenes across the top of the twelfth-century Byzantine icon (fig. 1) reproduce the imagery associated with these three feasts in the Byzantine world.

Early Middle Ages in the West

An important source for the eventual adoption of the cult of Anne in the West was the *Protevangelium,* reworked in Latin into a text usually known as the Pseudo-Matthew. Jan Gijsel, who has made an extensive study of the more than 130 surviving texts in medieval manuscripts, dates the original reworking, of which no manuscripts survive, to between A.D. 550 and 700.[24] Of the four text families into which the manuscripts fall, the first two, Gijsel's A and P, originate before 800. Text family A is prefaced by letters purporting to be written by Jerome and two of his contemporaries and attributing the text to Matthew, the translation into Latin to Jerome.[25] These are more likely to have been written by the actual translator working at the end of the fifth century, who presumably hoped that the forged letters would protect his translation from the papal prohibition of apocryphal infancy gospels. Gijsel's text family P does not include prefatory letters and deviates considerably from the original text.[26] Both of these versions of the Pseudo-Matthew circulated in the West, finding places in collections of saints' lives and serving as a source for writers.[27] The P version, for example, was reworked into rather elegant Latin distichs by Hrosthwitha, resulting in a long poem entitled *Historia nativitatis laudabilisque conversationis intactae Dei genitricis quam scriptam reperi sub nomine Sancti Jacobi fratris domini.* [28]

The cult of Anne in the West was probably fostered in the seventh century by refugees from the Muslim conquests. Some of these refugees attained influential positions, such as the Jerusalem bishop's son who was elected pope in 642, and their Eastern customs and feasts had a considerable impact. By the end of the seventh century, one Marian feast involving Anne, the Nativity of Mary, was being celebrated in Rome,[29] and a figure of Anne, the earliest known in the West, was painted in the Roman church of Santa Maria Antiqua, on the west wall of the presbytery, in about 650. Anne, standing, holds the infant Mary in her arms. Thus the earliest iconography of Anne in the West emphasizes her role as a mother. The resemblance to the Hodegetria—the Byzantine image of Mary as mother, holding the infant Christ and pointing to him (as in fig. 1)—is unmistakable and clearly deliberate. When Santa Maria Antiqua was redecorated in 705–7 under Pope John VII, "the panel with St. Anne was singled out as too precious (and possibly, also, too well preserved) to be covered over and . . . therefore it was retained and embodied, at considerable effort, in the new program."[30] The numbers of Eastern monks in Rome grew dramatically in the mid-eighth century as monks fled Byzantium to escape the persecutions of iconoclasts. After the iconoclastic Council of 754, iconophiles were attacked with physical violence and monasteries were closed. So many monks fled to Rome that "Paul I ordered that some Greek be introduced in the services so that the refugees would be able to follow the prayers."[31] Monks such as these must have continued to honor Anne as a holy mother, for in about 760 Anne was represented again in Santa Maria Antiqua, this time as one of three mothers—Anne, Mary, and Elizabeth—carrying infants.[32] Although Western art developed other ways of representing Anne as mother that more clearly differentiated her iconography from that of the Virgin, it continued to view Anne's maternity as her most important attribute. In fact, when, in the late Middle Ages, Anne becomes a frequently represented figure in the pictorial arts, she seldom appears alone; rather, her constant companion is her daughter, the Virgin Mary.

Anne thus enters the West as a mother, worthy of note because the birthday of the Virgin was deemed worthy of celebration. Other familial relationships implied in the New Testament were more problematic, and one of these would eventually involve Anne, namely, the proper understanding of the relationships among the three Marys. A ninth-century sermon for Easter Day states that three of the four Marys were sisters (Mary Magdalene is excluded), but no mention is made of their mother.[33]

A sweeping solution to the familial relationships of New Testament personages, a solution that protects the perpetual virginity of Mary, appeared as early as the mid-ninth century and apparently from the hand of the biblical commentator Haymo of Auxerre.[34] Connecting Jerome's comment that the brothers of the Lord were the sons of his mother's sisters with the notion that the three Marys were sisters, this writer draws the logical conclusion that Anne had three daughters named Mary and that their children were Jesus and his so-called brothers.

The full explanation accounts for other New Testament figures in a most economical way. The early death of Joachim is required, with his widow, Anne, and daughter, the Virgin Mary, surviving him. Since one of the Marys was called Mary Cleophas, her father must have been named Cleophas and must have been Anne's second husband. Since Jewish law asked the brother of the deceased to marry the surviving widow, Cleophas was Joachim's brother. James the Less, called a brother of Jesus in the New Testament, must therefore have been the son of Mary Cleophas. Elsewhere he is called son of Alpheus, yielding the "fact" that Mary Cleophas was married to Alpheus. Tradition assigned them another son, Joseph the Just. Cleophas also had the responsibility for the marriage of his niece and stepdaughter, Mary, for whom he found his own brother Joseph. Having tied so many threads, Cleophas died. The third Mary, called in the New Testament Mary Salome, must therefore have had a father named Salome, who was then of necessity Anne's third husband. James the Great and John the Evangelist, also called brothers of Jesus as well as sons of Zebedee, must have been the sons of Mary Salome, who was therefore married to Zebedee.

This notion of Anne's three marriages, or *trinubium*—which gives her the position of matriarch in a large, extended family called the Holy Kinship—appears in neither the cult nor the iconography of Anne in the East and is therefore a Western invention. The *trinubium* nonetheless had very little immediate impact in the West, and there is only scattered evidence for Anne's cult before the twelfth century. There was perhaps a vague sense of a conflict between the *trinubium* and the idea of the Immaculate Conception, which was growing in popularity as part of the rapidly developing cult of Mary. For example, Fulbert of Chartres champions the view that the purity of the Virgin's parents was surely incompatible with multiple parenthood. It was not fitting that they should be polluted by the propagation of more children.[35]

The feast of Anne's Conception of Mary appears especially early in England, where it was introduced in about 1030, probably under the influence of Greek monks from Italy.[36] Temporarily discontinued after the Norman Conquest, the feast was reestablished through the efforts of Anselm of Edmunsbury (d. 1148), who also influenced its introduction into Norman France. In preconquest England, the feast was understood as a celebration of Anne's conception of Mary, not, apparently, as advocating the doctrine of the Immaculate Conception.[37] The cult of Anne developed more slowly, for her feast day does not appear in preconquest calendars.[38]

The High Middle Ages

It is the twelfth century that represents, in the words of André Wilmart, "les débuts réel du culte de la *mater Matris* en Occident."[39] The same century also gave birth to two major controversies involving Anne. As Western theologians began to assimilate Anne into their views of sacred history, the character of her reception was shaped by their attitudes toward her conception of the Virgin and toward New Testament genealogy.

Until the twelfth century, theologians in the West were content with "vague formulations" in their references to Anne's conception of Mary.[40] But during the twelfth century the doctrine of the Immaculate Conception was explicitly formulated, first in England by Eadmer. It quickly became a matter of great controversy. Against strong English (as well as other) proponents of the feast, the voice of clear-thinking Bernard of Clairvaux rose in protest. Bernard asked how Mary's body could be exempt from Original Sin if she had been conceived by the concupiscence of her parents. Mirella Levi D'Ancona summarizes Bernard's logical conclusion: "If the exemption of Mary from Original Sin is required to explain the purity of the Conception of Christ, one would be obligated to believe the same thing of Anne and of all the female ancestors of the Virgin; the exemptions would have no end."[41] One might suspect that, being so deeply devoted to the Virgin, Bernard was repelled by the thought that Mary, rather than being uniquely pure, merely stood at the end of a line of pristine females.

The *trinubium* similarly aroused great controversy in the twelfth century. Not only had the views of Haymo of Auxerre been in circulation, but the *trinubium* had been taken up by no less important a figure than Peter Lombard. In his commentary on the Epistle to the Galatians, Peter expounds upon the text phrase by phrase. To explain the problematical passage "But other of the apostles I saw none, saving James the brother of the Lord" (1:19), Peter offers two explanations.[42]

First he restates the position of the *Protevangelium,* that James was a son of Joseph by a previous marriage, but, he says, "This is not certain, since Joseph is believed to have been a virgin." Then he describes Anne's three marriages, departing from the earlier explanation only in that he gives Mary Cleophas and Alpheus two additional sons, Simon and Jude. In the course of a long passage drawn from Augustine, in which examples are given of four different ways of using the word "brother" in the Hebrew Bible, it becomes clear that in Hebrew usage first cousins can be referred to as brothers. But Peter finally refuses to choose between these two possible explanations, concluding his commentary on Galatians 1:19 with this observation: "James, the brother of the Lord, ought to be understood either as one of the sons of Joseph by another wife, or as a blood relation of Mary his mother." Since Peter Lombard was the usual gloss on Paul in the Middle Ages, his discussion of the *trinubium* was widely read by students of theology, but it did not receive the unquestioning acceptance of his readers.

Identifying those who accepted the *trinubium* as "Salomites" because they took the Salome of Mark 15:40 and 16:1 to be a man (Anne's third husband and father of Mary Salome), anti-Salomites vigorously attacked the *trinubium.* Englishmen, perhaps because of their favoring of the Immaculate Conception, led the charge against the Salomites. Herbert of Bosham, for example, who calls Peter Lombard his master, dismissed the *trinubium* as "fabula" in a letter (ca. 1166) to Henry the Liberal, count of Champagne.[43]

Several manuscripts, the earliest of them contemporary with the Salomite controversy, include genealogical charts detailing the Holy Kinship (fig. 2), as does, for example, the *Imola Psalter* (fol. 11r), perhaps made in Winchester and dated after 1204.[44] The inclusion of the matrilineal genealogy in juxtaposition with the Tree of Jesse, the traditional image illustrating the patriarchal descent of Jesus, suggests that the patrons of these manuscripts were consciously stating their Salomite views. These manuscript illustrations demonstrate too the extension of the Holy Kinship to the "cadet line." According to this extension, Anne had a sister, Esmeria, whose daughter, Elizabeth, was the mother of John the Baptist. Esmeria's other child, a son, Eliud, was the ancestor of Saint Servatius, bishop of Tongres in the fourth century, whose cult flourished in the Low Countries.[45]

In the twelfth and thirteenth centuries, some authors, such as Peter

Fig. 2. *Diagram of the Holy Kinship,* miniature from the *Imola Psalter.*
Imola, Bibl. Comunale, MS. 100, fol. 10v. After 1204.
Photo: Biblioteca Comunale di Imola.

Comestor, continued to offer the *trinubium* as an explanation for the existence of Jesus' brothers, while others attacked it vehemently. Interestingly, Thomas Aquinas (1226–74) opposed both the *trinubium* and the Immaculate Conception. In his commentary on Galatians, Thomas cites evidence from Jerome, as the earlier anti-Salomites had done— specifically, the point that the name "Salome" is a woman's name, so the Salome of the New Testament could not have been the father of Mary Salome.[46] Against the doctrine of the Immaculate Conception, Thomas expounded the doctrine of Mary's Sanctification, holding that "while true that her parents conceived her in sin, according to the laws of human generation, when her sanctified soul joined her body in the womb of her mother Anne, it freed the body from impurity and restored it to that state of grace which it would have had naturally but for the Fall of Man."[47]

An especially complete summary of the anti-Salomite position was presented by Jean de Fribourg (Breisgau) in his *Defensorium beatae Annae*, written about 1300.[48] Jean, a Dominican, says that the inventors of ancient errors most lyingly (*mendosissime*) give Anne three husbands; in fact, she was content with one. Citing an impressive range of authorities, he proceeds to demolish the *trinubium* in four carefully argued chapters. Despite its cogency, Jean's work survives in only one manuscript, while by 1300 the *trinubium* had been incorporated into two works that enjoyed immense circulation: the *Legenda aurea (Golden Legend)* and two further versions of the Pseudo-Matthew.

According to Gijsel's study of the Pseudo-Matthew, a new version that arose in the second half of the eleventh century introduced further changes in this text. Eighteen chapters of childhood miracles of Jesus, a text that had existed separately, were now joined to the Pseudo-Matthew. In addition, a genealogy of the family of Mary, beginning "Anna et Esmeria," was included. The oldest manuscript of this version of the Pseudo-Matthew, which Gijsel calls Q, is dated to the twelfth century and does not contain this genealogy. The final version of the Pseudo-Matthew, Gijsel's R, revises the longer text but omits the prefatory letters, attributing the text to John the Evangelist, rather than to Matthew, but retaining the attribution of the translation to Jerome. Although the two oldest manuscripts of R date to the thirteenth and fourteenth centuries, Gijsel suggests that this variant may have been prepared as early as the twelfth century. Tischendorf published a late manuscript of R as his B, thereby introducing great confusion into scholarly understanding of the history of the cult of Saint Anne, as it is this version that gives the fullest account of Anne's three marriages.

The *trinubium* also became part of another widely circulated text, the *Legenda aurea*, where it forms part of the reading on the Nativity of the Virgin. Jacobus de Voragine, who compiled this legendary for the use of his own Dominican order, simply incorporated a large portion of one of the later versions of the Pseudo-Matthew to serve as this reading. From sermons based on this text and vernacular translations and adaptations of it, the *trinubium* reached a wide audience, for many of whom it became an accepted part of their understanding of biblical history.

Late Middle Ages

Due chiefly to the *Legenda aurea*, the late medieval Jesus is most significantly a product of a matrilineal descent system, rather than the patrilineal one of the Gospels. The *Legenda aurea*'s chapter "De nativitate beatae Mariae virginis" for the Nativity of the Virgin gently chides scriptural writers for their male chauvinism: "The nativity of the glorious Virgin Mary derives its origin from the tribe of Judah and the royal house of David. However Matthew and Luke do not describe the descent of Mary but of Joseph—who, nevertheless, was completely removed from the conception of Christ—because it is said that it was the custom of the Scriptures to construct a line of descent not of women, but of men. Most truthfully, nonetheless, the Blessed Virgin descended from the lineage of David."[49] As John Bossy observes about the inclusion of the Holy Kinship in the *Golden Legend*, "The value of this source was that it enabled Mary, and therefore Jesus, to appear in the world embedded in that plausible nexus of blood relations on which, though satisfying about her cousinage to Elizabeth and John the Baptist, the canonical gospels have such scanty and contradictory information."[50]

Both the Pseudo-Matthew and the *Golden Legend*, as well as their many vernacular translations and variants, put into wide circulation the entire story of Anne's life. Cycles of illustrations presenting the life of the Virgin, which began to appear in the twelfth century in the

West, often open with scenes from the life of Anne. For example, a German epic poem, "Driu liet von der maget," written by the Priest Wernher in 1172 and based on the Pseudo-Matthew, was very fully illustrated in an early-thirteenth-century manuscript.[51] The illustration of the angel's annunciation to Anne (fig. 3) indicates that the narrative held to the basic outlines already set in the *Protevangelium*. After Anne's lament, the angel appears to announce that she is with child. The angel continues: "You are now carrying beneath your heart that whose absence you have felt with sorrow, a child, a little daughter, so exalted, that none her equal ever has been or will be born, for she has been chosen to be princess of all the high hosts of heaven, for know this: she shall bear the one who is father to all the world, the son of God, the holy Christ."[52] The best-known treatment of the life of the Virgin that includes scenes from the life of Saint Anne is Giotto's fresco cycle in the Arena Chapel, Padua (1304–7), which includes an especially moving rendition of Anne's meeting with Joachim at the Golden Gate. The emotional interaction of the two figures is also stressed in the Meeting at the Golden Gate from the Buxtehude Altar, painted in the workshop of Master Bertram around 1410 (fig. 4).[53] This scene, symbolic of Anne's conception of Mary, was used by those supporting the doctrine of the Immaculate Conception (the "Immaculists") to represent their position.

Another important aspect of the cult of Anne as well as a virtual requirement for the development of her cult, at least partially independent of the cult of the Virgin, was the translation of some of her relics to the West. Louis Réau suggests that Anne's cult was stimulated by the Crusades, because through them her "pretended relics" ("prétendues reliques") were brought to the West. The veil of Saint Anne at the Cathedral of Apt, France, made it a center of pilgrimage,[54] and the head of Anne was presented to Chartres Cathedral by the Count of Blois on his return from the Fourth Crusade. The cartulary of the cathedral described the occasion: "The head of the mother was received with great joy in the church of the daughter."[55] The Dominicans at Mainz also had a head of Saint Anne until the early sixteenth century, when a mason stole it and took it to the Franciscans in Düren near Aachen, which subsequently became a pilgrimage site.[56] Frederick the Wise brought relics of Anne with him when he returned from a pilgrimage to the Holy Land. The reliquaries enshrining these

edaz fie die rede uolfprah. emen engel
fi gefah uor ir antlintze ften. di uorh
te begund fie durhgen. fie wider faz in z
harte: do fie in began anvvarten. ir fin fur
enwedele. fam uor dem winde di uedere. v
oh daz lovb gerne tut. der engil fwang ir
fin mut. uz den forgen alfo fwæren. mit
femftlichen gebæren. er gruzte die froen
fchone: mit der botfcaft trone. mit minne

ein kint von dem engel gefrowet fint

Gelobet fift wol ir gebiurt

Fig. 3. *Angel's Annunciation to Anne,* miniature from "Driu liet von der maget," by Wernher. Kraków, MS. Germ. oct. 109. 1172. Photo: Janusz Podlecki.

Fig. 4. Master Bertram, *Meeting at the Golden Gate,* from the Buxtehude Altar. Hamburg, Hamburger Kunsthalle. Ca. 1410. Photo: Elke Walford.

relics were illustrated on a page of a relic book made by Lucas Cranach the Elder and printed in Wittenberg in 1509 (fig. 5).[57]

During the thirteenth century the cult of Anne grew, and by the fourteenth century it was widespread. The Chronicles of Evesham report that the prior established a chapel dedicated to Anne before 1229. This was the first dedication to Anne in England.[58] Of the orders, the Carmelites first kept Anne's feast day, July 26, in the thirteenth century, and numerous other orders followed in the next two centuries. By the fourteenth century so many churches and dioceses celebrated the feast of Anne that "one may speak of a general distribution."[59] Papal approval of the feast in England on November 21, 1378, is usually associated with Anne of Bohemia, the new queen, as a compliment to her through the honoring of her name saint.

Introduction of a new feast meant its inclusion in liturgical books, where, depending on the elaborateness of the individual book, the text of the feast might well be accompanied by an illustration. In such books, the feast of Anne or prayers to Anne, if illustrated, most often show the scene of Anne teaching the Virgin to read, also called the Education of the Virgin. For example, in a book of hours of the Use of Sarum made in England in the last quarter of the fourteenth century, the feast of Anne was added in the Kalendar in red, and Anne is one of eight saints given an illustration on two facing pages at the end of the Kalendar (fig. 6).[60] Anne, wearing the peaked hood that identifies her as a widow, uses an open book to instruct her daughter. Anne is also featured prominently in illustrations for Marian feasts and in those for the Hours of the Virgin in books of hours. The full-page illustration for matins in the Hours of the Virgin in the *Playfair Hours,* a manuscript made in Rouen for use in England in the late fifteenth century, typically focuses on the Annunciation (fig. 7).[61] But four scenes in the border provide key episodes prior to the Annunciation, that is, the Meeting at the Golden Gate, the Nativity of the Virgin, the Presentation in the Temple, and the Marriage of Mary and Joseph—and all of these include Anne.

Although these developments indicate growing interest in Anne herself, she still received the most attention from those devoted to the *trinubium* or to the doctrine of the Immaculate Conception. Jean Gerson (1363–1429), chancellor of the University of Paris, supported both the Immaculate Conception and the Holy Kinship. In a sermon

Fig. 5. Lucas Cranach the Elder, *Relics of Saint Anne,* woodcut from the *Wittenberger Heiligtumsbuch.* Buch 581/82 S. 69, Kupferstichkabinett SMPK, Berlin. 1509. Photo: Jörg P. Anders.

Fig. 6. *Saints Christopher, George, Anne and the Virgin, and Mary Magdalene,*
miniature from an English book of hours. Oxford, Keble College, MS. 47,
fol. 7v. Last quarter of the fourteenth century. Photo by permission of the
Warden and Fellows of Keble College, Oxford.

Fig. 7. *Annunciation,* illustration to matins, Hours of the Virgin, in the *Playfair Hours*. Victoria and Albert Museum, MS. L. 475–1918, fol. 36r. Late fifteenth century. Photo by courtesy of the Board of Trustees of the Victoria and Albert Museum.

written for a Marian feast, Gerson quoted a mnemonic verse summarizing Anne's three marriages and naming her children and grandchildren. The verse, which begins "Anna tribus nupsit," is one of a number of such devices found by Max Förster in manuscripts from the eleventh century to the sixteenth. After 1400 the Holy Kinship took on a new and distinctive visual form in which Anne, her daughters, and their children, the last portrayed as infants and toddlers, inhabit a lush garden setting evocative of the *hortus conclusus* (fig. 8).[62] Anne the matriarch holds a prominent place in such compositions, as does her eldest daughter, Mary, the mother of Jesus.

Franciscans, Dominicans, and Carmelites defended the *trinubium,* and Franciscans, Carmelites, and Carthusians had all adopted the doctrine of the Immaculate Conception at least a century before it was proclaimed a dogma of faith in 1438 by the Council of Basel. Since the pope declared this council schismatic, its actions did not take effect, and controversy about the doctrine raged for most of the century. An image that became especially popular during the fifteenth century, Saint Anne with the Virgin and Child (*Anna Selbdritt*), gave visual expression to the doctrine.[63] A Franciscan pope, Sixtus IV, saw to the composition of an Office of the Immaculate Conception for the Franciscans in 1476, at least partially in the hope that his open support would quell the controversy over the doctrine, but continued strife persuaded him to issue a constitution in 1483 that forbade either side to accuse the other of heresy on pain of excommunication (*Grave nimis,* 1482).

The silencing of discussion about the Immaculate Conception along with papal approval of it seem to have contributed to a great rise in Anne's popularity in the late fifteenth and early sixteenth centuries.[64] Martin Luther, writing in 1537, noted that the cult had grown recently: "We invoke the help of the saints, creating one saint and deliverer after another. Thus we made saints of Anna and Joachim not more than thirty years ago."[65] Modern scholars, struck by the quick rise in the various aspects of Anne's cult, refer to the phenomenon of *Annalatrie*[66] and to Anne as the "fashionable saint" (*Modeheilige*) of the period.[67] The extreme was surely reached in a Spanish story recorded in 1511 of a woman devoted to both Anne and the Virgin but financially unable to continue giving money for both feasts. She resolved the issue by lighting candles to both, planning to maintain her

Fig. 8. Gert van Lon, *Holy Kinship,* center panel of *Holy Kinship Altarpiece.*
Münster, Westfälischer Kunstverein. 1510–20. Photo: Westfälisches
Landesmuseum für Kunst und Kulturgeschichte, Münster.

devotion to the one whose candle burned longer. After Anne's candle outlasted that of the Virgin, it was decided that Mary had honored her mother by deferring to her.[68]

The number of books about Anne in circulation provides further testimony to her popularity: "Seldom have any of the lives of the saints been so frequently reprinted as was the life of St. Anne, with a clear peak around 1500."[69] Peter Dorlant's *Historia perpulchra de Anna sanctissima,* published in Antwerp in about 1490, made an especial point of defending the *trinubium* by arguing that Anne should be considered as one of the women to whom the Old Law of the Hebrew Bible applied. Jan van Denemarken, whose life of Anne appeared in several languages and was reprinted into the nineteenth century, popularized the extension of the legend back to Anne's parents, Emerentiana and Stollanus, who lived on Mount Carmel.[70] In another tradition, also given wide circulation in early printed books, Anne's parents had the names Susanna and Isachar.[71]

An altarpiece made for the Carmelite church in Frankfurt summarizes the state of devotion to Saint Anne in the late fifteenth and early sixteenth centuries.[72] A brotherhood of Saint Anne first recorded in 1479 met at the Carmelite monastery in Frankfurt. In 1493 the brotherhood acquired a relic of Saint Anne's arm, and in 1494 Johannes Trithemius dedicated his *Tractatus de laudibus sanctissimae Matris Annae* to the brotherhood.[73] Finally, the brotherhood commissioned an altarpiece about Saint Anne from a painter in Brussels. The two wings of the altarpiece include sixteen individual paintings.

The sequence begins on the inner side of the left wing with a Tree of Esmeria, Anne's sister (fig. 9). Obviously based on the image of the Tree of Anne, which in turn derived from the Tree of Jesse, the painting borrows two other important ideas associated with Anne: matriliny and female literacy. From Esmeria's right shoulder grows a tree bearing first Elizabeth and then her son, John the Baptist. The tree rooted in her left shoulder leads to her son Eliud, his son Emiu, and, at the top, the episcopal saint Servatius.

Next the subject switches to the main branch of the family, that of Anne herself, as the next panel depicts Anne as a young girl being introduced to the Carmelites on Mount Carmel by her parents (fig. 10). According to Carmelite history, the Carmelites had been established on Mount Carmel since the time of Elias, and Emerentiana, Anne's

Fig. 9. *Tree of Esmeria*, from *Saint Anne Altarpiece*. Frankfurt am
Main, Historisches Museum. End of the fifteenth century.
Photo: Historisches Museum.

Fig. 10. *Saint Anne and Her Parents Visit Mount Carmel*, from *Saint Anne Altarpiece*. Frankfurt am Main, Historisches Museum. End of the fifteenth century. Photo: Historisches Museum.

mother, had sought their advice about whether or not she should marry. In a vision the Carmelites saw a tree with beautiful branches and interpreted the vision as referring to Emerentiana and her descendants. Anne and her sister Esmeria were thus the fruit of the marriage that the Carmelites advised, and it is natural that Anne was brought to meet the Carmelites. In the background a vignette shows the birth of Anne. In the next panel Emerentiana arranges the marriage of Anne to Joachim, while, in the background, Stollanus offers thanks to God (fig. 11). The scene of demons murdering young men in the right background refers to a story from the Book of Tobit in the Old Testament Apocrypha. The woman in the story is Sarah, who "had been given to seven husbands, and a devil named Asmodeus had killed them, at their first going in unto her" (Tob. 2:8). In response to prayers, God sent his angel Raphael to give Sarah in marriage to Tobias, son of Tobit, "for to him who feareth God is . . . [Sarah] due to be his wife: therefore another could not have her" (Tob. 7:12). In a transfer typical of hagiography, this story was first assigned to Emerentiana, and this painting implies its further transfer to Anne. In the following scene the wedding of Anne and Joachim takes place in front of the church portal whose tympanum contains the figure of Moses with the tablets of the law, a statement that this marriage takes place according to the law of Moses (fig. 12). The details of the wedding actually reflect approved practice at the end of the fifteenth century, when the painting was made.

The inner right wing presents four scenes from the married life of Anne and Joachim, which could serve as an exemplary model of marriage for the members of the brotherhood. The first of these scenes represents an incident that had been part of the *vita* of Anne as early as the *Protevangelium*—Anne and Joachim giving alms to the poor (fig. 13). Skipping over well-known episodes in the story, such as Joachim's expulsion, Anne's lament, the annunciations to Anne and Joachim, and the meeting at the Golden Gate, the visual narrative moves on to the Sacrifice of Anne and Joachim (fig. 14). This scene deviates from the narrative as expanded in the Pseudo-Matthew by including Anne in the painting. According to Pseudo-Matthew, after the angel had appeared to Joachim in the wilderness to tell him that he and Anne would have a child, the angel instructed Joachim to offer a sacrifice. Joachim obeyed, and the smoke rose to heaven.[74] Thus the scene took

Fig. 11. *Emerentiana Arranges the Marriage of Anne to Joachim*, from
Saint Anne Altarpiece. Frankfurt am Main, Historisches Museum.
End of the fifteenth century. Photo: Historisches Museum.

Fig. 12. *Wedding of Anne and Joachim,* from *Saint Anne Altarpiece.*
Frankfurt am Main, Historisches Museum. End of the fifteenth
century. Photo: Historisches Museum.

Fig. 13. *Anne and Joachim Give Alms to the Poor,* from *Saint Anne Altarpiece.* Frankfurt am Main, Historisches Museum. End of the fifteenth century. Photo: Historisches Museum.

Fig. 14. *The Sacrifice of Anne and Joachim,* from *Saint Anne Altarpiece.* Frankfurt am Main, Historisches Museum. End of the fifteenth century. Photo: Historisches Museum.

place in the wilderness, not in a temple in the presence of priests and observers, and not with Anne as an equal participant. Next Anne and Joachim are shown at table, an expansion of the indication in Pseudo-Matthew that they returned to their home after meeting at the Golden Gate (fig. 15). In the painting the details of their prosperous domestic life overshadow the hagiographically more important scene of the birth of Mary, shown in the right background. Finally, the inner right wing portrays the presentation of Mary in the temple, with an angel guiding the Virgin up the fifteen steps to the temple, where she is met by a priest (fig. 16). Again the focus is on the married couple, whose locked glances and expressive gestures communicate the depth of their feelings as they part with their child.

The outer wings of the Frankfurt altar turn from the historical life of Anne to her appearances in visions and her miracles. They begin in the upper left with the Vision of Elijah (fig. 17). According to a Carmelite exegesis of 3 Kings 18:42–45, Elijah's vision of the cloud that produced rain, ending a major drought, symbolized the Virgin herself. In the painting Elijah sees Anne hovering above the sea, with the Virgin and Child in a light-filled cloud above her. The next panel, showing Anne as a statue on an altar, with the figure of the Virgin in her womb (fig. 18), may be an illustration of the hymn for the feast of the Immaculate Conception, "Festum Mariae venerantes." In the hymn the authorities grouped reverently around the altar state their opinions as to the truth of the Immaculate Conception.[75] The two panels below illustrate two visions of Saint Colette in which Anne appeared to her. In the first, Anne introduces her glorious offspring to Colette in justification of her three marriages (fig. 19). In the second, Colette, praying before an altar whose altarpiece represents the Holy Kinship, sees Anne in heaven with a golden begging bowl, with which she solicits from the saints prayers to God on behalf of Colette (fig. 20).[76]

The outer left wing begins with a scene unique in art: a visit of the Holy Kinship to the Carmelites on Mount Carmel (fig. 21). It is surely meant to embody a vision devoutly wished for by contemporary Carmelites, for the Holy Kinship is represented as the altarpiece at the choir in the background, its stalls filled with Carmelites. Outside the church a procession led by a banner reading "Maria" and "Anna" encounters Anne with her daughters and children. It is as if their prayers

Fig. 15. *Anne and Joachim at Home,* from *Saint Anne Altarpiece.*
Frankfurt am Main, Historisches Museum. End of the fifteenth
century. Photo: Historisches Museum.

Fig. 16. *Presentation of the Virgin in the Temple*, from *Saint Anne Altarpiece*. Frankfurt am Main, Historisches Museum. End of the fifteenth century. Photo: Historisches Museum.

Fig. 17. *The Vision of Elijah*, from *Saint Anne Altarpiece*. Frankfurt
am Main, Historisches Museum. End of the fifteenth century.
Photo: Historisches Museum.

Fig. 18. *Saint Anne, Mother of the Immaculate Mary,* from *Saint Anne Altarpiece.* Frankfurt am Main, Historisches Museum. End of the fifteenth century. Photo: Historisches Museum.

Fig. 19. *The Vision of Saint Colette,* from *Saint Anne Altarpiece.*
Frankfurt am Main, Historisches Museum. End of the fifteenth
century. Photo: Historisches Museum.

Fig. 20. *Saint Colette's Devotion to the Holy Kinship,* from *Saint Anne Altarpiece.* Frankfurt am Main, Historisches Museum. End of the fifteenth century. Photo: Historisches Museum.

Fig. 21. *Saint Anne and Her Family Visit the Carmelites,* from *Saint Anne Altarpiece.* Frankfurt am Main, Historisches Museum. End of the fifteenth century. Photo: Historisches Museum.

had brought the altarpiece to life before their eyes and would seem, therefore, to offer a model of imaginative devotion to the viewer of the altarpiece. The next panel, illustrating three miracles of Elisha (fig. 22), has no direct reference to Saint Anne but reminds the viewer of the miraculous powers of one of the great founders of the Carmelite order. Below is represented a miracle of Saint Anne that shows her as the patron saint of women in childbirth (fig. 23). The story begins with a Hungarian youth, Procopius, whose initial successes in life gave way to such difficulties that he became a hermit. Having developed a great devotion to Saint Anne, he insisted that a golden necklace he discovered while digging a well be made into coins bearing the image of Anne. The king of Hungary complied and gave the first coin to his queen, who, alone in the woods when her labor began, called upon Anne and gave birth without difficulty. The king rewarded Procopius by making him an archbishop, and Procopius thanked Saint Anne by building churches, chapels, and monasteries in her honor. The key episodes of this tale are illustrated in the rather crowded painting. Finally, another female saint who, like Colette, experienced a vision of Anne is shown in the last panel (fig. 24). Seated in her study and intent on her reading, Bridget offers a model of devotion to the pious woman viewing the altarpiece. Her devotion is rewarded with the vision of Anne with the Virgin and Child that appears in the upper right. The vision implies that Anne will watch over Bridget even at her death, to which the scene directly below the vision refers.

Humanism and the Reformation

The great range of Anne's appeal as illustrated in the Frankfurt altarpiece would seem to have guaranteed that her cult would flourish in perpetuity, and indeed Anne remains an important saint in the Roman Catholic church, with special centers of devotion in Brittany and Canada. However, certain aspects of her cult were sharply curtailed. At the same time that the Frankfurt altarpiece was being made, humanists such as the German Trithemius and the French Lefevre d'Etaples became convinced that there was no historical basis for the *trinubium*.[77] Reformers eventually joined them, forcing Catholics to the defense. Thus Dr. Johannes Eck (1486–1543), professor at Ingolstadt, defended the *trinubium* when it was attacked by Luther. Finally,

Fig. 22. *Miracles of Elisha*, from *Saint Anne Altarpiece*. Frankfurt am
Main, Historisches Museum. End of the fifteenth century.
Photo: Historisches Museum.

Fig. 23. *Miracle of Saint Anne*, from *Saint Anne Altarpiece*. Frankfurt am Main, Historisches Museum. End of the fifteenth century. Photo: Historisches Museum.

Fig. 24. *Saint Bridget's Vision of Saint Anne,* from *Saint Anne Altarpiece.* Frankfurt am Main, Historisches Museum. End of the fifteenth century. Photo: Historisches Museum.

the Council of Trent (1545–63) forbade the *trinubium,* and the Holy Kinship disappeared as a subject in art late in the sixteenth century. The Council of Trent also had an impact on Anne's relation to the doctrine of the Immaculate Conception. The Council of Trent did not actually define the doctrine. However, the council's insistence in 1546 that the Virgin Mary was not included in the decree concerning original sin and that the constitutions of Sixtus IV were still valid obviously favored the Immaculate Conception, and works of art representing the Virgin of the Immaculate Conception appeared in great numbers in the seventeenth and eighteenth centuries. The council, however, reduced Anne's role, referring to the "misplaced devotion" that saw her as selected by God to be mother to the Virgin before the beginning of time. Thus Anne's status after the council was significantly diminished.

In the early sixteenth century Anne was especially popular in the lands where reformers were gaining ground. Martin Luther exemplifies the transition that reformers experienced in their attitudes toward Anne. In 1505, when Luther decided to become a monk, his vow was made to Anne, and he entered a monastery that had a brotherhood devoted to her.[78] First attacking the excesses of the church but preserving many of its doctrines, Luther in 1519 decried the dissolute practices of brotherhoods, not those whom they honored: "What have the names of Our Lady, St. Anne, St. Sebastian, or other saints to do with your brotherhoods, in which you have nothing but gluttony, drunkenness, useless squandering of money, howling, yelling, chattering, dancing, and wasting of time? . . . Although there is no day which is not dishonored by such doings, at least the festivals and the names of the saints should be spared."[79] Similarly, Luther encouraged the use of several traditional biblical themes in the visual arts, but with new interpretations.[80] By 1525, however, Luther had rejected all legendary material regarding the Virgin, which, of course, included all material regarding Anne.[81] Now the name of Anne still came easily to his lips, but only to be denounced. By 1530, in his "Exhortation to All Clergy Assembled at Augsburg," Luther could refer to "the idol [*Abgott*] St. Anne."[82] And in 1537 and 1538 Luther denounced "our false reliance on the saints and our idolatrous worship of them. . . . How many people sacrificed for St. Anne, although it is not certain whether such a person ever existed?"[83] Nonetheless, in 1543, struggling to create a genealogy for the Holy Family, Luther had to allow that a person who was Mary's mother was also Elizabeth's sister, "whom we want to allow to be Anne, as she is called everywhere."[84]

Thus our study of Anne has come full circle. For Protestants she became once again "the anonymous maternal grandmother of Jesus." Catholics continue to revere her as the mother of the Virgin, but her cult has never again reached the heights to which it soared around 1500, when she was a central figure both in the Holy Kinship and in the Immaculate Conception.

Saint Anne as Cultural Symbol in the Late Middle Ages

The story of Saint Anne was created to fill gaps in the biblical narrative; it was then given authority by theological discussions on matters of dogma; and finally it was absorbed into popular social practices of the late Middle Ages and early Renaissance. During the period from about 1350 to 1550, but especially from 1450 to 1550, Saint Anne became a cultural symbol of immense authority. The flourishing of the cult of Saint Anne calls for an explanation. Although this volume represents a broad range of fields, its narrow focus on Saint Anne is deliberate, for interdisciplinary approaches to a single figure can tell us much about the range of cultural roles she performed and give us access to this historically specific culture. In other words, we are using Saint Anne as a prism through which late medieval society may be refracted.

Among the cultural roles Anne performed are several directly linked to the narrative of her life, most importantly her function as intercessor for married women and mothers. Stephen Wilson comments that certain saints were known as "marrying saints," among them Saint Anne.[85] Jan van Denemarken's 1499 version of *Die historie van Sint-Anna* contains an extensive collection of examples showing that Anne offered particular protection to married people and knew how to convert poverty into marital prosperity.[86] She also promoted fertility on the basis of her miraculous conception of Mary in her old age. Juan de Robles's account of the miracles of Saint Anne (1511) describes a shrine at Tendilla, Spain, where "Saint Anne of Tendilla

rendered sterile women fertile."[87] Gail Gibson's essay fleshes out the
Spanish truism with an intimate portrait of fifteenth-century merchant families from East Anglia, for whom prayers to Saint Anne
were not empty devotional exercises but urgent pleas for offspring.
As mother saints, both the Virgin and her mother, Anne, were seen
as "particularly appropriate helpers for mothers with sick and injured
children."[88]

Metaphorically, too, Anne's *vita* stimulated a variety of visual and
verbal responses. In Francesca Sautman's essay the complex associations between Saint Anne and wood in folk and craft traditions are
richly explored. The noncanonical legend of Anne as the child abandoned in an eagle's nest and raised by a deer is connected not only to
many folklore motifs of wilderness but also to the theological symbol
of the sacred family tree that gives rise to Jesus and the apostles. As
a mystical symbol of creation from the living tree, Saint Anne was
patron of woodworkers.

From the most concrete to the most metaphorical level, Saint Anne
was associated with the idea of genealogy. She was mother and grandmother, founder of a sacred family tree, symbol of fertility and thus
the continuity of the generations. Pamela Sheingorn's essay examines
one of the chief images of Anne and her extended family, the Holy
Kinship group. Sheingorn argues that such images could negotiate
the shifts in the definition of the family that were taking place in the
fifteenth and sixteenth centuries. The family portrayed in the earliest
Holy Kinship pictures was clearly matrilineal, and, she notes, it is
tempting to read them as conscious rebuttals of the patriarchal Tree
of Jesse, which traced the lineage of Jesus through Joseph rather than
through Mary and Anne. Later representations of the Holy Kinship
cited by Sheingorn show a nuclear-family grouping, while still later
images give prominence to the husbands and fathers, especially in
their roles as educators of male children. Examination of images such
as the Holy Kinship as they change through time thus gives us access
to important shifts in gender roles and the formation of the family in
the early modern period.

In addition to functions growing out of her *vita,* Saint Anne took
on many of the tasks saints were expected to perform in late medieval
culture. For example, she was invoked in time of plague; prayers before an image of Saint Anne could give protection against the plague.[89]

Cures were sought at her shrines, and she was often the patron of a good death. A late-fifteenth-century French prayer (found in manuscripts from Rouen, Nantes, Paris, and Tours) calls on Anne "ma tres chere mere" for a kind of domino effect of spiritual benefits: she is to beg her daughter to ask her grandson to give the petitioner comfort at death—"memoire de la sure mort, et aprés celle mortelle vie, puissons estre en sa compagnie." [90]

Powers were often attributed to her because of events that had happened on her feast day, July 26. As happened with many saints, notable or catastrophic events taking place on Anne's day led to the institution of processions, feasts, or vigils, and Saint Anne's Day was marked by such commemorative rituals in many places. The villagers of Brea (near Madrid), noting that it had hailed several years in a row on Saint Anne's Day, took a vow to observe her vigil. Possibly suffering from the same storms, the nearby village of Buges set up the custom of giving a public dinner, or *caraidad,* on Saint Anne's Day. [91] Elsewhere in Spain, loggers sending timber from the mountains of Cuenca down the Guadiela River were amazed to see a log stand upright and burst into flame. In response to this sign, the mayors of many surrounding villages prudently decided to observe Saint Anne's Day as a nonworking holiday. The village of Argamasilla de Alba also read the signs: "It was vowed to observe Saint Anne's Day because in this town people used to work on that day, and it came to pass that several of those who worked on that day died." [92]

The essay by Roger Crum and David Wilkins in this volume traces the iconography of Anne as political symbol of the Florentine revolt against Walter of Brienne, which occurred on Saint Anne's Day, July 26, 1343. An altar in her honor was established within Orsanmichele, a civic building then under construction, and later an oratory chapel for her worship was built opposite Orsanmichele. In paintings as well, the image of Anne seems to have functioned to remind Florentines of the threat of tyranny. As Richard Trexler points out, however, the celebration of Saint Anne's Day in Florence after 1343 was a political statement made by only part of Florentine society, the merchant elite, who were commemorating their power over the artisan or working classes, who had been the chief supporters of Walter of Brienne. [93] It may not be totally accidental that Saint Anne tended to be appropriated by the wealthy bourgeoisie who formed the patrician oligarchies of many late medieval towns, for Anne and her husband, Joachim, were understood to be members of that class.

Part of the cult of any popular saint in the late Middle Ages was patronage of individuals with the same name. A. N. Galpern has given an example of how the name saint was to work:

> At Ervy, southwest of Troyes, an elderly donor had himself represented in a stained-glass window depicting the baptism of Christ, which he gave to the parish church about 1510. His name saint is with him. The saint has his hand on the old man's shoulder and his eye on someone in front and above him whom the window does not show. In the corresponding panel on the right, Saint Anne presents Anne the donor's wife to the unseen figure, while the woman's five daughters look on. . . . The essential function of the name saint, then, was to protect his dependents beyond the grave, and to intercede for them with the powers above.[94]

The function of intercession is also implied by a full page of illustrations of Saint Anne's three marriages in the *Bedford Hours,* commissioned by John of Lancaster, duke of Bedford, on his marriage to Anne of Burgundy in 1434. The largest painting, at the center of the page, is of Anne, the duchess of Bedford, kneeling in devotion before a large, seated Saint Anne beside whom stand the much smaller figures of her daughter, Mary, and grandson, Christ.[95] Many of the essays in this volume testify to the potent bond between individuals named Anne and Saint Anne. According to Myra Orth, even at the moment when the traditional narrative of Saint Anne and the *trinubium* was under severe attack by humanists at the French court, the patronage of Saint Anne was invoked for Queen Anne of Brittany.

Saintly patronage was extended not just to individuals or families but also to corporate groups such as brotherhoods. In towns most people belonged to several confraternities or brotherhoods, which had devotional, social, and charitable functions as well as craft or civic affiliations. Saint Anne was a popular patron of such organizations, perhaps because her status as a bourgeois wife and mother rendered her a particularly appropriate role model for confraternity members who were also in the comfortable, married, pious middle class.

The Saint Anne altarpiece described in part 2 of our Introduction was commissioned by a brotherhood of Saint Anne that met in the Carmelite monastery in Frankfurt, although its membership was pri-

marily composed of laymen, humanists, and merchants. Ton Brandenbarg makes a strong argument that Saint Anne was "the ideal model
of a spouse, mother and widow fitting into the pattern of norms and
values of the urban middle class. . . . In many ways she reflected the
ideals of the urban middle class."[96] Kathleen Ashley's essay argues that
the image of Anne in the N-Town plays fits the ideology of such a lay
religious guild. In N-Town, Anne represents godly wedlock in contrast to her role in two other late medieval plays, the Huy *Nativity* and
the Digby *Candelmas and Killing of the Children*. The latter plays present
Saint Anne in terms that suit their quite different social contexts; the
Anne that figures in the convent play from Huy, Belgium, is a wise
matriarch who instructs her daughters how to "read" the infant body
of Christ in the language of affective devotion, while the function of
Saint Anne to the town festival in East Anglia seems to be the representation of gender difference. Brandenbarg's argument that Anne
reflected the ideals of the middle class is too reductive for such a central
cultural symbol as Saint Anne. Certainly she could model middle-
class values, but she was equally available to the aristocracy for their
dynastic agendas. Francesca Sautman's essay also describes Saint Anne
as patron of carpenters on the basis of her mystical connection to trees
and wood, rather than her social exemplarity. Finally, ecclesiastical
patronage of Saint Anne should not be overlooked. The Carmelites,
in particular, had woven the story of Anne's birth to Emerentiana
and the iconography of the Holy Kinship into the history of their
order. The extensive altarpiece on Saint Anne was commissioned for
a Carmelite chapel, and the Huy *Nativity,* which dramatized the Holy
Kinship group of Anne and her three daughters, was written by a nun
in a Carmelite convent.

Whether or not we wish to engage class, gender, or institutional
ideology, images such as those of Saint Anne have no single essential "meaning" and certainly do not bear an unproblematic relation
to viewers' socioeconomic status or physiological sex. Indeed, the research and analyses in this Introduction and the essays that follow support a view of gender, for example, as a metaphor whose referent may
vary depending on who uses it, in what context, and who receives it.[97]
Saint Anne is a sign with shifting signifiers in late medieval culture.

We would suggest that the cult of Anne flourished in the fifteenth
and early sixteenth centuries precisely because her image has such a

range of possibilities, so that she could function symbolically to articulate the dilemmas and mediate the contradictions of the culture. Her power as a mediating symbol comes from the "fit" between her *vita* and the dilemmas of the period. As the matriarch of a multigenerational holy family, she was available to authorize the dynastic claims among rulers whose power was contested or the genealogical preoccupations of the bourgeoisie and, indeed, to represent the substantial benefits to be gained (in heaven as well as on earth) from being part of a large and well-connected family. As the miraculously pregnant older woman, she was a potent symbol of fertility. As the wife of Joachim, she represented holy wedlock to all those in the society who would not choose celibacy. As the thrice-married woman, she could be a site for working out the culture's ambivalence about the value of the active life and the changing roles of women. As the mother of Mary and the grandmother of Christ and the apostles, she modeled affective behaviors to a culture beginning to develop an ideology of the family.

Anne, more than any other saint who was popular during the late Middle Ages, embodied ideas of kinship, of connection, and of relationship. It is not surprising, therefore, that Saint Anne should prove so useful a mediating symbol for a culture whose major ideological and institutional formations were being profoundly reshaped. Validated by her holy status, Saint Anne represented new ways of thinking and new ways of behaving that were at odds with the dominant patterns of the early Middle Ages. Yet as connector, mediator, mother, kin, Anne represents the assurance that the new structures would cohere and would yield even richer benefits to those who lived within them.

APPENDIX: THE BOOK OF JAMES

1. *1*. In the "Histories of the Twelve Tribes of Israel" Joachim was a very rich (man), and he brought all his gifts for the Lord twofold; for he said in himself; What I bring in excess, shall be for the whole people, and what I bring for forgiveness [of my sins] shall be for the Lord, for a propitiation for me.

2. Now the great day of the Lord drew near, and the children of Israel were bringing their gifts. Then they stood before him, and Reubel [Reuben] also, saying: "It is not fitting for you to offer your gifts first, because you have begotten no offspring in Israel." *3*. Then Joachim became very sad, and went to the record of the twelve tribes of the people [and said]: "I have searched whether I am the only one who has not begotten offspring in Israel, and I have found of all the righteous that they had raised up offspring in Israel. And I remembered the patriarch Abraham that in his last days God gave him a son, Isaac." *4*. And Joachim was very sad, and did not show himself to his wife, but betook himself into the wilderness; there he pitched his tent and fasted *forty days and forty nights;* and he said to himself; "I shall not go down either for food or for drink until the Lord my God visits me; prayer shall be my *food* and drink."

2. *1*. Meanwhile Anna his wife uttered a twofold lamentation and gave voice to a twofold bewailing:

> "I will bewail my widowhood,
> and bewail my childlessness."

2. Now the great day of the Lord drew near, and Euthine [Judith] her maid-servant said to her: "How long do you humble your soul, since the great day of the Lord is near, and you ought not to mourn. But take this headband, which the mistress of the work gave me; it is not fitting for me to wear it, because I am [your] slave and it bears a royal mark."

3. But Anna said: "Away from me! I did not do this. It is the Lord who has greatly humbled me. Who knows whether a deceiver did not give it to you, and you have come to make me share in your sin!" Euthine [Judith] answered: "Why should I curse you because you have not listened to me? The Lord God has *shut up your womb,* to give you no fruit in Israel."

4. And Anna was very sad; but she put off her mourning garments, cleansed her head, put on her bridal garments, and about the ninth hour went into her garden to walk there. And she saw a laurel tree and sat down beneath it and implored the Lord, saying: "O God of our fathers, bless me and hear my prayer, as thou didst bless the womb of Sarah [our mother Sarah] and gavest her a son, Isaac."

3. *1*. And Anna sighed towards heaven, and saw a nest of sparrows in the laurel tree and immediately she made lamentation within herself:

> "Woe to me, who begot me,
> What womb brought me forth?
> For I was born as a curse before them all and before the children of
>   Israel,
> And I was reproached, and they mocked me and thrust me out of
>   the temple of the Lord.
> *2*. Woe is me, to what am I likened?
> I am not likened to the birds of the heaven;

for even the birds of the heaven are fruitful before thee, O Lord.
Woe is me, to what am I likened?
I am not likened to the unreasoning [dumb] animals;
for even the unreasoning [dumb] animals are fruitful before thee, O
  Lord.
Woe is me, to what am I likened?
I am not likened to the beasts of the earth;
for even the beasts of the earth are fruitful before thee, O Lord.

  3. Woe is me, to what am I likened?
I am not likened to these waters;
for even these waters gush forth merrily, and their fish praise thee,
  O Lord.
Woe is me, to what am I likened?
I am not likened to this earth;
for even this earth *brings forth its fruit in its season* and praises thee, O
  Lord."

4. *1*. And *behold an angel of the Lord came to her* and said: "Anna, Anna, *the
Lord has heard your prayer. You shall conceive and bear,* and your offspring shall be
spoken of in the whole world." And Anna said: "*As the Lord my God lives,* if I
bear a child, whether male or female, I will *bring it as a gift to the Lord my God,*
and it shall *serve him all the days of its life.*"

  2. And behold there came two messengers, who said to her: "Behold,
Joachim your husband is coming with his flocks; for an angel of the Lord
came down to him and said to him: 'Joachim, Joachim, the Lord God has *heard
your prayer.* Go down; behold, your wife Anna has conceived [*shall conceive*].' "
3. And Joachim went down and called his herdsmen and said: "Bring me ten
lambs without blemish and without spot; they shall belong to the Lord my
God. And bring me twelve [tender] calves for the priests and elders, and a
hundred kids for the whole people." *4*. And behold Joachim came with his
flocks, and Anna stood at the gate and saw Joachim coming and ran immediately and hung on his neck, saying: "Now I know that the Lord God has
greatly blessed me; for behold the widow is no longer a widow, and I, who
was childless, have conceived [shall conceive]."

  And Joachim rested the first day in his house.

  5. *1*. But the next day he offered his gifts, saying in himself: "If the Lord
God is gracious to me the frontlet of the priest will make it clear to me."

  And Joachim offered his gifts, and observed the priest's frontlet when he
went up to the altar of the Lord; and he saw no sin in himself. And Joachim
said: "Now I know that the Lord God is gracious to me and has forgiven all
my sins." And *he went down* from the temple of the Lord *justified, and went to
his house.*

2. And her six months [her months] were fulfilled, as (the angel) had said: in the seventh [ninth] month Anna brought forth. And she said to the midwife: "What have I brought forth?" And she said: "A female." And Anna said: "*My soul* is magnified this day." And she lay down. And when the days were fulfilled, Anna purified herself from her childbed and gave suck to the child, and called her Mary.

6. 1. Day by day the child *waxed strong;* when she was six months old her mother stood her on the ground to try if she could stand. And she walked [twice] seven steps and came to her bosom. And she took her up, saying: "*As the Lord my God lives,* you shall no more walk upon this ground until I take you into the temple of the Lord." And she made a sanctuary in her bedchamber, and did not permit anything common or unclean to pass through it. And she summoned the undefiled daughters of the Hebrews, and they cared for her amusement.

2. On the child's first birthday, Joachim made a *great feast,* and invited the chief priests and the priests and the scribes and the elders and the whole people of Israel. And Joachim brought the child to the priests, and they blessed her saying: "O God of our fathers, bless this child and give her a name renowned for ever *among all generations.*" And all the people said: "So be it, [so be it,] Amen." And they brought her to the chief priests, and they blessed her, saying: "O God of the heavenly heights, look upon this child and bless her with a supreme and unsurpassable blessing." And her mother carried her into the sanctuary of her bedchamber and gave her suck. And Anna sang this song to the Lord God:

> "I will sing praises to the Lord my God,
> for he has visited me and *taken away from me the reproach* of my enemies.
> And the Lord gave me the *fruit of righteousness,* unique and manifold
>   before him.
> Who will proclaim to the sons of Reubel [Reuben] that Anna gives
>   suck?
> [Hearken, hearken, you twelve tribes of Israel: Anna gives suck."]

And she laid the child down to rest in the bedchamber with its sanctuary, and went out and served them. When the feast was ended they went down rejoicing and glorifying the God of Israel.

7. 1. The months passed, and the child grew. When she was two years old, Joachim said to Anna: "Let us bring her up to the temple of the Lord, that we may fulfil the promise which we made, lest the Lord send (some evil) upon us and our gift become unacceptable." And Anna replied: "Let us wait until the third year, that the child may then no more long after her father and mother." And Joachim said: "Very well." 2. And when the child was three years old,

Joachim said: "Let us call the undefiled daughters of the Hebrews, and let each one take a lamp, and let these be burning, in order that the child may not turn back and her heart be enticed away from the temple of the Lord." And he did so until they went up to the temple of the Lord. And the priest took her and kissed her and blessed her, saying: "The Lord has magnified your name among all generations; because of you the Lord at the end of the days will manifest his redemption to the children of Israel." *3.* And he placed her on the third step of the altar, and the Lord God put grace upon the child, and she danced for joy with her feet, and *the whole house of Israel loved her.*

8. *1.* And her parents went down wondering, praising and glorifying the almighty God because the child did not *turn back* [to them]. And Mary was in the temple nurtured like a dove and received food from the hand of an angel.

NOTES

1. Two recent collections of essays both describe and assess the impact of this approach: Hunt, *New Cultural History,* and Veeser, *New Historicism.*

2. Conway, Bourque, and Scott, *Learning about Women,* Introduction, xxix. See also Showalter, *Speaking of Gender.*

3. For the assertion that the New Historicism has its roots in "the women's movement and the feminist theory and feminist scholarship which grew from it" (153), see Newton, "History as Usual?" 152–67.

4. For a group of essays that address the issue of the impact of gender studies on the disciplines, see O'Barr, *Women and a New Academy.*

5. For surveys of the public/private dichotomy, beginning with the Greeks, see Okin, *Women in Western Political Thought,* and Elshtain, *Public Man, Private Woman.* In a discussion of three recent feminist studies of nineteenth-century culture, Judith Newton comments: "In one basic way at least each of these books breaks with the ideological division of the world into 'public' and 'private,' man and woman, class and gender, and so works within a central insight of feminist theory, that public and private are not separate but intersecting" ("History as Usual?" 156).

6. Neuschel, "Creating a New Past," 16.

7. See, for example, the essays in Armstrong and Tennenhouse, *Ideology of Conduct.*

8. Showalter, *New Feminist Criticism,* 262.

9. Rose, *Women in the Middle Ages and the Renaissance,* xvii, xxii; see also essays by Joan Ferrante, Elaine Tuttle Hansen, and Michelle Freeman in Erler and Kowaleski, *Women and Power in the Middle Ages.*

10. Ferguson, Quilligan, and Vickers, eds., *Rewriting the Renaissance,* xxii.

11. Spelman, *Inessential Woman.*

12. See Turner, *Forest of Symbols,* and the discussion in Bynum, "Introduction: The Complexity of Symbols," 1–20.

13. Miles, *Image as Insight,* especially 82–93.

14. For general studies of Saint Anne and treatments of important aspects of her *vita,* or cult see Aurenhammer, *Lexikon der christlichen Ikonographie;* Charland, *Madame Sainte Anne* and *Le Culte de Sainte Anne;* Kleinschmidt, *Die heilige Anna;* Lafontaine-Dosogne, *Iconographie de l'enfance de la Vierge;* Lechner, "Sippe, heilige"; Künstle, *Ikonographie der christlichen Kunst;* Réau, *Iconographie;* Schaumkell, *Der Kultus der heiligen Anna;* and Schiller, *Iconographie.*

15. Delooz, "Sociological Study," 196.

16. For an English translation and references to editions of the Greek text, see Cullman, "Protevangelium of James"; see also Strycker, "La Forme." For the beginning chapters of the *Protevangelium,* which deal with Anne, see the Appendix. The excerpt is taken from Cullman, "Protevangelium of James," 374–78.

17. For a discussion of the icon in the context of Marian iconography, see Schiller, *Ikonographie,* 37–38.

18. "This feast was in origin principally a commemoration of the annunciation to Joachim and Anna of the conception of Mary, as related in the apocryphal *Protevangelium,* but it included also the miracle of the conception in a sterile pair and the passive conception of Mary" (Clayton, "Feasts," 211).

19. Our translation from Jerome, *De perpetua virginitate, adversus Helvidium,* PL 23:193–216. For a discussion of Jerome's views, see Blinzler, *Die Brüder,* 142–44.

20. Cullman, "Protevangelium of James," 368.

21. Lafontaine-Dosogne, *Iconographie de l'enfance de la Vierge* 1:25.

22. See Vailhé, "La Fête de la Vierge"; Kishpaugh, *Feast of the Presentation;* and Coleman, *Campaign for the Feast.*

23. Jugie, *L'Immaculée conception,* 135.

24. Gijsel, *Pseudo-Matthäus,* 12.

25. "It is a strange irony that this work, in which the story of Joseph's first marriage still retains its place, should have been put out as a translation attributed to Jerome, of all people" (Cullman, "Protevangelium of James," 406).

26. Gijsel, *Pseudo-Matthäus,* points to severe problems in the widely used Tischendorf edition of the Pseudo-Matthew, but Tischendorf must still be consulted since Gijsel does not provide a critical edition. See also Philippart's review of Gijsel.

27. Clayton, "Aelfric," 289.

28. For an English translation, see Hroswitha, *Nondramatic Works.* For a discussion of Hroswitha's use of the Pseudo-Matthew, see Gijsel, "Textfamilie."

29. Clayton, "Feasts," 213.

30. Nordhagen, *Frescoes,* 89.

31. Savas, *Icon and Logos,* 34; on the introduction of the cult of Anne in the West, see Lampen, "Vereering der H. Moeder Anna," and Bannister, "Cultus of St. Anne."

32. For illustration, see Croce, *Biblioteca sanctorum,* fig. 1272.

33. The failure of the sermon to mention Anne leads de Gaiffier to suggest that it predates the *trinubium:* "N'est-ce pas pour expliquer que les 'trois Marie' étaient soeurs, qu'est née la légende du *Trinubium Annae?*" ("Le Trinubium," 298).

34. Haymo, *Historiae,* cols. 823–24. Earlier scholarship gives this document to Haymo of Halberstadt (d. 853). De Gaiffier makes a rather tentative re-attribution to Haymo of Auxerre, whose commentaries are dated to 849–60. He also reproduces the relevant passage.

35. Fulbert, "In ortu," col. 526.

36. Clayton, "Feasts," 226.

37. "The feast of the Conception of Mary (not the Immaculate Conception) was introduced in England c. 1030 (not, as Wrenn states, c. 1000), as a commemoration of the events surrounding Mary's conception in the apocryphal accounts of this, not to make a doctrinal point. It commemorated the angel's appearance to Joachim and Anna and his annunciation of Mary's birth. There is no suggestion in any pre-Conquest text that Mary was preserved free of original sin; this idea was formulated for the first time by Eadmer in the twelfth century" (Clayton, "Aelfric," 288).

38. Wilmart, "Les Compositions d'Osbert," 264.

39. Ibid., 261.

40. D'Ancona, *Iconography of the Immaculate Conception,* 7.

41. Ibid., 8.

42. Our translations from Peter Lombard, *Collectaneorum,* cols. 101–2.

43. Smalley, "Commentary," 38. Maurice, prior of Kirkham, an Augustinian house in Yorkshire, wrote two anti-Salomite tracts between 1161 and 1181 (James, "Salomites," 287–97).

44. For a recent discussion of this manuscript, see Morgan, *Early Gothic Manuscripts,* 1.

45. On Servatius, see Boeren, *Jocundus,* and Koldeweij, *Sente Servas.*

46. Albert, Parent, and Guillemete, "La Legende," 169, citing *Comm. in ep. ad Gal.* cap. 1, lect. 5.

47. D'Ancona, *Iconography of the Immaculate Conception,* 9.

48. The complete text is reproduced in Albert, Parent, and Guillemette, "La Legende."

49. "Nativitas gloriosae virginis Mariae ex tribu Juda et regia stirpe David

duxit originem. Matthaeus autem et Lucas non generationem Mariae, sed Joseph describunt, qui tamen a conceptione Christi penitus alienus fuit, quia consuetudo scripturae dicitur fuisse, ut non mulierum, sed virorum generationis series texeretur. Verissime tamen virgo beata ex progenie David descendit" (Jacobus, *Legenda aurea*, 585).

50. Bossy, *Christianity in the West*, 9.

51. This manuscript, formerly Berlin MS. germ. oct. 109, is now in the Jagellonian Library in Kraków, where it retains the designation MS. germ. oct. 109. For a recent description of the manuscript, see the entry (by Elisabeth Klemm) in *Regensburger Buchmalerei* (57–58). The entire cycle of illustrations, along with a modern German translation of the poem, was published in 1925 in Degering, *Des Priesters*. For a recent discussion of the illustrations, see Messerer, "Illustrationen," 447–72.

52. Degering, *Des Priesters*, 29.

53. See Plotte, *Meister Bertram*, 11–13, 19–20.

54. "L'une des plus célébres était le voile de sainte Anne dont s'enorgueillissait la cathédrale d'Apt, près d'Avignon, qui prétendait posséder le corps de la mère de la Vierge apporté en Provence par la Madeleine et son frère Lazare: ce n'est en réalité, comme le prouvent les inscriptions qu'on y a déchiffrées, qu'un tissu arabe en lin et soie, fabriqué en Egypte à la fin du XIe siècle pour un calife de la dynastie des Fatimides" (Réau, *Iconographie* 3:91). See also Danigo, "Culte de Sainte Anne."

55. Mâle, *Religious Art in France*, 317.

56. Brandenbarg, "St Anne and Her Family," 102–3.

57. Düfel, *Luthers Stellung*, 35.

58. Stéphan, "Cult of St. Anne," 75. We are grateful to Maryanne Kowaleski for supplying us with this reference.

59. Kleinschmidt, *Die heilige Anna*, 132.

60. On this manuscript, see Parkes, *Medieval Manuscripts*, 215–23, and Sandler, *Gothic Manuscripts*, cat. 146.

61. See Watson, *Playfair Hours*.

62. For a discussion of the Holy Kinship altarpiece illustrated in figure 8, see Pieper, *Die deutschen*, 293–98.

63. See Beck, "Eine frühe," and Gohr, "Anna Selbdritt." For a summary of the iconography of the Immaculate Conception and further references, see Fournée, "Immaculata Conceptio."

64. For a detailed study of the cult of Anne in one region, see the study by Carl Nagel, who concludes, "Das bunte Mosaikbild der Annenverehrung, das sich vor uns aufgetan hat, zeigt in der Vielfalt und Stärke ihrer Erscheinungen, wie die Mark [Brandenburg] auch an dieser neuen Bewegung der Volksfrömigkeit sehr kräftig teilnimmt" ("Die St.-Annen-Verehrung," 48).

65. Luther, "Sermons on the Gospel of St. John," 347. This is most probably a reference to the feast of Joachim, created and assigned to March 20 by Pope Julius II (1443–1513).

66. Réau, *Iconographie* 3:91.

67. Düfel, *Luthers Stellung,* 35.

68. Christian, *Local Religion,* 240, citing chapter 12 of Juan de Robles, *La vida y excelencias r miraglos de santa Anna y dela gloriosa nuestra señora santa Maria fasta la edad de quatorze años: Muy devota y contemplativamente copilada* (Seville: Jacobo Cromberger, 1511), BNM R/31.

69. Brandenbarg, "St Anne and Her Family," 101.

70. Both of these writers are discussed at some length in ibid.

71. Tervarent, "La Suzanne," 25–27.

72. The following interpretation of the altarpiece relies heavily, though not exclusively, on Tervarent, "Le Rétable de Sainte Anne."

73. Brandenbarg, "St. Anne and Her Family," 113–16.

74. "Tunc Ioachim accepit agnum immaculatum et dixit ad angelum: Ego non ausus essem offerre holocaustum deo, nisi tua iussio daret mihi pontificium offerendi. Et dixit ei angelus: Nec ego te ad offerendum hortarer nisi uoluntatem domini cognouissem. Factum est autem cum offerret sacrificium, simul cum odore sacrificii quasi cum fumo perrexit ad caelum" (Pseudo-Matthew 3:5, as in Gijsel, *Pseudo-Matthäus*).

75. Fournée, "Immaculata Conceptio," cols. 177–78.

76. Colette's vision of Anne is discussed at length in this volume in the essay by Kathleen Ashley.

77. For an extended discussion of the demise of the *trinubium,* see this volume's essay by Myra Orth.

78. Düfel, *Luthers Stellung,* 35.

79. Luther, "Blessed Sacrament," 68–69.

80. See Andersson, "Religiöse Bilder." See also, in this volume, the essay by Pamela Sheingorn for a discussion of a reused woodcut of the Holy Kinship by Cranach.

81. "Desgleichen fabeln und fragen haben uns unsere lerer auch gemacht, von Christi und Maria geschlecht und des narrenwercks viel mehr" (Düfel, *Luthers Stellung,* 163, quoting vol. 17, pt. 1, p. 109, l. 29 of the Weimar edition of the complete works of Luther).

82. Luther, "Exhortation," 28.

83. Luther, "Luther's Exposition," 22.

84. "Im Gegensatz dazu steht allerdings der Versuch des Reformators, bei den Auseinandersetzungen mit der Juden in der Schrift 'Vom Schem Hamphoras und vom Geschlecht Christi' (1543) dennoch eine Genealogie der heiligen Familie zu geben. Über das verwandtschaftliche Verhältnis zwischen

Maria und Elisabeth äussert Luther hier: 'Auch spricht der Engel Gabriel, Luce. I., das Elizabeth sey Marie Mume oder gefreundtin. Das kan nicht wol anders sein, denn das Marien mutter sey Elisabeth Schwester gewest, die wollen wir lassen sein Anna, wie sie uberal genennet ist'" (Düfel, *Luthers Stellung*, 163).

85. S. Wilson, *Saints and Their Cults*, 16.

86. Brandenbarg, "St Anne and Her Family," 110.

87. Christian, *Local Religion*, 245.

88. Ibid., 98.

89. Translator's note in Luther, "Personal Prayer Book, 1522," 43:11.

90. Rézeau, *Les Prières aux saints*, 31–32.

91. Christian, *Local Religion*, 33.

92. Ibid., 37–38.

93. Trexler, *Public Life*, 222.

94. Galpern, *Religions of the People*, 45.

95. Fol. 257, reproduced in Thomas, *Golden Age*, 85.

96. Brandenbarg, "St Anne and Her Family," 121.

97. For a stimulating discussion of these ideas, see Pollock, *Vision and Difference*, esp. 6–17, 30–41.

BIBLIOGRAPHY

Albert, G., J. M. Parent, and A. Guillemete. "La Légende des trois mariages de sainte Anne: Un Texte nouveau." *Etudes d'histoire, littéraire, et doctrinale du Xiiie siècle*. 1st ser. (1932): 165–84.

Anderson, Bonnie, and Judith Zinsser. *A History of Their Own: Women in Europe from Prehistory to the Present*. Vol. 1. New York: Harper and Row, 1988.

Andersson, Christiane D. "Religiöse Bilder Cranachs im Dienste der Reformation." In *Humanismus und Reformation als Kulturelle Kräfte in der Deutschen Geschichte*, ed. Lewis W. Spitz, 43–79. Veröffentlichen der Historischen Kommission zu Berlin 51. Berlin: de Gruyter, 1981.

Armstrong, Nancy, and Leonard Tennenhouse, eds. *The Ideology of Conduct: Essays in Literature and the History of Sexuality*. New York: Methuen, 1987.

Aurenhammer, Hans. *Lexikon der christlichen Ikonographie*. Vol. 1. Vienna: Hollinek, 1959–60.

Baker, Derek, ed. *Medieval Women*. Oxford: Basil Blackwell, 1978.

Bannister, H. M. "The Introduction of the Cultus of St. Anne in the West." *English Historical Review* 18 (1903): 107–12.

Beck, Herbert. "Eine frühe rheinisch-maasländische Anna Selbdritt-Gruppe im Liebighaus." *Städel-Jahrbuch* 8 (1981): 67–78.

Bell, Susan Groag. "Medieval Women Book Owners: Arbiters of Lay Piety and Ambassadors of Culture." In *Women and Power in the Middle Ages,* ed. Mary Erler and Maryanne Kowaleski, 149–87. Athens: University of Georgia Press, 1988.

Blinzler, Josef. *Die Brüder und Schwestern Jesu.* Stuttgart: Verlag Katholisches Bibelwerk, 1967.

Boeren, P. C. *Jocundus: Biographe de Saint Servais.* The Hague: Nijhoff, 1972.

Bossy, John. *Christianity in the West, 1400–1700.* Oxford: Oxford University Press, 1985.

Brandenbarg, Ton. "St Anne and Her Family: The Veneration of St Anne in Connection with Concepts of Marriage and the Family in the Early Modern Period." In *Saints and She-Devils: Images of Women in the Fifteenth and Sixteenth Centuries,* ed. Lène Dresen-Coenders, 101–27. London: Rubicon Press, 1987.

Bridenthal, Renate, Claudia Koonz, and Susan Stuard, eds. *Becoming Visible: Women in European History.* 2d ed. Boston: Houghton Mifflin, 1987.

Bynum, Caroline Walker. *Holy Feast and Holy Fast: The Religious Significance of Food to Medieval Women.* Berkeley and Los Angeles: University of California Press, 1986.

———. "Introduction: The Complexity of Symbols." In *Gender and Religion: On the Complexity of Symbols,* ed. Caroline Walker Bynum, Stevan Harrell, and Paula Richman, 1–20. Boston: Beacon Press, 1986.

Charland, Paul-Victor. *Le Culte de Sainte Anne en Occident, second période: De 1400 (environ) à nos jours.* Quebec: Imprimerie Franciscaine Missionaire, 1921.

———. *Madame sainte Anne et son culte au moyen âge.* 2 vols. Paris: Picard et Fils, 1911–13.

Christian, William A., Jr. *Local Religion in Sixteenth-Century Spain.* Princeton: Princeton University Press, 1985.

Clayton, Mary. "Aelfric and the Nativity of the Blessed Virgin Mary." *Anglia* 104 (1986): 286–315.

———. "Feasts of the Virgin in the Liturgy of the Anglo-Saxon Church." *Anglo-Saxon England* 13 (1984): 209–33.

Coleman, William E., ed. *Philippe de Mézières' Campaign for the Feast of Mary's Presentation.* Toronto: Pontifical Institute of Medieval Studies, 1981.

Conway, Jill K., Susan C. Bourque, and Joan W. Scott. *Learning about Women: Gender, Politics, and Power.* Ann Arbor: University of Michigan Press, 1989. Originally published in *Daedalus* 116 (1987).

Corstanje, Charles van, Yves Cazaux, Johan Decavele, and Albert Derolez. *Vita Sancta Coletae (1381–1447).* Leiden: Brill, 1982.

Costa, Dominique. *Sainte Anne.* Nantes: Musée Dobrée, 1966.

Croce, E. *Biblioteca sanctorum* 1:1276–95.

Cullman, Oscar. "The Protevangelium of James." In *Gospels and Related Writings,* vol. 1 of *New Testament Apocrypha,* ed. Edgar Hennecke and Wilhelm Schneemelcher, trans. R. McL. Wilson, 370–88. Philadelphia: Westminster, 1963.

D'Ancona, Mirella Levi. *The Iconography of the Immaculate Conception in the Middle Ages and Early Renaissance.* New York: College Art Association, 1957.

Danigo, J. "Le Culte de Sainte Anne." *Sanctuaires et pèlerinages* 9 (1963): 49–64.

de Gaiffier, Baudouin. "Le Trinubium Annae." *Analecta Bollandiana* 90 (1972): 289–98.

Degering, Hermann. *Des Priesters Wernher drei Lieder von der Magd.* Berlin: Wegweiser, 1925.

Delooz, Pierre. "Towards a Sociological Study of Canonized Sainthood in the Catholic Church." In *Saints and Their Cults: Studies in Religious Sociology, Folklore, and History,* ed. Stephen Wilson, 189–216. Cambridge: Cambridge University Press, 1983.

Düfel, Hans. *Luthers Stellung zur Marienverehrung.* Göttingen: Vandenhoeck and Ruprecht, 1968.

Elshtain, Jean Bethke. *Public Man, Private Woman: Women in Social and Political Thought.* Princeton: Princeton University Press, 1981.

Erler, Mary, and Maryanne Kowaleski, eds. *Women and Power in the Middle Ages.* Athens: University of Georgia Press, 1988.

Ferguson, Margaret W., Maureen Quilligan, and Nancy J. Vickers, eds. *Rewriting the Renaissance: The Discourses of Sexual Difference in Early Modern Europe.* Chicago: University of Chicago Press, 1986.

Förster, Max. "Die Legende vom Trinubium der hl. Anna." In *Probleme der englischen Sprache und Kultur: Festschrift Joh. Hoops zum 69. Geburtstag,* ed. Wolfgang Keller, Germ. Bibl. 2, 20. Heidelberg: Karl Winter, 1925.

Fournée, J. "Immaculata Conceptio." In *Lexikon der christlichen Ikonographie,* ed. Engelbert Kirschbaum, vol. 2, cols. 338–44. Freiburg: Herder, 1970.

Fulbert of Chartres. "In ortu almae virginis Mariae inviolatae." PL 141: 325–31.

Galpern, A. N. *The Religions of the People in Sixteenth-Century Champagne.* Cambridge: Harvard University Press, 1976.

Gijsel, Jan. *Die unmittelbare Textüberlieferung des sogenannte Pseudo-Matthäus.* Verhandelingen van de Koninklijke Academie voor Wetenschappen, Letteren en Schone Kunsten van Belgie. Klasse der Letteren. Vol. 43, no. 96. Brussels: Koninklijke Academie, 1981.

———. "Zu Welcher Textfamilie des Pseudo-Matthäus Gehort die Quelle von Hrotsvits Maria?" *Classica et Mediaevalia* 32 (1980): 279–88.

Gohr, Siegfried. "Anna Selbdritt." In *Die Gottesmutter: Marienbild in Rheinland und in Westfalen,* ed. Leonhard Küppers, 1:243–54. Recklinghausen: Aurel Bongers Recklinghausen, 1974.

Haymo of Auxerre. *Historiae sacrae epitome.* PL 118:817–74.

Hroswitha. *The Nondramatic Works of Hroswitha.* Trans. S. M. Gonsalva Wiegand. Saint Meinrad, Ind.: Abbey Press, 1936.

Hunt, Lynn, ed. *The New Cultural History.* Berkeley and Los Angeles: University of California Press, 1989.

Jacobus a Voragine. *Legenda aurea vulgo historia Lombardica dicta.* Ed. Th. Graesse. 1890. Reprint. Osnabrück: Zeller, 1969.

James, M. R. "The Salomites." *Journal of Theological Studies* 35 (1934): 287–97.

Jerome. *De perpetua virginitate, adversus Helvidium.* PL 23:193–216.

Jugie, Martin. *L'Immaculée Conception dans l'Écriture Sainte et dans la tradition orientale.* Rome: Officium Libri Catholici, 1952.

Kirshner, Julius, and Suzanne Wemple, eds. *Women of the Medieval World.* Oxford: Basil Blackwell, 1985.

Kishpaugh, Sister Mary Jerome. *The Feast of the Presentation of the Virgin Mary in the Temple: An Historical and Liturgical Study.* Washington, D.C.: Catholic University of America Press, 1941.

Kleinschmidt, Beda. *Die heilige Anna: Ihre Verehrung in Geschichte, Kunst und Volkstum.* Düsseldorf: Schwann, 1930.

Künstle, Karl. *Ikonographie der christlichen Kunst.* 2 vols. Freiburg: Herder, 1926.

Koldeweij, A. M. *De gude Sente Servas.* Assen: van Gorcum, 1985.

Lafontaine-Dosogne, Jacqueline. *Iconographie de l'enfance de la Vierge dans l'empire byzantin et en Occident.* 2 vols. Brussels: Académie royale de Belgique, 1964–65.

Lampen, Willibrord. "Vereering der H. Moeder Anna in de Middeleeuwen." *Historisch Tydschrift* 2 (1924): 221–43.

Lechner, M. "Sippe, heilige." In *Lexikon der christlichen Ikonographie,* ed. Engelbert Kirschbaum, vol. 4, cols. 163–68. Freiburg: Herder, 1972.

Luther, Martin. "The Blessed Sacrament of the Holy and True Body of Christ, and the Brotherhoods." Trans. Jeremiah J. Schindel, rev. E. Theodore Bachmann. In vol. 35 of *Luther's Works,* ed. E. Theodore Bachmann, 45–73. Philadelphia: Muhlenberg Press, 1960.

———. "Dr. Martin Luther's Exposition of the Fourteenth, Fifteenth, and Sixteenth Chapters of the Gospel of St. John." Trans. Martin H. Bertram. In vol. 24 of *Luther's Works,* ed. Jaroslav Pelikan. Saint Louis: Concordia Publishing House, 1961.

———. "Exhortation to All Clergy Assembled at Augsburg." Trans. Lewis W. Spitz. In vol. 34 of *Luther's Works,* ed. Lewis W. Spitz, 3–61. Philadelphia: Muhlenberg Press, 1960.

———. "Personal Prayer Book, 1522." Trans. Martin H. Bertram. In vol. 43

of *Luther's Works,* ed. Gustav K. Wiencke, 3–45. Philadelphia: Fortress Press, 1968.

———. "Sermons on the Gospel of St. John, Chapters 1–4." Trans. Martin H. Bertram. In vol. 22 of *Luther's Works,* ed. Jaroslav Pelikan. Saint Louis: Concordia Publishing House, 1957.

Mâle, Emile. *Religious Art in France: The Thirteenth Century.* Ed. Harry Bober, trans. Marthiel Matthews. Princeton: Princeton University Press, 1984.

Messerer, Wilhelm. "Illustrationen zu Wernhers 'Drei Liedern von der Magd.'" In *Deutsche Literatur im Mittelalter: Kontakte und Perspektiven, Hugo Kuhn zum Gedenken,* ed. Christoph Cormeau, 447–72. Stuttgart: J. B. Metzlersche Verlagsbuchhandlung, 1979.

Miles, Margaret. *Image as Insight: Visual Understanding in Western Christianity and Secular Culture.* Boston: Beacon Press, 1985.

Morgan, Nigel J. *Early Gothic Manuscripts, 1190–1250.* Vol. 4 of *A Survey of Manuscripts Illuminated in the British Isles.* London: Harvey Miller, 1982.

Muller, Ellen. "Saintly Virgins: The Veneration of Virgin Saints in Religious Women's Communities." In *Saints and She-Devils: Images of Women in the Fifteenth and Sixteenth Centuries,* ed. Lène Dresen-Coenders, 83–100. London: Rubicon Press, 1987.

Nagel, Carl. "Die St.-Annen-Verehrung in der Mark Brandenburg am Vorabend der Reformation." *Jahrbuch für Berlin-Brandenburgische Kirchengeschichte* 41 (1966): 30–51.

Neuschel, Kristin B. "Creating a New Past: Women and European History." In *Women and a New Academy: Gender and Cultural Contexts,* ed. Jean F. O'Barr, 8–21. Madison: University of Wisconsin Press, 1989.

Newton, Judith Lowder. "History as Usual?: Feminism and the 'New Historicism.'" In *The New Historicism,* ed. H. Aram Veeser, 152–67. New York: Routledge, Chapman, and Hall, 1988.

Nochlin, Linda, and Ann Sutherland Harris. *Women Artists, 1550–1950.* New York: Knopf, 1976.

Nordhagen, Jonas. *The Frescoes of John VII (A.D. 705–707) in S. Maria Antiqua in Rome. Acta ad Archaeologiam et Atrium Historiam Pertinentia* 3 (1968).

O'Barr, Jean F., ed. *Women and a New Academy: Gender and Cultural Contexts.* Madison: University of Wisconsin Press, 1989.

Okin, Susan Moller. *Women in Western Political Thought.* Princeton: Princeton University Press, 1979.

Parkes, M. B. *The Medieval Manuscripts of Keble College, Oxford.* London: Scholar, 1979.

Peter Lombard. *Collectaneorum in Epistolas S. Pauli. In Epistolam ad Galatas.* PL 192: 94–170.

Petroff, Elizabeth, ed. *Medieval Women's Visionary Literature.* Oxford: Oxford University Press, 1986.

Philippart, Guy. "Le *Pseudo-Matthieu* au risque de la critique textuelle." *Scriptorium* 38 (1984): 121–31.

Pieper, Paul. *Die deutschen, niederländischen, und italienischen Tafelbilder bis um 1530*. Westfälisches Landesmuseum für Kunst und Kulturgeschichte Münster. Landschaftsverband Westfalen-Lippe. Münster: Aschendorff, 1986.

Plotte, Hans. *Meister Bertram in der Hamburger Kunsthalle*. Hamburg: Kunsthalle, 1973.

Pollock, Griselda. *Vision and Difference: Femininity, Feminism, and the Histories of Art*. London: Routledge, 1988.

Réau, Louis. *Iconographie de l'art chrétien*. 3 vols. in 6 parts. Paris: Presses Universitaires de France, 1955–59.

Rézeau, Pierre. *Les Prières aux saints en français à la fin du moyen âge*. Prières a un Saint Particulier et aux Anges, vol. 2. Geneva: Librairie Droz, 1983.

Regensburger Buchmalerei. Ed. Florentine Mutherich. Munich: Prestel, 1987.

Rose, Mary Beth, ed. *Women in the Middle Ages and the Renaissance*. Syracuse: Syracuse University Press, 1986.

Sandler, Lucy Freeman. *Gothic Manuscripts, 1285–1385*. Vol. 5 of *A Survey of Manuscripts Illuminated in the British Isles*. 2 vols. London: Harvey Miller, 1986.

Savas, Daniel J. *Icon and Logos: Sources in Byzantine Iconoclasm*. Toronto: University of Toronto Press, 1986.

Schaumkell, E. *Der Kultus der heiligen Anna am Ausgange des Mittelalters*. Freiburg-Leipzig, 1893.

Schiller, Gertrud. *Ikonographie der christlichen Kunst: Maria*. Gütersloh: Gerd Mohn, 1980.

Showalter, Elaine, ed. *The New Feminist Criticism: Essays on Women, Literature, and Theory*. New York: Pantheon Books, 1985.

———, ed. *Speaking of Gender*. New York: Routledge, 1989.

Smalley, Beryl. "A Commentary on the *Hebraica* by Herbert of Bosham." *Recherches de theologie ancienne et médiévale* 18 (1951): 29–65.

Spelman, Elizabeth V. *Inessential Woman: Problems of Exclusion in Feminist Thought*. Boston: Beacon Press, 1988.

Stéphan, (Dom) John. "The Cult of St. Anne in Exeter." *Transactions of the Devonshire Association* 97 (1965): 74–76.

Strycker, Emile de. *La Forme la plus ancienne du Protévangile de Jacques*. Brussels: Société du Bollandistes, 1961.

Tervarent, Guy de. "La Suzanne du Tympan de Bergame." In *Les Enigmes de l'art du moyen âge*, 25–27. First series. Paris: Les Éditions d'Art et d'Histoire, 1938.

———. "Le Rétable de Sainte Anne au Musée de Francfort." In *Les Enigmes de l'art du moyen âge*, 35–46. Second series. Paris: Les Éditions d'Art et d'Histoire, 1941.

Thomas, Marcel. *The Golden Age: Manuscript Painting at the Time of Jean, Duke of Berry.* New York: George Braziller, 1979.

Tischendorf, Constantin. *Evangelia Apocrypha.* 2d ed. Leipzig, 1876.

Trexler, Richard. *Public Life in Renaissance Florence.* New York: Academic Press, 1980.

Tufts, Eleanor. *Our Hidden Heritage: Five Centuries of Women Artists.* New York: Paddington Press, 1974.

Turner, Victor. *The Forest of Symbols: Aspects of Ndembu Ritual.* Ithaca, N.Y.: Cornell University Press, 1967.

Vailhé, S. "La Fête de la Vierge à Jerusalem au Ve siècle." *Le Museon* 56 (1943): 1–33.

Veeser, H. Aram, ed. *The New Historicism.* New York: Routledge, Chapman, and Hall, 1988.

Watson, Rowan. *The Playfair Hours.* London: Victoria and Albert Museum, 1984.

Wilmart, André. "Les Compositions d'Osbert de Clare en l'honneur de sainte Anne." 261–86. In *Auteurs spirituels et textes dévots du moyen âge latin,* 1932. Reprint. Paris: Études Augustiniennes, 1971.

Wilson, Katharina M., ed. *Medieval Women Writers.* Athens: University of Georgia Press, 1984.

Wilson, Stephen, ed. *Saints and Their Cults: Studies in Religious Sociology, Folklore, and History.* Cambridge: Cambridge University Press, 1983.

Saint Anne in Folk Tradition

Late Medieval France

FRANCESCA SAUTMAN

olk culture and, in particular, folk religion are a rich field of human experience in which attitudes toward health, work, family, nature, time, and the hereafter are not easily separated but, rather, intersect and inform each other. The cult of the saints plays a major role in such a culture, providing the community with specific protectors for places, crops, and professions and intercessors for the entire range of human illness.

In this context, it is to be expected that the grandmother of Christ would be invoked with great fervor and that her patronage would extend to a variety of areas. Because Saint Anne is a relative latecomer to medieval religious practices, her popular cult may seem less widespread than her position in the Christic family tree would suggest. Nevertheless, it is quite considerable and presents the very interesting characteristic of being one of the most coherent and, in some areas, such as the Celtic domain, the most syncretic of hagiographic cults.

Saint Anne's cult and imagery are excellent examples of how folk culture apprehended a profoundly abstract notion: Time. It is through figures such as Anne that the ever-waning quality of human life and the harsh reality of the irreversible passing and disappearing of things are made more familiar and less threatening and, on the symbolic plane, are eventually conquered. Anne's late childbearing through divine intervention is the most powerful element in that portrayal. However, all her other functions, as patron of women in childbirth, of woodworkers, seamstresses, and seafarers, her connection to mines, to the grapevine, to water points and the tenuous regulation of drought, generated by a combination of elements from her *vita* and her place in the calendar, as well as her powerful genealogical associations, all have significant symbolic content and connect remarkably well with each other.

Examining the different areas in which Saint Anne's cult operated enables one not only to document its particular aspects but also to present a clear example of the manner in which the cult of the saints in the Middle Ages was not a haphazard, arbitrary, and fanciful medley of unrelated fragments, a judgment that reflects our twentieth-century biases rather than truly grasps the paramount role of symbolic thinking in past cultures.

To undertake this task, we will have to base ourselves largely on Saint Anne's *vita*. Her legend was widely known throughout the Middle Ages in several traditions that center around her belatedly fertile marriage to Joachim. These have been discussed extensively elsewhere and will not be elaborated on here.[1]

Yet there is another, less well known variant of Saint Anne's *vita* that is very relevant to the study of popular manifestations of her cult. A bizarre French text known as *Le Romanz de Saint Fanuel et de Sainte Anne et de Nostre Dame et de Nostre Seigneur et de ses Apostres,*[2] which is preserved in manuscripts of the thirteenth and fourteenth centuries, gives details of the ancestry and birth of Saint Anne that are not taken up in any established tradition. The longtime devotee of Saint Anne's cult, the Abbé Charland, discards these details as mere "merveilleux grotesque."[3] A close scrutiny of the text shows, however, that the story of Saint Fanuel is important because it corresponds to numerous folktale themes and motifs.

It tells us that Saint Anne was never "d'ome engenree." She had no biological mother, and Saint Fanuel (whose name must derive from Phanuel, father of Anne the Prophetess, in Luke 2:36–38) assumed that role: "La porta si longuement / Si com mere fait son enfant."[4]

This legend begins in Abraham's orchard, near Jerusalem, where there is a shoot from the Tree of Life given to him by God after God removed it from the Garden of Eden. On that stem blooms a flower so beautiful that it defies description, a flower guarded daily by an angel. When the tree was planted in Abraham's orchard, God appeared to him explaining the mystery of the tree and of its destiny:

Tu as .i. arbre plante chi,
Ge i serai crucifiez
Et escopis et laidengiez
Si i serai covert de sanc
Qui descendra aval mon flanc
Et de ceste flor ci naistra
.i. chevalier qui portera
La mere a icele pucele,
Dont Jhesu Crist fera s'ancele.[5]

One day Abraham's lovely twelve-year-old daughter walks in the garden. Seeing the splendid flower, she cannot refrain from picking it, but the flower

geta si grant our
que del flair que ele geta
la pucelete en engroissa.[6]

The parents are infuriated at their pregnant daughter, but the innocent, cognizant of divine matters, maintains that she remains a virgin and faces the stake. Covered with flowers and surrounded by birds, she is vindicated and gives birth to Fanuel.

Fanuel grows to be a pious, righteous man. He owns apples of such virtue that they are capable of curing any sick person, even a leper, who tastes them. One day King Fanuel is peeling apples to feed the sick and, finding a bit of juice left on the knife, he casually wipes it on his thigh. A new marvel takes place: the holy man's thigh "engroissa," causing him much pain, which all the doctors of the land cannot explain. He eventually gives birth, so to speak, to a girl named Anne. Horrified by such an aberration, he orders a faithful servant to take her to the woods and kill her. As the knight prepares to do his duty, a dove rests on his shoulder and tells him of the girl's wondrous destiny. Frightened, he disposes of her in the nearest place: an empty eagle's nest.

Time passes, and the child Anne reaches the age of ten, raised by a magnificent deer whose antlers are budding with flowers. The king goes out hunting with his retinue, and his seneschal, Joachim, chases down the deer. As he prepares to strike it, little Anne enjoins him from her treetop not to touch the deer and identifies herself:

> Anne, dist el, m'apele hon,
> et si sui grant et parcreue
> je ne vi onques le mien pere
> mes ge voi cha venir ma mere
> Dites li tost que vieigne a mi
> si me mete jus de cest ni.[7]

When the mother in question, namely, Fanuel, appears, Anne re-iterates her command, and, charmed by her beauty and wisdom, the seneschal, Joachim, asks to marry her. From here on the story follows the tradition of the *Protevangelium*.[8]

The folklore analogues in this story are so numerous and so suggestive that they can only be alluded to briefly here. First, the story contradicts the Christian conception of the Virgin Birth by ascribing it in an unorthodox manner to one other than the Virgin Mary. This was a theological issue raised about Saint Anne since some claimed that she bore Mary without her husband.[9] Instead it follows the non-Christian theme of the miraculous birth of the hero (motif T510) expressed in a number of folktale motifs,[10] such as conception through smelling a flower (T532.1.1) or eating an apple (T511.1.1, D1347.1), which also have a wonderful curative power (D1338.3.1, D1342.2, and D1500.1.5.1). The judgment of the innocent mother-to-be is a favorite theme in hagiography as well as romance; we find it in the life of Saint Fursy[11] and in the story of Merlin, whose popularity is roughly contemporary with our legend. Both Fursy and Merlin are Celtic, and miraculous births are frequent in Celtic folklore; thus a good question for further study is whether or not folk motifs show that the Fanuel story, in spite of its biblical setting, is of Celtic character.

Most striking is the resemblance of our story to folktale type 705,[12] where a king's son finds a speechless maiden in a bird's nest and marries her, but their children are stolen away, and he rejects her. He then must solve the riddle "A fish was my father, a man was my mother," whose answer is that a man eats a magic fish meant for his wife, becomes pregnant, and has a girl child cut out of his knee (Scandinavian, Slavic, Irish, Greek, German). It is not unrelated to a particularly important tale type, already well attested to in the Middle Ages: type T706, "The Mannekinne," or "Maiden without Hands,"[13] in which the young woman is very often discovered by her future husband in a tree (N711.1). The order to kill an unwanted child or disliked relative and the servant's last-minute remorse are familiar to us from the Oedipus story, Boccaccio's "Ginevra," and Perrault's "Sleeping Beauty," as well as from numerous folktales (K512.2.2).

Anne's confinement to a tree is linked to the crucial medieval theme of the wild man, a creature human in appearance but extraordinarily hairy and strong, whose animal "other" or double was the bear[14] and who was often associated, in text and in iconography, with a deer. There are several medieval stories in which this connection appears, the main one being the life of Merlin,[15] where the enchanter is wild man–deer and lives in "Esplumoir," or bird's nest castle. In other, less well-known texts, an abandoned child is brought up or accompanied by a deer.[16] Wild people also existed in tree-climbing form and even in bird form, inverting Plato's axiom that "man is a bipede without feathers."[17] The most illustrious example is, of course, Nebuchadnezzar, whose premonitory dream was fulfilled when he became a wild creature, growing eagle feathers and birds' talons: "And he was driven away from among men, and did eat grass like an ox, and his body was wet with the dew of heaven ["et rore caeli corpus eius infectum est"]; till his hairs grew like the feathers of eagles, and his nails like birds' claws" (Dan. 4:30).

The work of French ethnologist Claude Gaignebet has shed the most light on this figure, showing that the fall into wildness is usually a sign of punishment and mark of pollution, in Nebuchadnezzar's case underscored by the choice of the Latin "infectum est" in the Vulgate.[18] This state is also linked to the calendar and to time in reverse, as the wild man of myth and folklore appears at certain periods of the year, such as Carnival, May 1, and Canicula (dog days under the reign of Sirius).[19] Brought up by a deer in an empty eagle's nest, Anne is shown here as a little wild girl with omniscient qualities out of proportion to her age, a child born of a man rather than a woman, one who has grown up extremely quickly ("grande et parcreue")—all traits well in keeping with the theme of time in reverse.

Since Anne's feast day is on July 26 or, in medieval Paris, on July 28,[20] she fits into the canicular period, which reaches its height with the rise of Sirius, Canis Major, around the middle of July. During that period there is a nefarious conjunction between the sun, Sirius, and the Milky Way that endangers the lives of man, beast, and vegetation.[21] The rising of Sirius has been linked to the combined feast of

Saint Christopher and Saint James on July 25, and the cult of these two saints is very relevant to the story of Saint Anne in *Le Romanz de Saint Fanuel*. Saint Christopher was a prototypical wild man, a giant who devoured men before he became a Christian and who was known in Eastern tradition to have been "dog-headed." After he had been converted, Christopher became a guide of souls.[22] Saint James was Anne's grandson, according to the *trinubium* tradition, and the Milky Way, with the constellation of the dog at its southern end and that of the eagle at its northern end, was the celestial reflection of the road to Compostella or "Road of Saint James" traveled by his pilgrims.[23] Saint James was connected to the mysteries of the builders, in particular those initiates who called themselves children of "Maître Jacques." [24] Indeed, a further connection between what seems like fantasy in *Le Romanz de Saint Fanuel* and the cult of Saint Anne is her patronage of woodworkers, who frequently represent the wild man, "the man of the woods," in their carvings. Furthermore, the complexity of the fanciful Saint Fanuel story and the point that such tales cannot be discarded as mere fruit of arbitrary imagination are underscored by the existence of both eagle and deer as Christological symbols.[25]

The obviously composite nature of this story and its total isolation from other traditions about Saint Anne make us wonder about its diffusion. An interesting factor is that it is attested to in eight different manuscripts, not all containing the same sets of texts. A particularly enlightening comment comes from a version of Wace's poem on the Conception of Our Lady, which does not contain the Saint Fanuel episode: instead, the copyist takes issue with it, interjecting that Anne, born in Bethlehem:

> De flour ne fu pas engenree
> Ce saichies vos certainement
> mais d'oume conseue charnelment
> Celles et ci soient confondu
> qui croient le roumans qui fu
> qui dist que de flour iert venue
> sainte Anne et engenue.[26]

This comment indicates that the Fanuel story was already old ("le roumans qui fu"), was circulating at the time this manuscript was copied, and was known well enough in that milieu to warrant countering.

All the versions of Saint Anne's life, whether the acceptable *Prot-evangelium* group, the Servatius legend, or the Fanuel story, do have something in common. They stress the questions of ancestry and descendance, making Saint Anne the focal point of the sacred lineage of Mary and Jesus. It is, in my view, this concept of lineage that explains why the tradition of the *trinubium,* or Anne's subsequent marriages to Cleophas and Salome, although criticized by church fathers, found grace in the eyes of medieval religious authorities such as Peter Lombard and William Durandus.[27] By marrying three times, Anne gives life to a holy progeny, the two other Marys, and, through them, to James the Less and the Great, John the Evangelist, Simon, and Jude. All become the offshoots of one sacred tree of which Anne is the root: "Jessae stirps hanc protulit / Ceu vitis alma palmitem," as the breviary of Chartres celebrated her.[28] This family tree made it possible to at once dramatize the nature of Jesus as man and develop mystical symbolism from images known to all.

The cult of the Three Marys, which was of great importance in many parts of medieval France, not only in Provence, extolled indirectly the holy virtues of Saint Anne's later fruition. The veneration of the two Marys, Jacobus and Salome, the "faithful friends" of Christ, and the story of their dramatic arrival, along with other holy fugitives, on the shores of Provence were quite old, since Caesarius of Arles founded a convent in their honor in 542. It remained active throughout the Middle Ages, with numerous pilgrims flocking to their Provençal shrine, including the ailing Bishop of Nantes in 1332 and, in the middle of the fifteenth century, King René of Provence, who was to order the excavation of their remains.[29]

The relationship of the Three Marys to Anne has been, at times, confusing, although many indications reinforce that association. In Chartres Cathedral a small chapel dedicated to the Three Marys was later renamed for Saint Anne, and the paintings commissioned in 1448 by King René of Provence for the chapel of Notre-Dame-de-la-Mer included the Holy Family, Joachim and Anne and the two Marys with their children. Yet the identity of the Three Marys is far from settled; for some the Three Marys included the Virgin Mary herself, while for others the third was Mary Magdalene. It is possible that the "anti-trinubium" tendency was responsible, at least in part, for favoring the Magdalene's role in the group by lessening the image of the three daughters of Anne. This problem was directly addressed in a vision of

Saint Colette, who, having criticized Saint Anne's triple marriage, saw her appear with her noble progeny, thus amply justifying her conjugal history.[30] In any event, it cannot be said that the Magdalene's inclusion in the group is a late or even a typically Provençal phenomenon, since both interpretations coexist in contemporary records.[31]

There seems, however, to be another connection between the cult of Saint Anne and that of her progeny, one justified by their common link to water. In Provence the cult of the Marys was connected to the sea, a theme that also appears in Saint Anne's cult—for instance, in the episode in which Hugh of Lincoln became her devotee while threatened by a storm at sea and, in more recent folklore, on the western coasts of France. The Carmelite Jean de Venette wrote a forty-thousand-verse poem in honor of the two Marys. The poem was reproduced in a shortened version in early printed books in which the poet calls them the "Marys of the sea."[32] The presence in the Provençal church of a Gallo-Roman *cippus* dedicated to the Junos and misread by medieval hagiographers to designate the Three Marys, the presence of an underground spring, and the existence of the terms "Three Marys" and "Three Good Marys" in other parts of France all point to the recovery of an ancient triadic cult. This may be reinforced by the fact that Saint Sara, the servant of the Marys worshiped as a special cult figure by the Gypsies, was already known at the time of King René's archaeological digs in 1448, and her bones were piously preserved in a separate reliquary with the remains of the ancient altar.[33]

Saint Anne's connection to the idea of lineage has yet another very important meaning in popular medieval tradition. Among many other patronages, she was invoked by woodworkers, especially by joiners and turners. The small lead tokens studied by Forgeais for the late Middle Ages and linked to guilds and societies include at least one example of Anne instructing the Virgin on one side, with the compass and other measuring instruments of the woodworker on the other.[34] Some claim that this association, not obvious for a female saint, is based on the profession of her son-in-law Joseph. Others see it as based on the notion that she made the first true tabernacle.[35] However, in both cases the very important association of visual and verbal symbols in popular religion is overlooked. Joseph's cult, although certainly practiced at an earlier date, was not made obligatory until the seventeenth century, and there is no reason to invoke such a lateral relationship.[36]

More simply put, Anne is root of a tree whose wood produces the flower of Mary and the grape of Christ. She herself was associated with the grapevine from the time of John Damascene, who says in his "Homilia in nativitatem Beatae Mariae Virginis" that she brought forth a most fertile vine, producing a delicious grape that provides mortals with nectar for eternal life.[37] The litanies of the Church at Apt, which claimed to have Anne's relics from the time of Charlemagne—a claim hotly contested by the Bollandists[38]—call her "root of Jesse, fertile tree, vine loaded with fruit." In more recent times, the bust of Saint Anne was decorated by the Apt parishioners with new grapes that were distributed to the sick and called "grapes of Saint Anne."[39] Saint Anne's feast is during a time when the picking of early grapes and their offering as "premices" was a well-practiced custom throughout France, more precisely a little later, on the feast of Saint Sixtus (August 6) or the feast of the Transfiguration.[40] That Saint Anne was linked to this ritual is therefore an important observation for the history of folk liturgy as well as of her own cult. Indeed, her link to wine and its symbolism was ever present in her iconography, where she so often appeared in a bright red cloak.[41]

In vernacular poetry Anne was referred to as a variety of trees or vegetation. The late-fifteenth-century poet Molinet calls her bough, cypress, cedar, rosebush, branch, tree trunk, rod, as opposed to a sterile and dried-out tree, devoid of fruit, flower, or leaf, which were associated with Joachim.[42] Thus Saint Anne brings the woodworkers under the protection of her sacred lineage. Woodworking, like so many other trades in which raw matter was transformed into art or technology, was marked by a mystical relationship between the wood, the tool, and the technique. It is truly a living tree, wood made of sacred flesh, that Anne offers to the craftsman's skill.

The long orison that Molinet wrote in honor of Anne contains an important passage that seems to be a "signature" of the woodworkers. In the verse, "a toy nous nous appoions / nous qui l'anne manions," *l'anne* can signify a measuring instrument or a tool used by joiners, called the *bedanne* or *bec d'anne*, referring to the "beak," not of a donkey, as one might think, but of a female duck (*cane*), derived from the Latin *anas, ane* in Old French.[43] Of course, Molinet, a *rhetoriqueur* particularly fond of puns and double entendres, knew that the word would also connote its homonym *âne*, donkey.

Although it is commonly felt that the *compagnons'* rites cannot be truly documented before the seventeenth century, fragments of earlier information do exist, such as Molinet's poem. It artfully plays on, or carves into the text, the multiple meanings of the word *anne*, in its many spellings, which combine the harmony of the year, proportion, measuring, old wine and grapes, possibly a medicinal and magical plant (the *aulnée* or *inula*) as well as a tree (the *aulne*, or alder) used to make dark-colored dyes, and the pun on the joiners' tool.[44] Although he is writing a serious orison to Saint Anne, Molinet, whose work is quite often very bawdy and quite irreverent, had to take into account the most obvious facetious connotations of the ambiguous word *anne*, which would not be lost on his contemporaries.

One such connotation is the donkey, which in the iconography of the Flight into Egypt carries the Virgin as she carries the Child, just as Saint Anne holds the Virgin who holds the Child and "carries" them both symbolically in her womb (fig. 1).[45] One of the numerous facetious etiologies that grace modern French folklore also combines Saint Anne with her artisans and the pun on the donkey. The joiners, wanting their own patron saint, went to heaven to ask for Saint Peter's help. Seeing the five pilgrims, he called them "cinq ânes" (five jackasses), and the puzzled suppliants concluded on the way back that he meant "Sainte Anne."[46]

The ass was important in rituals of reversal, such as the derisive *assouade*, or riding the donkey backward. The ass's presence was also felt in the calendar, because it feeds on a canicular plant, the thistle, and is also present at the other end of the year, at the manger of the Nativity.[47] Furthermore, Molinet, by his complicated punning on the word *anne*, evokes the unmentionable, the obscene anus, which plays a part in the scatological secret rituals of the *compagnons*.[48] Molinet may thus have been alluding to artisans' hidden rituals, in which they indeed manipulated ("manions") various overlapping meanings of the word, using his poetic prerogative to stress homonymy and connotation rather than literal meaning.

Another important connection can be made: the woodworkers, by their skill and sense of proportion, turn dead wood into something lasting, giving time the imprint of duration. Their secret rites, however unappealing they may seem to outsiders, also confer a sacred meaning on the time needed for the workman's skills to mature, since his sometimes brutal, often repulsive initiation rites are what seal his

Fig. 1. *Saint Anne Trinitarian,* woodcut from *Heures à l'usage d'Angers,* printed by Simon Vostre. Estampes, Bibliothèque Nationale, Paris. Sixteenth century. Photo: Bibliothèque Nationale, Paris.

adherence to the group of master workmen. It is quite apparent that Saint Anne is herself a very rich figure of time in reverse—both in her traditional story of the aged mother and in the Saint Fanuel episode —as well as an important calendar marker. Indeed, in addition to her feast during the Canicula, she was also honored on the feast of the Nativity of the Virgin, September 8, when she was commemorated for producing the most sacred fruit of that grape harvest time. Also, the conception of the Virgin took place around December 8, which is the period of Advent and the onset of winter.[49] All the important moments of her cult and her legend as well as her iconography, where she is represented as an old woman (see, for example, fig. 1), underscore her relationship to symbolic time. It is in that manner that Molinet chose to express his devotion to her, putting his word play to work on the theme:

> Ton nom est Anne et en latin Anna;
> Dieu tout puissant qui
> justement t'anna [formed]
> Veult qu'a l'anne [the year] tu soyes comparee;
> Quatre quartiers une tres juste anne [year] a,
> Quatre lectres en ton nom amena
> Par quoy tu es juste et bien mesuree. . . .
> S'on le retourne Anna tousjours on trouve.[50]

That Saint Anne was truly present in the daily tasks of woodworkers is seen in an expression used in Paris workshops: a mixture of strong glue and sawdust, employed to fix holes in planks, was called "Saint Anne's brains."[51] It is also manifest in the maintenance of her cult later on by the *compagnons* at a time when Saint Joseph's cult had become more widespread. In modern popular usage, her feast day was observed by the wood-carvers and joiners of Liège,[52] and in Villedieu-les-Poêles, Normandy, ironworkers observed her feast one day, followed by the St.-Anne-de-Bois, celebrated on the Monday following July 26 by the joiners, followed again by a holiday of lacemakers who celebrated "the little girl."[53]

Saint Anne was also connected to the religious activities of women in many ways; one of these was her patronage of sewing and embroidery. She was patron to seamstresses, linen workers, and lacemakers in many parts of Europe. In Italy, she was revered by embroiderers, who kept her feast day by abstaining from work lest their labor be destroyed, a practice also followed by washerwomen.[54] For a woman, sewing a vestment is tantamount to creating a body or its partial image. Saint Anne's patronage of sewing activities cannot be ascribed simply to her model role as good parent, since iconography represented that function by showing her teaching the Virgin Mary to read. Rather, as in the case of the woodworkers, there is a mystical bond between the craftsman's or craftswoman's gesture and the creative role of the saint. The origin of this patronage can be traced at least to a late medieval poem in praise of the Virgin, which says that she was the "robe inconsutile" (or robe "devoid of seams") that enveloped the Logos made flesh and that Anne and Joachim pulled the white silk threads used to make this seamless dress, of which there was an example in the cult of the Virgin, reputed to have grown with the Child Jesus.[55] The mystical tone of the poem cannot obscure the fact that thread and sewing were powerful sexual images:

> Anne dressa la trayme sans couppeure
> Et Joachim par humble affection
> Fournist the soye et matiere si pure
> Quel neust jamais tache d'infection.[56]

In the sixteenth century the German monk Trithemius wrote a long tribute to Saint Anne in which he extolled and defended her cult. It includes an exhaustive list of all the healing and curative powers that were attributed to her: she cured those who suffered from melancholia, protected those who were among enemies or thieves, freed persons in chains and in jails, saved those who were in danger at sea, chased away pestilence, and helped women in labor. She could also be invoked to guard against sudden death and to assist the dying.[57] Her later role against the plague was manifest in the iconography of the Dominican *Pestblätter* and in inscriptions on bells that also served to protect crops. In the little town of Chevain, in the diocese of Paris, a sixteenth-century statue of Saint Anne was invoked against whooping cough, the protection against which was a function normally ascribed to the Virgin.[58]

Among the complex manifestations of her cult, a link to water both as healing agent and as agent in agricultural rituals stands out as very important. Saints' lives that contain mentions of cephalophoria point to connections between the head of a saint and water points, springs, and wells.[59] It is therefore interesting to note that the most famous relic in France was Saint Anne's head, sent by the Count of Blois from Constantinople to Chartres in 1205. In honor of this relic, a statue was placed at the northern portal and a window was made under the stained-glass rose; the figure of Saint Anne in that window is the largest figure in the whole cathedral, its head measuring over half a meter.[60]

Water consecrated to Saint Anne's worship was credited with wonderful healing value in France, Italy, England, and Germany. It was used to lessen fevers, to help parturients and those who had lost their minds,[61] and, in Germany, to guard against the mumps.

To better understand this theme of Anne's cult, it is useful to consider examples of more recent folk custom in France that provide clear links with her medieval role. For instance, at the spring of Montbrun, Anne was beseeched to give milk to nursing women and animals.[62] According to one observer, she has been represented naked to the waist and breast-feeding the Virgin Mary.[63] This can be confirmed with at least one example of medieval iconography, an illustration of the Nativity of the Virgin on folio 344v of BN MS. lat. 757, a Franciscan book of hours and missal dated 1380 (fig. 2), which indeed shows Anne lying in bed with head covered but breasts bared. There may be a relation to the peculiar relic that the inquisitor Bernard Gui claimed to have seen in Limoges: "Sanctae Annae mamilla habetur veneratur et manifeste ostenditur infra crystallum in ecclesia S. Annae in loco sic ab ipsa Anna denominato."[64]

In the village of Champfremont (Mayenne), a shepherd saw his ram kneeling in one place, dug up the ground, and found a statue of the saint and a spring. A chapel was erected on the spot, purportedly chosen by the saint herself in the seventeenth century.[65] In Brie, near Vitry, there is dedicated to Saint Anne a sacred spring whose waters are reputed to cure eyes, throat, and fevers, and the spring was the locus of a pilgrimage on July 26 and September 8 for a very long time. A legend of 1794 tells that a man who wanted to displace her statue was blinded and that the water began to run red as blood. In the forest of Villefermoy there is an old fountain sacred to Saint Anne where worshipers sought cures for fevers and infertility with gifts of money left on the stone near the spring.[66]

St.-Pair-sur-Mer (Normandy) also has its well of Saint Anne, its

Fig. 2. *Nativity of the Virgin Mary. Franciscan Book of Hours and Missal.*
Bibliothèque Nationale, Paris MS. lat. 757, fol. 344v. 1380.
Photo: Bibliothèque Nationale, Paris.

pure, fresh water located only a few meters away from the sea. It
held a pilgrimage, probably started in the early nineteenth century, of
women from Granvilliers, sailors' wives, marching in silence on her
feast day to pray for their men away at sea. Near Gorges, Saint Anne
of the Swamps was invoked for rain, while in nearby Le Plessis, dry
weather was requested from Saint Anne of the Woods.[67] In a completely different region, Isère, Saint Anne was also invoked against
fevers at La More, and, elsewhere, to dispense rain and dry weather. At
La Roche, people would make a barefoot procession to her chapel in
the desert of Valjouffroy, and her statue was bathed in the headwaters
of the Bonne River.[68] Such connections with water were known in
other parts of Europe, with the famous well of Saint Anne of Buxton,
the chapels of Saint Anne in the Willows and Saint Anne in the Wodde

near Bristol, and the miraculous springs of Mulfingen in Germany and in Belgium.[69]

In many areas, Anne was a saint of women. Her iconography from the Middle Ages to the sixteenth century represented her as the center of a family group, seated with her daughter, or, very frequently, as Anne who holds the Virgin who holds the Child, either one on each knee or with the Virgin and Child on her lap.[70] This theme evolved into some very unusual but revealing manifestations, such as "Saint Anne Trinitarian," of which a clear example appeared in the printed *Hours of Simon Vostre,* usage of Angers (see fig. 1): Saint Anne stands in the center of the composition, her breasts and stomach marked by a flaming sun, and the Virgin and Child appear inside her womb. In Germany the Trinitarian theme gave rise to the proliferation of *Selb-dritt* pictures, "herself making a third," which came under Luther's attacks.[71]

In many ways the cult and iconography of Anne repeated those of the Virgin (as with the Chevain statue)—for instance, she was often present in printed rosary illustrations once that usage was instituted for the Virgin.[72] Anne's feast days were also associated with the Marian ones, not only on September 8, the Nativity of the Virgin, an obvious link to Anne's own story, but at all "feasts and solemnities of Our Lady" (for example, at the monastery of L'Isle Barbe, which claimed to have her oldest relics).[73] This repetition should not be ascribed to lack of imagination, because the accretion of aspects of the Marian cult to Saint Anne's fulfills an important function in the symbolism of time. Indeed, Anne and Mary become associated as two faces of divine womanhood, the very young and the very old, both becoming mothers by divine intervention. In a sense, the iconography of the two women and Child, showing the Virgin herself as a little, or very young, girl held by Saint Anne, concentrates the symbolism of motherhood on her figure, the largest in the group.[74]

Thus one of Anne's best-known functions in popular religion was assisting women in labor, a belief kept alive even into this century in, for instance, the Abruzzi region of Italy.[75] This role appeared in medieval prayers, as in the following fifteenth-century example: "Anne la prophète enfanta Samuel le prophète. Saincte Elisabeth enfanta Sainct Jehan Baptiste. Saincte Anne enfanta la benoite Vierge Marie Mere de Dieu. La benoiste Vierge Marie sans douleur et sans paine enfanta le doulx benoist Jhesucrist Sauveur et rachetteur de tout le monde. Par les sainctes prieres de ceulx ci et de tous les sains et sainctes de paradis nostre Seigneur veuillez delivre ceste creature. Amen."[76] A note in the manuscript underscores that this is an actual prayer ritual, adding, "Quant la femme est au fort de son travail, on doit dire sur elle les parolles qui ensuivent" ("When the woman is at the height of her labor, one must say the following words over her").

Fecundity is also the theme of two other prayers, both from the sixteenth century. One stresses the victory over sterility so dramatically retold in the *Protevangelium:* "O benoiste et eureuse dame saincte Anne, qui apres que long temps fuz sterille en ta vieillesse et hors d'age de concepvoir, par la voulenté et bonté divine. . . ."[77] The other, addressed to both the Virgin and her mother, emphasizes numbering and proliferation: "Autant qu'il y a de gouttez d'eaue en mere et de grains de saublons, et de fruictz d'arbres et de feuilles et d'estoilles du ciel et d'esprit angelicques, autant de fois avouecq vostre filz vous salue, tres chaste vierge Marie."[78]

Although these aspects of Saint Anne's cult are fragmentary, they do trace a litany of folk religion in the late Middle Ages with its many facets. In spite of the relative lateness of her cult, Saint Anne appears as an ancient figure of motherhood and time in which many traditions culminate.

She is Anna, root and stem of the Tree of Jesse, of the lineage of Christ, source of the strong wood that craftsmen bend in multiple shapes and erect in proud, lasting foundations, vine of the mystical grape.

She is Anna, first mother in the family of Christ, protector of women in childbed, the sterile tree who bore fruit in the autumn of her age.

She is Anna who raises her daughters in womanly skills, sewing the envelope of flesh of the human body and the vestments that adorn it.

She is Anna, spring of life, healer and eternal giver, invoked to cradle the harvests that need water, but also dryness, and that are reaped in the days of her feasts.

She is Anna, whose name spells out harmony, proportion, the beginning and the end, the year in its entirety, the passage of time and its ceaseless mystery of redemption, the fruitful old woman who is a figure of Time herself.

NOTES

1. See this volume's Introduction, by Kathleen Ashley and Pamela Shein-gorn.

2. This text was edited by Camille Chabanneau in 1889.

3. Charland, *Trois Légendes,* 321.

4. "There he carried her so long / Just as a mother carries her child" (Chabanneau, *Romanz,* lines 445–46). The translation is mine, as are all other translations from Old French Latin to English in this text.

5. Chabanneau, *Romanz,* lines 80–88.

> You have planted a tree here.
> I will be crucified on it
> And beaten and insulted,
> And on it I will be covered with blood
> Which will run down my side.
> And from that flower will be born
> A knight who will bear
> The mother of that maiden
> Of whom Jesus Christ will make his servant.

6. "The flower gave out such a great [strong] odor / That from the scent it gave out / The young maiden became pregnant" (Chabanneau, *Romanz,* lines 120–22).

7. Chabanneau, *Romanz,* lines 560–65.

> Anne, she says, they call me,
> And although I am big and have grown,
> I never saw my own father.
> But I do see my mother coming here.
> Tell her now to come to me
> And take me down from this nest.

8. This entire episode covers lines 35–596 of the *Romanz.*

9. *Acta sanctorum,* July 26, 237. This point was already refuted by Epipha-nus as early as the fourth century. See Molinet, "Oroison a Madame Saincte Anne," line 68, in *Faictz et dictz:* "Vous conchutes [la Vierge Marie] sans tache originelle." See also the manuscript illustration of Joachim, Anne, and the Immaculate Conception in the *Hours of Catherine of Cleves,* pl. 91 (Pierpont Morgan MS. M. 917, p. 145). In this miniature we can see golden rays ema-nating from God the Father toward Anne's womb as she stands modestly beside Joachim. The border design, as Plummer suggests, is made of leaves of "uterine shape."

10. Thompson, *Motif Index.* All motif numbers are taken from this work, which classifies motifs first by letter, in alphabetical order, then by number.

Interesting analogues to the virgin birth of Fanuel, where the mother of the saint or hero swallows an object (ball, insect, star), are to be found in Heist, "Hagiography, Chiefly Celtic," 130–31.

11. Corblet, *Diocèse d'Amiens* 1:234–87.

12. Aarne and Thompson, *Types of the Folktale*. All types are taken from this work, where they are classified by number. The possibility of a relationship between the story of Saint Fanuel in the *Romanz* and Arabic folktales brought back during the Crusades is discussed in an article by Gaston Huet, "Une Légende religieuse du Moyen Age: Le *Roman de St. Fanuel*."

13. For a discussion of tale type 706 in relation to medieval literature, see Gaignebet and Lajoux, *Art profane,* 109, 129, which gives an essential commentary for understanding the connection of the tale type to the theme of ritual purification and to the symbolism of trees; see also Velay-Vallantin, "La Belle sans mains."

14. See the late medieval novel *L'Histoire du noble Valentin et Orson* (first published in Lyon, by Jacques Maillet, in 1489); the legend of the bear stealing a woman has been studied by Fabre in "L'Ours ravisseur." On the relation between bear and wild man, the cult of Saint Blasius, February rituals, and the mythic shepherd, see Gaignebet, *A plus hault sens,* 154–231.

15. A new and important mythological and folkloric reading of the *Histoire de Merlin* is given in Gaignebet and Lajoux, *Art profane,* particularly in the chapter "Les Mythes."

16. For an example of a child brought up in the forest and accompanied by a deer, see the *chanson de geste* in *Doon de Mayence,* edited by Pey, lines 414–98, 1714–15, 4366–4813. I have discussed these texts in my dissertation, "'L'Epopée taisible'" (University of California at Los Angeles, 1978).

17. In Gaignebet and Lajoux, *Art profane,* 100–101, there is a very suggestive discussion of Nebuchadnezzar as an "eagle-man." This discussion is continued in Gaignebet, *A plus hault sens* 1:157, 2:215, with further comment and illustration. See also a very important article by Donatien Laurent, "Le Gwerz de Skolan." For examples of wild men who are not hairy and live in trees or shrubbery, see Husband, *Wild Man,* 93 (no. 19), 143 (no. 37), 163 (no. 45), 164 (no. 108), 165 (no. 109), which are all fifteenth-century German; p. 119, fig. 72, shows a wild woman with a stag.

18. *Infectum* comes from *inficior,* which means at once to touch, to wet, to soil, and to infect. Thus Nebuchadnezzar has been touched by the dew and in some way "contaminated" by a form of sacrality that translates into his fall from grace and physical degradation.

19. Gaignebet and Lajoux, *Art profane,* 92–93, and Gaignebet, *A plus hault sens* 1:165–69.

20. Perdrizet, *Le Calendrier parisien,* 188.

21. On Canicula and the Milky Way, see the discussion of Pliny in Gaigne-bet and Lajoux, *Art profane*, 70–71.

22. See Saintyves, "L'Origine" and *St. Christophe*.

23. Gaignebet and Lajoux, *Art profane*, 173b, 261–63.

24. Ibid., particularly the section "Notre-Dame-de-Semur," 270–75; see Gaignebet, *A plus hault sens* 1:107–8, for the role of Saint James in masonic symbolism.

25. See Beigbeder, *Lexique des symboles*, and Sarolli, *Prolegomena*, 2, chap. 2.

26. Chabanneau, *Le Romanz*, quotes this text in his introduction.

> Of a flower she was not engendered,
> This you must know for sure,
> But by a man conceived carnally.
> May they be confounded, those men and women,
> Who believe the story that was,
> Which says that from a flower came
> Saint Anne and was engendered.

27. Durand, *Rational* vol. 5, book 10, section 42; Latini, *Li Livres* 1:64.

28. Charland, *Trois Légendes*, 362.

29. Cintrat, *Les Trois Marie*, 7, 50, 71; Mazel, *Les Saintes-Maries-de-la-Mer*, 107.

30. Cintrat, *Les Trois Marie*, 26; Mazel, *Les Saintes-Maries-de-la-Mer*, 107. See also the discussion of Colette's vision in Kathleen Ashley's essay in this volume.

31. Careful scrutiny of the history of the cult shows the complexity of the question. The Virgin Mary was very frequently associated with the Marys, her sisters—for instance, by the fraternity of Notre-Dame-de-la-Mer, which in its foundation article of 1315 invokes the Virgin Mary and Saints Mary Salome and Mary Jacobus, without mention of Mary Magdalene (Mazel, *Les Saintes-Maries-de-la-Mer*, 128–29). However, the association with the Magda-lene could be fairly early and not exclusively Provençal, as can be seen from the following examples. Although, according to the bishop Peter of Nantes, in the breviary of Aix and in many others, the feast day of the Marys was on May 25, in the vicinity of Chartres, at Mignières (site of an important pilgrimage to them), the first celebration was actually on May 22, for Mary Jacobus, followed by the second on July 22, feast of the Magdalene, and by the third feast on October 22 (Cintrat, *Les Trois Marie*, 7).

In 1210, Gervaise of Tilbury spoke of the entire fugitive group from Bethany alighting from their boat and raising an altar to the Virgin Mary in the place where the church of Notre-Dame-de-la-Mer was to be, but William Durandus of Mende only mentions the Marys, alone with Magdalene and

Martha, raising an altar to the Virgin (Chaillan, *Les Saintes Maries*, 43). In 1279 Charles II, discovering the relics of the Magdalene, attempted to find those of the two Marys, which does indicate a relationship between their cults (Chaillan, *Les Saintes Maries*, 51). A fourteenth-century breviary lists the feast days of the two Marys and of the Magdalene together, as do missals as old as the tenth century (Chaillan, *Les Saintes Maries*, 46). In the thirteenth century, Ludolph the Carthusian wrote a mystical commentary on the Three Marys wherein Mary Magdalene was the first stage, that of penance (Cintrat, *Les Trois Marie*, 48). In 1347, Bishop Foulques of Paris wrote instructions allowing forty days of indulgence to those who celebrate the Marys, dated on the eve of the feast of Mary Magdalene (Cintrat, *Les Trois Marie*, 71). In 1491, Louis de Béaumond, bishop of Paris, had relics of the two Marys enclosed inside a silver reliquary head of the Magdalene, which was preserved in the Church of La Madeleine until 1630 (Lamoureux, *Les Saintes Maries*, 102).

32. Lamoureux, *Les Saintes Maries*, 203–4.

33. Ibid., 107.

34. Forgeais, *Collection des plombs*, série 1, *Méreaux des corporations de métiers* (1862), under "menuisiers"; Coussée, *Légendes, croyances*, 154. A chapel built in 1823 on the territory of Roncourt is dedicated to Saint Anne and decorated with the compass and square.

35. "Tu es l'arche que Dieu voult composer / Pour son tres sainct temple en toy reposer" (Molinet, "Orison," verses 121–22, in *Les Faictz et dictz*). See also Charland, *Trois Légendes*, 354.

36. Perdrizet, *Le Calendrier parisien*, 188.

37. "Vitis uberrima ex Anna pullulavit, uvaque suavissima effloruit, potum nectaris terrigenis fudens in vitam aeternam" (John Damascene, "Homilia," col. 674, sec. 847–49).

38. *Acta sanctorum*, col. 254.

39. Terris, *Sainte Anne d'Apt*, 30–31.

40. Van Gennep, *Manuel de folklore français*, vol. 1, part 5, 2390–93.

41. See, for instance, in Paris, Bibliothèque Nationale, lat. 10540, fol. 58v; lat. 1156, fol. 12v; and lat. 919, fol. 24. See also *Hours of Catherine of Cleves*, p. 292 (pl. 143), or the painting of Saint Anne by Masaccio at the Uffizi in Florence (n. 8386).

42. Molinet, "Orison," verses 30–33 and passim, in *Les Faictz et dictz*.

43. Gaignebet must be credited for stressing the connection between the tool and the word *anne*. For *bec d'anne* see Godefroy, *Dictionnaire*, complément, 8:310. The mythological connection between duck, donkey, and goose (*cane, âne*, and *oie*) is pointed out by Coussée, *Légendes, croyances*, 126.

44. See entries for *anne, aisne*, and *aine* in Godefroy, *Dictionnaire*, vol. 1.

45. Tristan, *Le Monde à l'envers*, 36, mentions an alchemical meaning to this motif.

46. Certeux, "Les Pourquoi," 368; this story circulated widely, for it was also known in the town of Y, which received Saint Anne's patronage with the same pun. See Debrie, "Traces," 33.

47. Eating thistles, which bloom in the hottest months, is an insignia of the ass-cuckold (as in Coquillart's "Monologue des Perrucques," in *Oeuvres*, 280); the Greek name for thistle, *dipsacos*, is also related to thirst (Gaignebet and Lajoux, *Art profane*, 275). The full symbolism of the jackass in medieval tradition is the subject of a thorough and novel investigation in Anne Witte's forthcoming dissertation (City University of New York).

48. Gaignebet and Lajoux, *Art profane*, 204–29.

49. On the feast of the Immaculate Conception of the Virgin Mary, see Perdrizet, *Le Calendrier parisien*, 273.

50. Molinet, "Oroison," lines 151–64, in *Les Faictz et dictz*. Because of the multiple puns and spelling ambiguities, it is very difficult to translate this passage, and an attempt to do so confirms the old saying "traduttore, traditore." In the following, slightly clearer passage, brackets indicate words based on "Anne."

> Your name is Anne and in Latin Anna;
> God all mighty who
> justly [formed] you
> Wants you to be compared to the [year].
> Four quarters a very just [year] has.
> Four letters in your name he brought.
> That is why you are just and well measured. . . .
> If one turns it around, always Anna will be found.

51. Perdrizet, *Le Calendrier parisien*, 188.

52. Charland, *Madame Sainte Anne*, 177.

53. Seguin, *En Basse-Normandie*, 57.

54. *Enciclopedia cattolica*, "Anna," article by Toschi.

55. Estienne, *Apologie* 2:134.

56. "Anne set up the warp without break, / And Joachim by humble affection, / Provided the silk and such pure matter, / That it never was spotted with infection" (Charland, *Trois Légendes*, 316). The text is difficult and the translation therefore not totally literal.

57. Trithemius, *De laudibus*, chap. 14.

58. Schaumkell, *Der Kultus der heiligen Anna*, 16–17, 27; Perdrizet, *Vierge de miséricorde*, 100–101. On Chevain, see Gaignebet, *A plus hault sens* 1:120.

59. Fromage, "Couples sacrés," 16–18.

60. Perdrizet, *La Calendrier parisien*, 188.

61. *Enciclopedia cattolica; Dictionnaire de spiritualité* 1:671.

62. Cadet, "Les Divinités féminines," 27.

63. Lascaux, "Une Christianisation," 78.

64. "The breast of Saint Anne is kept, venerated, and visibly shown inside a crystal in the church of Saint Anne in the place named for the same Anne" (*Acta sanctorum*, col. 257).

65. Delavigne, "La Source de Ste. Anne," 94.

66. Iablokoff, "Le Canton de Chastelet," 85.

67. Seguin, *En Basse-Normandie*, 50.

68. Van Gennep, *Folklore du Dauphiné* 2:350.

69. Charland, *Madame Ste. Anne*, 160–74.

70. See Barbier de Montault, Masseron, and Vincens.

71. See the essay by Pamela Sheingorn in this volume; see also Schaumkell, *Der Kultus der heiligen Anna*, 17, 26–27.

72. Perdrizet, *Vierge de miséricorde*, 220.

73. Le Laboureur, *Les Masures*, 299–301.

74. The negative value ascribed to old women in medieval and even in later tradition would call for extensive commentary. It overlaps with a medical conception of the noxious quality of old women and also a more lay perception of the barren but lecherous hag, taken up by, among others, Eustache Deschamps or the well-known fourteenth-century *Vetula*. To these, accusations of witchcraft add a dimension while owing much to this primary perception. Thus the cult of Saint Anne as mother (Dante himself makes her a prominent mother figure in the Rose, *Paradiso* 32:133–35) and fruitful old woman is remarkable in the medieval context and raises many interesting questions about her associations with such non-Christian figures as the Celtic Anu or the Roman Anna Perenna. Anna, the old woman, and scatology have been addressed by Claude Gaignebet in radio conferences on *France Culture*.

75. This information was provided by Alfredo Di Scipio, whose mother was a midwife. See also Gatto-Trocchi, *Fiabe abruzzesi*, 11, for an invocation, naming Saint Anne, to protect the newborn.

76. "Anne the prophetess bore Samuel the prophet. Saint Elizabeth bore Saint John the Baptist. Saint Anne bore the blessed Virgin Mary, Mother of God. The blessed Virgin Mary without pain and without trouble bore the sweet blessed Jesus Christ Savior and redeemer of the whole world. By the holy prayers of these and of all the saints of paradise, our Lord please deliver this creature. Amen" (Sonet, *Répertoire*, no. 77).

77. "O blessed and happy lady Saint Anne, who, after having been sterile a long time, in your old age and past the time to conceive, by divine will and goodness . . ." (ibid., no. 1284).

78. "As many as there are drops of water in the sea and of grains of sand,

and of fruits of the trees and of leaves and stars of the sky and of angelic spirits, as many times along with your son I hail thee, very chaste Virgin Mary" (ibid., no. 91).

BIBLIOGRAPHY

Aarne, Antti, and Stith Thompson. *The Types of the Folktale. Folklore Fellows Communications* no. 184. Helsinki: Academia Scientiarum Fennica, 1961.

Barbier de Montault, Xavier. *Oeuvres complètes.* 16 vols. Poitiers: Blais, Roy, et Cie, 1889–1902.

Beigbeder, Olivier. *Lexique des symboles.* St-Léger-Vauban: Zodiaque, 1969.

Cadet, A. "Les Divinités féminines des fontaines." *Bulletin de la Société de mythologie française* 127 (1982): 23–31.

Certeux, A. "Les Pourquoi des métiers." *Revue des traditions populaires* 8 (1893): 368.

Chabanneau, Camille, ed. *Le Romanz de Saint Fanuel et de Sainte Anne et de Nostre Dame et de Nostre Seigneur et de ses Apostres.* Paris: Maisonneuve et Charles Leclerc, 1889.

Chaillan, Msgr. M. *Les Saintes Maries de la Mer: Recherches archéologiques et historiques avec documents des fouilles du XVe siècle.* Aix/Marseille: A. Dragon/Tacussel, 1926.

Charland, Victor. *Les Trois Légendes de Madame Saincte Anne.* Montreal: Charland et Cie, 1898.

————. *Madame Ste. Anne et son culte au moyen âge.* Paris: Picard, 1911.

Cintrat, Abbé. *Les Trois Marie* [sic]: *Notice historique sur le pélerinage de Mignières, le culte et la vie des Saintes Marie Jacobé, Marie Salomé, et Marie-Madeleine.* Chartres: Imprimerie de Notre-Dame, 1895.

Cocheris, Hippolyte François Jules Marie, ed. *La Vieille; ou Les dernières amours d'Ovide Poème français du XIVe siècle; traduit du latin de Richard de Fournival par Jean Lefèvre.* Paris: Auguste Aubry, 1861.

Coquillart, Guillaume. *Oeuvres.* Ed. Charles d'Héricault. 2 vols. Paris, 1857.

Corblet, Jules. *Hagiographie du diocèse d'Amiens.* 3 vols. Paris: J.-B. Dumoulin, 1868–72.

Coussée, Bernard. *Légendes, croyances, et traditions en Douaisis.* Douais: Chez l'Auteur, 1982.

Debrie, R. "Traces de légendes hagiographiques et autres en Picardie." *Bulletin de la Société de mythologie française* 125 (1982): 26–35.

Delavigne, R. "La Source de Ste. Anne." *Bulletin de la Société de mythologie française* 93 (1974): 94.

Dictionnaire de spiritualité ascétique et mystique. Vol. 1. Paris: Beauchesne, 1937.

Durand, Guillaume. *Rational des divins offices.* 5 vols. Ed. and trans. Charles Barthélémy. Paris: Louis Vivès, 1854.

Enciclopedia cattolica. 12 vols. Città del Vaticano: Ente per l'Enciclopedia cattolica e per il Libro cattolica, 1949–54.

Estienne, Henri. *Apologie pour Hérodote.* 2 vols. Ed. Le Duchat. La Haye: Henri Scheurleer, 1735.

Fabre, Daniel. "L'Ours ravisseur dans les mirabilia et les histoires naturelles." *Via Domitia* 11 (1962): 54–60.

Forgeais, A. *Collection des plombs historiés trouvés dans le Seine.* 5 vols. Paris: Chez l'Auteur et Aubry, 1862–66.

Fromage, Henri. "Couples sacrés et micro-géographie dans le légendaire français." *Bulletin de la Société de mythologie française* 96 (1975): 13–40.

Gaignebet, Claude. *A plus hault sens: L'Esotérisme charnel et spirituel de Rabelais.* 2 vols. Paris: Maisonneuve et Larose, 1986.

Gaignebet, Claude, and Jean-Dominique Lajoux. *Art profane et religion populaire au moyen âge.* Paris: Presses Universitaires de France, 1985.

Gatto-Trocchi, Cecilia. *Fiabe abruzzesi.* Milan: Arnoldo Mondadori, 1982.

Godefroy, Frederic. *Dictionnaire de l'ancienne langue française et de tous ses dialectes du IXe au XVe siècle.* 10 vols. 1888. Second reprint. Vaduz: Kraus, 1965.

Heist, William W. "Hagiography, Chiefly Celtic, and Recent Developments in Folklore." In *Hagiographie, cultures, et sociétés, IVe–XIIe siècles,* Centre de Recherches sur l'Antiquité Tardive et le Haut Moyen Age, Paris 10. Paris: Etudes Augustiniennes, 1981.

Hours of Catherine of Cleves. Ed. John Plummer. New York: Braziller, 1977.

Huet, Gaston. "Une Légende religieuse du Moyen Age: Le *Roman de St. Fanuel.*" *Revue de l'Histoire des Religions* 84 (1921): 230–51.

Husband, Timothy. *The Wild Man.* New York: Metropolitan Museum of Art, 1980.

Iablokoff, Mme. "Le Canton du Chastelet en Brie." *Bulletin de la Société de mythologie française* 90 (1973): 77–90.

John Damascene. "Homilia in nativitatem Beatae Mariae Virginis." Ed. Jacques-Paul Migne. *Patrologia graeca,* vol. 96.

Lamoureux, Chanoine. *Les Saintes Maries de Provence: Leur vie et leur culte.* Avignon: Aubanel Frères, 1898.

Lascaux, Michel. "Une Christianisation du culte de Vénus: La chapelle Ste. Agathe à Langon." *Bulletin de la Société de mythologie française* 117 (1980): 71–78.

Latini, Brunetto. *Li Livres dou tresor.* Ed. Francis Carmody. 1948. Reprint. Geneva: Slatkine, 1975.

Laurent, Donatien. "La Gwerz de Skolan et la légende de Merlin." *Ethnologie française* 1, nos. 3–4 (1971): 19–54.

Le Laboureur, Claude. *Les Masures de l'abbaye royale de l'Isle Barbe*. Paris: Jean Couterot, 1681.

L'Histoire du noble Valentin et Orson. Lyon: Jacques Maillet, 1489.

Masseron, Alexandre. *Sainte Anne*. L'Art et les Saints, no. 19. Paris: Henri Laurens, 1916.

Mazel, A. *Les Saintes-Maries-de-la-Mer et la Camargue*. Vaison-la-Romaine: Bonne Presse du Midi, 1950.

Molinet, Jean. *Les Faictz et dictz*. Vol. 2. Ed. Noël Dupire. Paris: SATF, 1936.

Perdrizet, Paul. *La Vierge de miséricorde: Etude d'un thème iconographique*. Paris: Bibliothèque des Etudes Françaises d'Athènes et de Rome, fasc. 101, 1908.

———. *Le Calendrier parisien à la fin du moyen âge*. Paris: Les Belles Lettres, 1933.

Pey, M. A., ed. *Doon de Mayence*. Paris: F. Vieweg, 1859.

Saintyves, Pierre. "L'Origine de la tête de chien de Saint Christophe." *Revue anthropologique* 34 (1924): 336–83.

———. *St. Christophe successeur d'Anubis, d'Hermès, et d'Héraclès*. Paris: Nourry, 1936.

Sarolli, Gian Roberto. *Prolegomena alla 'Divina Commedia.'* Florence: Olschki, 1971.

Sautman, Francesca. " 'L'Epopée taisible.' " Ph.D. diss., University of California at Los Angeles, 1978.

Schaumkell, E. *Der Kultus der heiligen Anna am Ausgange des Mittelalters*. Altenburg: Stephan Geibel, 1893.

Seguin, Jean. *En Basse-Normandie et Haute-Bretagne: Saints guérisseurs, saints imaginaires, dévotions populaires*. 2d ed. Avranches: Chez l'Auteur, 1929.

Sinclair, Keith Val, ed. *Tristan de Nanteuil*. Assen: Van Gorcum, 1971.

Sonet, Jean. *Répertoire d'incipit de prières en ancien français*. Geneva: Droz, 1956.

Terris, Paul. *Sainte Anne d'Apt: Ses traditions, son histoire d'après les documents authentiques*. Avignon: F. Seguin Ainé, 1876.

Thompson, Stith. *Motif Index of Folk Literature*. 6 vols. Bloomington: Indiana University Press, 1955–58.

Tristan, Frédéric. *Le Monde à l'envers*. Paris: Hachette-Massin, 1980.

Trithemius, Johann. *De laudibus sanctissimae matris Annae*. 1494, Bibliothèque Nationale, Res. 1550.

Van Gennep, Arnold. *Le Folklore du Dauphiné*. Vol. 2. Paris: Librairie Orientale et Américaine, 1933.

———. *Manuel de folklore français contemporain*. Vols. 1–5. Paris: Picard, 1951.

Velay-Vallantin, Catherine. "La Belle sans mains: conte nouveau." *Bulletin du Cermeil* 1, no. 2 (July 1984): 12–20.

Vincens, Charles. *De l'iconographie de Sainte Anne et de la Vierge Marie*. Paris: Imprimerie Chaix, 1891.

Saint Anne and the Religion of Childbed

Some East Anglian Texts and Talismans

GAIL MCMURRAY GIBSON

h agiography is about recurrence. As David Jeffrey has observed (invoking Gregory of Tours), "It is better to talk about the life of the saint than the lives of the saints."[1] The saintly typology that comes first to mind, the recurrent Christ-likeness that pressed its pattern upon the Western narrative and dramatic tradition and upon saints from Antony of the desert to Francis of Assisi and far beyond, was a suffering and redemptive critique of the world, a saint's life that invited marveling wonder but rarely emulation. Only sanctity at a fiercely heroic level made of man or of woman this kind of saint; many marveled, but few stripped off their shoes and their fathers' clothes to join the martyrdom of writing in flesh again and again those uncompromising words of Matthew's gospel, "If you would be perfect." But there is paradox in a second truth about medieval saints, and that is that their cults were not just about the lives of the saints but also about the lives of the supplicants. Medieval men and women venerated saints for reasons of urgent and practical utility, honoring them to the extent that their story was not only Christ-likeness but also life-likeness, to the extent that saintly trials and triumphs touched and made safe or comprehensible their own lives as carnal human creatures. Heroic sanctity was a myth about the surely uneasy progress

of every human life and the living of it; it was the human, uneasy
progress that made saints and their talismans things to be believed in
and hoarded at all costs.

So it is that this essay about a saint begins with a found object, a
fourteenth-century Nativity alabaster relief that lay hidden beneath
the chancel floor of the parish church of Holy Trinity at Long Melford,
Suffolk (fig. 1), until it was discovered in the eighteenth century by
workmen doing repairs on the church.[2] The Long Melford Nativity
(fig. 2) represents the Virgin Mary reclining in her childbed and attended by a midwife. Joseph is there, too, nodding his head in an old
man's sleep, but focused in adoration of the Madonna and the Christ
Child in her lap are the Three Kings, crowned surrogates for the
parish believers who hid this image in Long Melford church in risky
defiance of the iconoclasm of Reformation edict. That this simple alabaster carving—of all the sculptures once displayed in the splendid
"wool" church of Long Melford Holy Trinity—was the one that was
saved both demands explanation and forces the eloquence of subter-
fuge upon its otherwise conventional Nativity iconography. What the
Long Melford alabaster as found object argues is what the midwife
argues. Far from her apocryphal gospel of beginning, Salome, the
midwife who doubted, now stands believing and attending at Mary's
bedside, touching with a human hand the mystery of Incarnation, but
her hand touches also the mystery, terrifying and necessary, of childbed itself. In the Middle Ages, the dynastic urgency of conceiving
heirs always grappled with the physical danger of childbirth, but even
the physical perils were overshadowed by the appalling practice in
some parishes of refusing burial in holy ground to pregnant women
or women who had died in the throes of childbirth, still thought to be
contaminated by the bodily fluids of lustful generation that church-
wardens feared would desecrate the churchyard.[3] Physical and spiritual danger and the desperation that sought blessing on the travailing
womb are, I think, why the Long Melford Nativity carving was the
most urgent to pray before and to save, and that same human need is
almost certainly the most essential fact of medieval affective piety for
both the mother Mary and that even more experienced motherer—
Mary's own, Saint Anne.

Yet it is curious that although scholarly controversy has raged for
years, for example, over whether the late medieval Saint Anne's Day

Fig. 1. Holy Trinity Church, Long Melford, Suffolk. Late fifteenth century (west tower rebuilt 1898–1903). Photo: G. M. Gibson.

Fig. 2. *Nativity and Adoration of Magi,* alabaster relief found at and preserved in Holy Trinity Church, Long Melford, Suffolk. Fourteenth century. Photo: G. M. Gibson.

spectacles recorded in the cathedral and municipal records at Lincoln
were plays or elaborate stage machines or floats or silent tableaux[4]
(distinctions surely far more important to modern drama historians
than to the medieval audiences who watched them), such controversy
has ignored and obscured an essential question: *why* Saint Anne's feast
was deemed such an important day for communal celebration (not
only at Lincoln but elsewhere, most notably in Suffolk and Norfolk,
in the East Anglian towns that have given us the Saint Anne plays of
the N-Town cycle of mystery plays and the Saint Anne's Day plays
in the Digby manuscript), why, indeed, the day of Saint Anne could
function for the medieval theater of public streets as a counterpart to
that other summer festival of bodily grace and reassurance, Corpus
Christi.

Although the official recognition of the cult of Saint Anne in
England did not come until 1382 (when, on the occasion of King
Richard II's marriage to Anne of Bohemia, Pope Urban VI ordered
that the feast of the new queen's name saint be observed in the English
church), and although the feast of the mother of the Virgin was not a
required holy day for the universal Catholic church until 1582, there is
evidence of considerable medieval English devotion to the mother of
the Virgin, especially in East Anglia. Abbot Anselm (1121–48) of Bury
Saint Edmunds, Suffolk, is credited with being the first to celebrate in
medieval England the feast of the mother of the Virgin,[5] and Anselm's
Suffolk contemporary, Osbert of Clare, is known for the enthusiasm
with which he wrote, from his Augustinian priory at Clare, letters
and treatises urging reverence of Saint Anne and observance of the
feast of Saint Anne's Immaculate Conception of Mary.[6] By 1309, long
before Richard's marriage to Anne of Bohemia, there was already a
parish confraternity of Saint Anne at Bury Saint Edmunds, and, in
the crypt of the abbey church at Bury, there was a chapel dedicated
to Saint Anne's Immaculate Conception.[7] By the fifteenth century
there were dozens of Saint Anne guilds and altars in East Anglian
parish churches. In the 1460s at East Harling, Norfolk, for example,
an heiress named Anne Harling (a member of the bookish crowd presided over by Chaucer's granddaughter, Elizabeth Chaucier, duchess
of Suffolk) founded a chantry chapel dedicated to Saint Anne in the
north aisle of Harling parish church.[8] We know from the will of Long
Melford church's most important fifteenth-century patron, a wealthy

Fig. 3. Kentwell Manor, from the late medieval kitchen and moathouse that formed part of the Clopton estate of Lutons. Photo: Royal Commission on the Historical Monuments of England.

clothier and onetime sheriff of Suffolk and Norfolk named John Clopton, that Long Melford, too, had a Saint Anne altar and that Clopton bequeathed a fine red vestment to it.[9] Neither the Saint Anne's altar nor the stained-glass window of Saint Anne leading the Virgin Mary by the hand, presented by John Clopton to Long Melford church,[10] survive today, nor did anything survive of the Elizabethan rebuilding but the old kitchen and moathouse of the Clopton manor house at Lutons (fig. 3), where once stood the Clopton family chapel that we know was dedicated to Saint Anne.[11] As the hidden Long Melford alabaster reminds us by its very surprising presence, time and iconoclasm have left all too well their effects on visual evidence of English medieval popular devotion.

Where East Anglian popular devotion to Saint Anne does still reveal itself is in a group of texts, once apparently a separate quire, bound into the fifteenth-century commonplace book of Robert Reynes of Acle, a Norfolk village eleven miles east of Norwich. Like John Clopton of Long Melford, Robert Reynes was an important patron of his parish church and a man who had developed a proprietary interest in the affairs of his local community. Like Clopton, Reynes was a prominent layman with close ties to a local monastic house. In the case of Robert Reynes, that monastery was not a great and royally favored Benedictine abbey such as Bury Saint Edmunds, where Clopton and his father before him had been honored by lay brotherhood status, but Weybridge Priory, the small house of canons regular that had been founded at Acle by the Bigod family and that was the meeting place for the Acle confraternity of Saint Anne.[12] Robert Reynes's commonplace book contains a whole series of texts concerning Saint Anne that appear to be a register of texts for public recitation at guild festivities.[13] The most important of these is a poem of 460 lines on "þe worchepe of sent Anne in thys tyme of ʒeere."[14] The Acle poem presents for the edification of "this gylde"[15] the same kind of redemptive prologue, traced from the womb of Saint Anne to the womb of Mary, that we can see dramatized in the N-Town *contemplatio* plays or celebrated in John Lydgate's aureate hymns on the mother of the Virgin.[16] All of these texts are wondering celebrations of a miraculous redemption that has been directed backward beyond the Holy Child in Mary's womb to the conception of Mary herself. But, significantly, there are two other preoccupations in the Acle guild poem that help clarify the meaning of the Saint Anne guild and its festival celebrations of Saint Anne.

First of all, the Reynes commonplace book confirms that the popular cult of Saint Anne in fifteenth-century Norfolk, as elsewhere, was an undisguised celebration of family ties and the relationships of human kinship. If the life of the archetypal medieval saint, Saint Francis, was about radical repudiation of family ties in favor of a barefoot and homeless brotherhood of mendicants, then Saint Anne, just as archetypically, was the saint who asserted the opposite, humanly consoling message not only that is the heart where the home is but that it is in the family where holiness can be found. The poem in the Reynes commonplace book has no sooner called for silence than it begins to tell the complicated and somewhat gossipy story of Saint Anne's family tree ("Summe wyll askyn of Sent Anne who was her ffadyr")[17] and the improbable medieval legend of Anne's three husbands (she marries Cleophas and Salome in turn after Joachim's death and has a trinity of daughters all named Mary). Three other entries in the Robert Reynes commonplace book also concern the holy lineage of Anne, including a brief Latin line that seems to be a mnemonic device for remembering the exotic names of Saint Anne's parents ("Est tuus Anna pater Izakar, Nazaphat tua mater").[18] Far from being "learned Latin notes," as Rosemary Woolf has called the very similar marginal comments in the N-Town cycle manuscript detailing the genealogy of Saint Anne and Joachim,[19] these litanies of Holy Family history, rendered in the dogged verse of a parish commonplace book, prove English fascination with the same Holy Kinship theme that is so ubiquitous in fifteenth- and sixteenth-century Continental altar paintings.[20]

But, most of all, what the Acle guild poem rather ingenuously makes clear is that Saint Anne and her husband, Joachim, are a merchant's saints par excellence; pregnant Saint Anne was, to be sure, but she was never barefoot. Saint Anne and Joachim were "ryght ryche folke,"[21] the poet tells us approvingly, as he transforms ascetic gospel and saintly paradigms by his enthusiastic bourgeois piety. This is no Saint Anne of Franciscan poverty but a Saint Anne who, with her multiple husbands and her doting and dutiful daughters, appears in this poem as a rich and pious widow on a fifteenth-century tomb monument, her modishly dressed family lined up in birth order beside her and shown with clasped, bejeweled hands. The Acle poem closely follows the canonical history of the life of Saint Anne in the *Golden Legend* but adds elaboration and emphases that make of Saint Anne a model East Anglian matron, tending to her tithes, her alms basket, and her prayer book. This is sanctity envisioned as a busy, comfortable, and pious life in which only the temporary martyrdom of childlessness must be suffered—to be overcome in the fruitful triumph of becoming the grandmother of God. It is difficult to imagine a saint with more obvious popular appeal.

It was a versified life of this merchant's saint that Osbern Bokenham (ca. 1392–1445) wrote for Katherine Denston, the half sister of the prominent Suffolk clothier John Clopton. The "Vita Sanctae Annae matris Sanctae Mariae" is actually one of thirteen Middle English verse lives of women saints known to have been written by Osbern Bokenham, an Augustinian friar from Clare Priory, near Long Melford, and an admiring disciple of Suffolk's much better known poet-monk, John Lydgate. (In a self-conscious prologue to one of his saints' lives, Bokenham writes that Pallas Athena has informed him that he has arrived too late for her to bestow her aureate verses, since all the "most fresch flourys" of rhetoric have already been gathered by Gower, Chaucer, and Lydgate; rejected by his muse, Bokenham laments that he thus has no choice but to tell his saint's life in plain verse, "aftyr the language of Suthfolk speche.") [22] In 1447, apparently shortly after Bokenham's death, his versified saints' lives in "Suthfolk speche" were gathered together into a manuscript anthology by one of his patrons, Friar Thomas Burgh of Cambridge, to be given to a "holy place of nunnys that þei shulde haue mynd on hym & of hys systyr Dame Betrice Burgh." [23] The Burgh anthology, still existing in a single manuscript in the British Library (MS. Arundel 327), was edited in 1938 by Mary Sergeantson for the Early English Text Society as *Legendys of Hooly Wummen.*

What are most interesting about Bokenham's legends of holy women are their gossipy prefaces and epilogues. Each exemplary narrative is framed by Bokenham's characteristically rambling and name-dropping explanations of the circumstances and patronage of each poem. The prologue to Bokenham's "Life of Saint Mary Magdalene," for example, tells us that, at the urging of Elizabeth Howard de Vere (who was countess of Oxford and, with her husband, chief patron of Bokenham's priory at Stoke-by-Clare), he had just begun a poem on Saint Elizabeth of Hungary, whose life "to alle wyvys myht a merour be." [24] He happened to be talking one Twelfth Night, in 1445, to Lady Isabel Bourchier, the daughter-in-law of Lydgate's former patroness, Ann, countess of Stafford. As Lady Isabel and this social-climbing friar sit chatting and watching Isabel's four sons "busy with their revel and their daunsyng," they begin to speak of Bokenham's poem-in-progress for the countess of Oxford. Bokenham describes how Lady Isabel, somewhat petulantly insisting that she has had for a long time "synguler devocyoun" to Saint Mary Magdalene, entreats him to put aside for a while his life of Saint Elizabeth of Hungary in order to create a translation in English verse of the life of Mary Magdalene "for my sake / . . . & for reverence of her." [25] The peevish competition for Bokenham's attentions between Lady Isabel of the staunchly Yorkist Bourchier family and the local Lancastrian matriarch, Elizabeth de Vere, is not so amusing in hindsight; Elizabeth de Vere's husband and son would be arrested and beheaded at the Tower of London in 1462 on a charge of treasonous correspondence with

Margaret of Anjou to plot a landing of Lancastrian troops on the east coast of Suffolk.[26] Here, in Bokenham's poem of a saint, a Twelfth Night revel is the setting for family rivalry that will spill over into the turbulent dynastic politics of the Wars of the Roses.

Thankfully, not all the Suffolk and Norfolk families mentioned in Bokenham's poems were linked by violence. Most were connected by the intimacies of business, kin, and friendship rather than those of hostility,[27] and all but one of Bokenham's saints' lives (a life of Saint Margaret requested by Friar Burgh) were commissioned by women. Like Katherine Denston, these patronesses were the wives and daughters of the local landed gentry, wealthy cloth merchants, and prominent civil servants of this flourishing East Anglian regional culture. Most were commissions made to honor a name saint or a special patroness with whom the women were identified in private and public devotional practice. Bokenham rendered poems intended to perform explicitly stated and practical functions: to teach and edify (as did the life of Saint Elizabeth of Hungary, who is to be a "merour" to all wives), to entertain (as did the extravagant adventures of Bokenham's "Life of Saint Mary Magdalene," engendered at the Twelfth Night revel, which make good escapist reading and bombastic theater in the Digby play of *Mary Magdalene*), but especially to perform, by the power exchange of talismanic magic, the specific intercessions and protections begged by the pious woman whose name or whose pious prayers linked her to the glorified saint. Bokenham's role was also to create texts that would perform in turn the glorification of the patroness and of her kin.

But Osbern Bokenham's texts and their circumstances make clear that the local East Anglian politics of family were as complexly connected and encoded as the dynastic politics of the Crown. John Clopton, in fact, would be arrested along with Elizabeth de Vere's family on suspicion of Lancastrian treason but, unlike them, was allowed to return to his home at Long Melford, where he seems to have made some hasty political realignment: Yorkist white roses appear conspicuously in his surviving donor portrait in the Long Melford church built by his cloth fortune. Among the celebrated stained-glass windows of Melford church, Clopton placed not only his own portrait but also portraits of his sons and daughters, his ancestors, and his friends and important associates, some of them kinsmen by marriage, some of

them as connected as kin in the power alliances of this close East
Anglian neighborhood. A portrait of Katherine Denston must have
been there among the Cloptons at Long Melford; the stained-glass
images of her daughter (fig. 4) and of her husband, John, still survive
in the clerestory windows of the north aisle.[28] In 1474 John Denston,
an important Suffolk civil servant and landowner, along with his son-
in-law, Sir John Broughton, founded a college and chantry at Denston
church and rebuilt his own parish church in a perpendicular style much
influenced by (indeed, in token competition with) Long Melford's
grandeur (fig. 5). In Denston Saint Nicholas, Katherine and John Denston still lie together within a canopy tomb placed at the north side of
the chancel, their stone effigies carved as decaying corpses in funeral
shrouds (fig. 6).[29]

If Katherine Denston's tomb sculpture speaks a sermon on her
death, her life is as eloquently commemorated by Bokenham's verse
life of Saint Anne. And it is in the facts of Katherine Denston's life
and in the creating circumstances of the poem of the life of Saint Anne
that I think the most articulate example of Bokenham's hagiography
of kinship can be found. The facts we know are these: Katherine's
mother, Margery Drury, had died young in 1420, leaving William
Clopton to take as his second wife Margery Francis, who bore his
son, John, in 1422. Katherine was still a child when her stepmother
died, evidently while giving birth to the second Clopton daughter,
Elizabeth, two years later.[30] Her half brother, John Clopton, grew up
to become patriarch of the Clopton kin, a man preoccupied in life
—and in prospect of death—by extraordinary concern for his family
and family name; inscriptions bearing the Clopton family name are
carved into every knapped-flint wall of Long Melford church.[31] John
Clopton's will is full of allusions to material objects hallowed by the
holiness of kinship; each heirloom is bequeathed along with the com-
mandment that it continue to be handed down in the "blode of Clopton." Such is the condition, for example, that accompanies Clopton's
bequest of a brooch "with the iii perlis and iii stones" to a daughter-
in-law; she must leave it in turn to his grandson Fraunces "or to some
issue male of my sonne Willyams, so that it may contynewe in the
blode of Cloptons."[32]

The Clopton heirs were alternately named William and John for
generations, but Anne was the name of Katherine Clopton Denston's

Fig. 4. Norwich Glass Workshop, *Donor Portrait of Anne Denston,* in a
window in the north aisle of Holy Trinity Church, Long Melford, Suffolk.
Late fifteenth century. Photo: G. M. Gibson.

Fig. 5. Church of Saint Nicholas, Denston, Suffolk. Late fifteenth century. Photo: Royal Commission on the Historical Monuments of England.

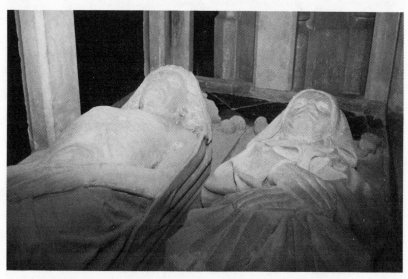

Fig. 6. *Cadaver Tomb of John and Katherine Denston,* Church of Saint Nicholas, Denston, Suffolk. Ca. 1500. Photo: Margaret Statham.

only child. And for Katherine Denston, commissioning a poem of the life of Saint Anne was surely no Twelfth Night whim. Bokenham's poem was commissioned not only to honor the saint, who was a special patron of the Clopton family, but also to instruct her namesake, Anne Denston. (Nor could it have been lost on young Anne Denston that Saint Anne's husband, Joachim, was "a ryche man & of gret dignyte.")[33] But Osbern Bokenham's life of Saint Anne was most especially a text heavy with its own sacramental function. In his awkward and stiffly aureate Suffolk verse, Bokenham wrote for Katherine Denston an incantational text invoking childbirthing grace and protection, invoking from the saint of long-sought childbirth—the saint who had been finally glorified with triumph over the womb —safe delivery of the male issue that Katherine (alas, fruitlessly) hoped would continue the name of Denston and the kin of Clopton. Bokenham's "Vita S. Annae" culminates in prayerful supplication for Saint Anne's protection of the Denstons in this world and in the world to come, but especially with a prayer that reveals the essential purpose of Katherine's commission and of Bokenham's poem. May Saint Anne, Osbern Bokenham implores,

> Prouide, lady, eek þat Ion denstone
> & kateryne his wyf, if it plese þe grace
> Of god aboue, thorgh þi merytes a sone
> Of her body.[34]

Bokenham's text, in fact, seems to have been written to perform precisely the same kind of talismanic function as the hidden Long Melford alabaster of Mary in childbed: both give image and name to the holy births that blessed and redeemed the carnal yearning for the immortality of humankind. Daughter of mothers dying in childbirth, mother of a daughter called Anne, Katherine Denston asks of Bokenham creative writing in the most primary sense, for Bokenham's poem on the life of Saint Anne both invokes the mothering saint as answer to his patroness's fear and longing and offers the hope that the dark and painful mystery of childbed might be transfigured by grace. Sleeping at her husband's side in her stone shroud, Katherine Denston surely remembers.

NOTES

This essay is for Annie.

1. Jeffrey, "English Saints' Plays," 72.

2. On the Long Melford alabaster and other English fourteenth-century Nativity alabasters of similar iconography, see Cheetham, *English Medieval Alabasters*, 18–19.

3. See Erickson, *Medieval Vision*, 196–97.

4. See especially Nelson, *Medieval English Stage*, 100–118.

5. In 1328 the provincial council of Canterbury attributed the feast of the Immaculate Conception to Anselm, although there is evidence that the feast had been celebrated and subsequently forgotten in preconquest England. See Bishop, *Liturgica historica*, 238–59.

6. See *Letters of Osbert of Clare*, 11–13.

7. Redstone, "Chapels, Chantries, and Gilds in Suffolk," 75.

8. Anne Harling's will specified that she be buried in this "chapell of Seint Anne, joyned to the chaucell of the churche . . . in Estharlyng, in the tombe wt my late worshipfull husbond, Sir William Chamberleyn, accordyng to my promyse made unto hym afore this time" (*Testamenta eboracensia* 4:149).

9. *Visitation of Suffolke* 1:37. A 1529 inventory from Long Melford church mentions "a Candlestick of 10 branches before St. Ann" and a hutch and painted altarcloths from Saint Anne's chapel (Parker, *History of Long Melford*, 84–85).

10. Woodforde, *Norwich School of Glass Painting*, 112.

11. Parker, *History of Long Melford*, 170.

12. *Commonplace Book of Robert Reynes of Acle*, 35–36, and Taylor, *Index monasticus*, 27.

13. *Commonplace Book of Robert Reynes*, 12.

14. Ibid., 196–228. The particularity of the Reynes text and its guild occasion is underscored by another manuscript version of the poem, MS. Harley 4012, which pointedly omits the reference to Saint Anne guild and replaces "þe worchepe of sent Anne in thys tyme of ʒeere" with the general phrase "in any tyme of ʒer." See *Middle English Stanzaic Versions of the Life of Saint Anne*, 126 (line 453).

15. *Commonplace Book of Robert Reynes*, 228.

16. See *Minor Poems of John Lydgate*, 130–33.

17. *Commonplace Book of Robert Reynes*, 200.

18. Ibid., 194.

19. Woolf, *English Mystery Plays*, 309. See also *N-Town Plays*, fol. 37.

20. Fragments of an East Anglian Holy Kinship window survive in the parish church of Saint Peter Mancroft in Norwich, where a Saint Anne guild worshiped (see Woodforde, *Norwich School of Glass Painting*, 21). Paintings of

Saint Anne's daughters and grandsons also survive on a fifteenth-century rood screen in the Norfolk parish church of Ranworth (see Cautley, *Norfolk Churches*, 233–34, and Lasko and Morgan, *Medieval Art in East Anglia*, 49).

21. *Commonplace Book of Robert Reynes*, 110.

22. Bokenham, *Legendys of Hooly Wummen*, 111.

23. Ibid., 289.

24. Ibid., 138.

25. Ibid., 139.

26. Parker, *History of Long Melford*, 44.

27. On some of the connections between East Anglian literary patrons recorded in contemporary documents, see Moore, "Patrons of Letters," 82–93.

28. Woodforde, *Norwich School of Glass Painting*, 108. An inscription in Long Melford church urged the passerby to "pray for the soul of John Denston and for the happy state of Catherine his wife, daughter of [William] Clopton, Esq. and of Anne Broughton, daughter and heir of the aforesaid John and Katherine" (see Moore, "Patrons of Letters," 83).

29. Fleming, "St. Nicholas' Church, Denston, Suffolk," 10–11.

30. Woodforde, *Norwich School of Glass Painting*, 101.

31. See Pevsner, *Suffolk*, 344–45.

32. *Visitation of Suffolke* 1:36.

33. Bokenham, *Legendys of Hooly Wummen*, 45.

34. Ibid., 57–58.

BIBLIOGRAPHY

Bishop, Edmund. *Liturgica historica*. 1918. Reprint. Oxford: Clarendon Press, 1962.

Bokenham, Osbern. *Legendys of Hooly Wummen*. Ed. Mary S. Sergeantson. EETS, o.s., no. 206. 1938. Reprint. London: Kraus Reprints, 1971.

Cautley, H. Munro. *Norfolk Churches*. 1949. Reprint. Ipswich: The Boydell Press, 1979.

Cheetham, Francis. *English Medieval Alabasters*. London: Phaidon and Christie's Limited, 1984.

The Commonplace Book of Robert Reynes of Acle: An Edition of Tanner MS. 407. Ed. Cameron Louis. New York and London: Garland Publishing Company, 1980.

Erickson, Carolly. *The Medieval Vision: Essays in History and Perception*. New York: Oxford University Press, 1976.

Fleming, Irene J. R. "St. Nicholas' Church, Denston, Suffolk." Halstead, Suffolk, n.d. Visitors' guide.

Jeffrey, David L. "English Saints' Plays." In *Medieval Drama*, ed. Neville

Denny, 69–89. Stratford-upon-Avon Studies, no. 16. London: Edward Arnold, 1973.

Lasko, P., and N. J. Morgan, eds. *Medieval Art in East Anglia, 1300–1520.* Norwich: Jarrold and Sons, 1973.

Lydgate, John. *The Minor Poems of John Lydgate, Part 1.* Ed. Henry Noble Mac-Cracken. EETS, e.s., no. 107. 1911. Reprint. London: Oxford University Press, 1962.

The Middle English Stanzaic Versions of the Life of Saint Anne. Ed. Roscoe E. Parker. EETS, o.s., no. 174. London: Oxford University Press, 1928.

Moore, Samuel. "Patrons of Letters in Norfolk and Suffolk, c. 1450." *PMLA* 28 (1913): 82–93.

Nelson, Alan. *The Medieval English Stage: Corpus Christi Pageants and Plays.* Chicago: University of Chicago Press, 1974.

The N-Town Plays: A Facsimile of British Library MS. Cotton Vespasian D VIII. Ed. Peter Meredith and Stanley J. Kahrl. Leeds Medieval Drama Facsimiles, no. 4. Ilkey, Yorkshire: Scholar Press, 1977.

Osbert of Clare. *The Letters of Osbert of Clare.* Ed. E. W. Williamson. London: Oxford University Press, 1929.

Parker, Sir William. *The History of Long Melford.* London: Wyman and Sons, 1873.

Pevsner, Nikolaus. *Suffolk.* Rev. Enid Radcliffe. Harmondsworth and New York: Penguin Books, 1975.

Redstone, V. B. "Chapels, Chantries, and Gilds in Suffolk." *Proceedings of the Suffolk Institute of Archaeology and Natural History* 12 (1904): 1–87.

Taylor, Richard. *Index monasticus; or, The Abbeys and Other Monasteries, Alien Priories, Friaries, Colleges, Collegiate Churches, and Hospitals with Their Dependencies Formerly Established in the Diocese of Norwich and the Ancient Kingdom of East Anglia.* London: Richard and Arthur Taylor, 1821.

Testamenta eboracensia: A Selection of Wills from the Register at York. Vol. 4. Ed. James Raine. Surtees Society, no. 53. Durham: Andrew and Company, 1869.

The Visitation of Suffolke, Made by William Hervey, Clarenceux King of Arms, 1561, with Additions from Family Documents, Original Wills, Jermyn, Davy, and Other MSS., Etc. Vol. 1. Ed. Joseph Jackson Howard. London: Samuel Tymms and Whittaker and Company, 1866.

Woodforde, Christopher. *The Norwich School of Glass Painting in the Fifteenth Century.* London: Oxford University Press, 1950.

Woolf, Rosemary. *The English Mystery Plays.* Berkeley and Los Angeles: University of California Press, 1972.

Image and Ideology

Saint Anne in Late Medieval Drama and Narrative

KATHLEEN ASHLEY

T he iconography of Saint Anne has been one of the least-
studied contexts for late medieval spirituality and drama,
although the flourishing of the cult of Anne, mother of the
Virgin Mary and grandmother of Christ, coincides with the period
of the religious drama's greatest efflorescence—the late fifteenth and
early sixteenth centuries. The veneration of Anne, who could be the
patron of such specifically female activities as childbirth, may seem to
give a feminized slant to fifteenth-century religious experience. However, the figure of Anne was available for many nongendered purposes
within late medieval culture. Furthermore, even as a gendered image,
Anne does not always have the same "meaning."

   To explore the complexity of late medieval gender symbolism, I
will offer a comparative analysis of three plays, each associated with
the cult of Saint Anne in a distinctive way. The first is a Nativity play
written by a Belgian nun and performed in her convent at Huy, near
Liège.[1] The Huy Nativity dramatizes a visit by Anne and her other
two daughters to Mary shortly after the birth of Christ. The English
N-Town cycle, whose institutional auspices are unknown, although
it appears to be the product of East Anglian piety, dramatizes the conception of Mary and her birth to Anne and Joachim within a section
of the manuscript marked by Marian devotion.[2] The third play, the
Digby manuscript play of Candelmas Day and the killing of the chil-

dren of Israel, is set within the communal celebration of Saint Anne's Day and represents, by contrast, a strikingly male perspective in the comedy of the young soldier Watkyn, who is afraid of the militant mothers.[3]

I will connect the representation of Anne in each play with a particular social context: the lay religious guild (N-Town), affective piety and female mysticism (Huy), and the ritualization of gender separateness by town ceremonial (Digby). I aim to explore late medieval theater as a site of cultural production in which conflicting social ideologies could be dramatically displayed and perhaps symbolically resolved, and I will argue that cultural symbols such as Saint Anne are less a means of representing a meaning than an opportunity to perform it. In other words, it's not so much what a symbol *expresses* as what it *triggers*. The image of Saint Anne and references to her legend are symbolic triggers for activating ideological formations within specific social genres for specific social groups.

The Huy Nativity

Unlike Saint Anne's appearance in the birth and childhood of Mary in the N-Town cycle, which was authorized by narrative traditions based on the apocryphal Gospels, her role in the Huy Nativity play is highly unusual. How, then, do we explain her prominence in the scene wherein she arrives with her other two daughters on a postpartum visit to Mary?

An analysis of "tone" may offer a lead. The language of the scene is humanly affectionate but at the same time elevated. It combines a recognition of the human relationships of mother to daughter, mother to son, mother-in-law to son-in-law, and sister to sister with an explicit acknowledgment that the birth of Christ is part of the divine plan for incarnation and salvation. The word "humaine" weaves through the scene—"char humaine" (lines 183, 206), "humaine nature" (line 209), "humaniteit" (lines 218, 223)—as the metaphorical fulcrum: it is through humanity, human flesh, that God meets men and women. The human familial relationships displayed in the play become the means by which the incarnational plan works, both as drama and as theology. Thus, when Saint Anne arrives, Mary greets her with joy and kisses her mother and sisters. Joseph also salutes her as "dame de grant digniteit," full of "bonteit," and he is greeted in return for his "saint bonteit," which has earned him the privilege of guarding the Son of God and his mother. Human dignity and amiability provide a structure for the plan of incarnation.

Next, Anne asks her beloved daughter to tell them all about the birth experience, but this gossipy human interaction is suffused with the miraculous details of the painless delivery, which signals Mary's perpetual virginity and her awareness that the child she sees in the flesh is the Son of God (lines 177–90). When Anne asks to see the child, Joseph carries him to Mary, who sits him on her knee for Anne, Marie Jacob, and Marie Salome to worship as both their human relative and divine God. Anne speaks to the baby as "suy vostre indigne grandame" (line 210), while Marie Jacob worships him as "tresdouls cusin" (line 216), noting the great love that had led him to take their humanity. Then Anne addresses Mary as "Queen of heaven and earth," asking her to tell her poor mother ("vostre poure mere," line 227) further details of the birth of Christ. Mary then details the adoration of the angels, the shepherds, and the three Magi, all of whom recognized the divine essence joined with humanity (lines 255–56). Anne confirms that all this occurred following biblical prophecies, but her other two daughters ask their sister Mary to look at her son, who is laughing and looking back at them with his beautiful eyes, as if he recognizes them (lines 272–75).

Contemporary feminist film theory has called attention to the male gaze that demeans and dehumanizes women, turning them into objects.[4] Here the gaze of the adoring grandmother and aunts on the baby confirms his beauty and lovableness, first as human infant and then, as interpreted by Anne, as the fulfillment of the prophecy of David, as the most beautiful being ever born of a mother ("c'est la plus belle forme d'home, que oncque de mere nasqui," line 283). He is, Anne says, "Dieu et home" (line 289).

This adoring female gaze upon the body of Christ and his reciprocal look of recognition at the worshiper are central to late medieval religious traditions of affective piety, which grew out of the Franciscan emphasis on the Incarnation. It is central to the lyric genre, especially in lyrics of the Nativity and Passion spoken by or to Mary. Often there are references, for example, to the beauty of Christ's infant body, which contrasts with the suffering and discolored body hanging on the cross.[5] In the late Middle Ages the gaze upon the incarnate body provides the metaphorical language of mystical visions, especially those of women mystics.[6]

In the Huy play, although it is her daughters who call attention to the reciprocal gaze that characterizes adoration, Anne is the figure of authority who shows how to read physical images within a meditative context. It has been pointed out recently that, within late medieval spirituality and associated with the rise of female mysticism, is a gendering of meditative techniques. Richard Kieckhefer notes the distinction that was made between contemplative prayer, "in which one discards all images and concepts and surrenders oneself to the flow of spontaneous illumination," and meditative prayer, "with its discursive reflection on images and events (drawn largely from the life of Christ)."[7]

Although both types of prayer originated in the monasteries, in the late Middle Ages contemplative prayer came to be associated with monastic mysticism, while meditative recreation of biblical scenes burgeoned within lay spirituality. André Vauchez suggests that such image-based meditation was characteristic of the mystical experiences of women,[8] and Elizabeth Petroff says that, "for many women, devotional meditations of this kind pass imperceptibly into visions."[9]

Late medieval piety is a societywide phenomenon, but it is striking how often its characteristic *forms* were attributed to the needs of the "weaker sex"—women. Religious images had traditionally been defended as texts for the unlettered that encouraged religious understanding, but they were often specifically designed for women. The meditative technique outlined and demonstrated in the fourteenth-century *Meditations on the Life of Christ* was addressed to a nun, a Poor Clare, by a Franciscan. The *Meditations* provided the model for numerous handbooks of meditation, including Ludolph the Carthusian's *Vita Jesu Christi*. In a brilliant essay, Christiane Klapisch-Zuber has analyzed the part played by religious objects, such as dolls and other toys, in exciting the imaginations of women and children: "By the contemplation of these objects, by their manipulation in play, ritual or dramatic fantasizing, these souls of 'weaker' and more 'malleable' constitution were led to a spiritual vision of the sacred verities."[10]

Images of the infant Christ with his mother, attended by female relatives and servants, might seem most appropriate to the piety of those who had shared the experience of motherhood, but they appear to have been common in the mystical devotions of nuns as well. The *Meditations on the Life of Christ* models this affective devotion to the infant Christ for its monastic reader: "You too, who lingered so long, kneel and adore your Lord God, and then his mother, and reverently greet the saintly old Joseph. Kiss the beautiful little feet of the infant Jesus who lies in the manger and beg his mother to let you hold him a while. Pick Him up and hold Him in your arms. Gaze on his face with devotion and reverently kiss Him and delight in Him. . . . Then return Him to the mother, and watch her attentively as she cares for Him assiduously and wisely, nursing him and rendering all service, and remain to help her if you can." [11]

In a play written by one of the nuns of the convent,[12] acted by and for nuns, the celebration of the female Holy Kinship group has a special relevance. The language of incarnational devotion in the Huy Nativity bears out the claim, made by Caroline Bynum and other scholars of medieval spirituality, that in women's piety the humanity of Christ is emphasized more than devotion to the Virgin,[13] while most recognition goes to Mary for her physical role as bearer of the incarnate God. The Virgin Mary and her mother, Saint Anne, are honored in the Holy Kinship image as women through whose bodies the divine plan is accomplished. Especially inspirational to nuns in a convent, this powerful image was not confined to only female contexts but was widely accessible. This highly gendered image modeled a type of affective piety for late medieval society as a whole. It was a type of piety in which the physical image could give rise to contemplation, in which the physical body was vehicle for the divine, in which there was no conflict between earth and heaven—only a functional harmony.

The N-Town Mary Play

A second locus for the appearance of Saint Anne I consider is the N-Town cycle, a manuscript of plays whose exact performance context is unknown (if, in fact, they were ever performed), since no external records link it to a particular city—unlike the Chester or York cycles in England or Passion plays and *mystères* on the Continent. The manuscript seems to be a composite cycle of plays from Creation to Judgment Day, including an Old Testament group, a Passion play, and, most importantly for our purposes, a group of plays on the early life of Mary, which were derived from the apocryphal materials on the conception, nativity, and betrothal of the Virgin, materials that had been incorporated into the *Legenda aurea* and its vernacular offspring.[14]

If one takes into account these textual sources for the apocryphal legend of Saint Anne and her three marriages, known as the *trinubium,* the appearance of Anne in the section of the N-Town cycle on the early life of the Virgin is a matter of no surprise. But where the Huy Nativity, in the dignified and powerful matriarchal figure of Saint Anne, authorizes a type of affective and feminized reading of earthly images, the N-Town Anne articulates at least as many problems as she solves.

The genealogy of Anna and Joachim, laid out in table form, fills the folio in which the Mary play begins. The prologue has a *contemplacio* figure who describes the matter of the plays to follow: the conception of Mary, her appearance at the temple as a small child, her marriage to Joseph, and her meeting with Elizabeth. In the first scene, Joachim is thrown out of the temple by Isakar, the high priest, because he and Anna are barren. In the second, an angel assures Joachim that Anna will have a child in her old age, and the couple meet at the Golden Gate, where, according to the iconography of the Immaculate Conception, which the play promotes, Mary was conceived by their "clene kiss." In the fourth scene, Mary is dedicated to a life of virginity in the temple, and in the fifth she and Joseph are persuaded to marry, against their wishes to remain virgins. The parliament of heaven, where the Incarnation is debated, inaugurates the next sequence of plays on the Nativity of Christ.

Anne is portrayed in N-Town in her full genealogical regalia as the necessary link in the Holy Kinship to which Jesus belongs. She is a loving wife and mother—indeed, she, Joachim, and Mary represent an idealized family group. But perhaps more profoundly, the figure of Anne mediates the social contradictions implicit in this drama.

If there is one theme that ties the plays of the N-Town cycle together, it may be the concern, verging on obsession, with purity and holiness. The language I use here is anthropologist Mary Douglas's, who discusses "pollution beliefs" as expressions of a moral order that is beyond social morality. Of the Hebrew idea of holiness, she says, "Holiness means keeping distinct the categories of creation. It therefore involves correct definition, discrimination and order. Under this head all the rules of sexual morality exemplify the holy. Incest and adultery are against holiness, in the simple sense of right order. Morality does not conflict with holiness but holiness is more a matter of separating that which should be separated than of protecting the rights of husbands and brothers." [15]

N-Town is filled with purgation rituals, which reestablish the purity of the central characters. Paradigmatic of this type of "cosmology," in Douglas's terminology, is Joachim's exclusion from the temple. It is a matter not of what Joachim has *done* but of his violating through barrenness the conditions of admittance to the temple. His presence pollutes and violates the temple. Holiness, not virtue, is at issue here, where the temple is the symbol of all holy places and bodies. Similarly, N-Town stages a trial of Joseph and Mary for adultery, complete with grotesque "detractors." It has been taken as satire, but it is more accurately a demonstration of the purity of Joseph and Mary than an examination of the limits of the social system. The clean body of Mary is a central symbol in the whole cycle but especially in the sequences portraying Mary's childhood and betrothal and the Nativity of Christ.

On the basis of this "cosmology" of purity, it could be argued that the N-Town cycle might have belonged to an East Anglian religious guild with both lay and clerical membership and strong ecclesiastical ties. This is an argument that others familiar with the cycle have also made recently, although on grounds different from mine. Peter Meredith, for example, speculates that a Norfolk religious guild provided "exactly the right setting for the kind of devotional tone that the *Mary Play* has." He discusses the commonplace book of Robert Reynes, with materials (a poem in honor of Saint Anne, notes on Anne's parentage, genealogies of Mary) compiled for a guild dedicated to Mary and her mother, materials reminiscent of the content of N-Town.[16] The family imagery and the relative lack of dramatic interest in representing social differentiation within good and evil groups support the probability that the plays were created for a religious guild whose group identity was strong but whose language of "brotherhood," "sisterhood," and family kinship downplayed social distinctions among members. Saint Anne functions here as one of the mediator figures of the cycle, who resolve contradictions acutely felt by guild members in this late medieval society. The growth of lay piety, with its intense devotionalism, often generated difficulties wherein modes and values from a monastic context (such as contemplation or chastity) were now appropriated by people outside the religious orders. Questions arose about how far laypersons could go in private meditation and devotional practices without official clerical guidance. Was it now possible to combine the ideal of chastity with the married state and poverty with the active life? These are live and troublesome issues for many within the culture, especially laywomen.

The *trinubium* of Anne, which had been constructed in order to neatly relate Christ and all the apostles in the narrative of his human life, clearly became problematic, among theologians and laypersons alike, for this reason. To begin with, marriage itself ranked lower than virginity in the medieval hierarchy of holiness. Margery Kempe, the fifteenth-century visionary and would-be saint, was tormented by her married state; she records several conversations with the Lord in her spiritual autobiography, or "Book," in which she explicitly raises the problem of being a holy person and a contemplative when one is engaged in the active life of marriage and family. She is especially troubled when she becomes pregnant, saying that her condition is incompatible with her visionary calling. Jesus tells her, "Rest assured that I love wives also, and especially those wives who would live chaste if they might have their will and do all they can to please me as you do. For though the state of maidenhood be more perfect and more holy than the state of widowhood, and the state of widowhood more perfect than the state of wedlock yet I love you, daughter, as much as any maiden in the world." [17] The subject obviously torments Margery, for she returns to it in several of her conversations, but she is always reassured by Christ: "Because you are a maiden in your soul, I shall take you by the one hand in heaven, and my mother by the other, and so you shall dance in heaven with other holy maidens and virgins, for I may call you dearly bought and my own beloved darling." [18]

What is explicit in Margery Kempe's unsuccessful case for sainthood is a subtext in other narratives of the period. In a society where many who were not in monasteries aspired to holiness, the traditional boundaries between the contemplative and active lives were being renegotiated. Saint Anne is a symbolic means for that renegotiation to take place in the fourteenth and fifteenth centuries. According to a structuralist understanding of mythical processes, by which incompatible realities are symbolically resolved in a figure that combines the contradictory alternatives, she was an appropriately ambivalent figure to provide that mediation. Saint Anne represented not just the marital state but the thrice-married state, thus violating social norms in a flamboyant way. At the same time, she was essential to the story of Mary's Immaculate Conception and the new interest in the genealogy of the Holy Family. She could be, in other words, the ideal mediating figure for a society in transition from ideals of chastity and contemplation to the elevation of marriage and the active life.

It is related that Colette of Corbie refused to pray to Saint Anne because she was appalled by Anne's three marriages. Colette even chastised her own mother for marrying twice, though her mother replied acerbically that Colette would not have been born otherwise. Colette replied that she was sure God would have seen to it that she was born to some near relation.[19] When Colette prayed, it was to saints renowned for their virginity. "On account of that she hardly ever, or never, referred for asking of help to blessed Anna, genetrix of holy Mary. But because she prayed so fervently in God's presence, once Anna appeared to her with glorious ornaments bringing with her all her glorious progeny, her three most glorious daughters, and her noble son. . . . And in this apparition, the glorious Anna manifested to her that although she had several times copulated in marriage no one in the whole church militant and triumphant was so adorned for his progeny and honored with fame." As a result of this vision, Colette realized the potential for multiple intercessions through Anne and her numerous offspring, so she founded special chapels and devotions to Anne in her convents.[20]

In a culture that had valued virginity and seen marriage as a necessary evil, the three marriages of Anne were a potential scandal and required justification. A culture in which Saint Anne could be so popular was clearly one undergoing a transition, and Saint Anne was an apt symbolic mediator of the contradictions of that transition, functioning as symbol for the contested issue of marriage in late medieval society.

The emerging ideology of marriage is closer to the surface in

N-Town than in the Huy Nativity, no doubt because it is not being dramatized within the confines of the convent (where earthly marriage, after all, is not a live issue) but is instead connected with the dramatic activities of a lay religious guild. Through the figure of Anne, the dilemma of those who wanted to lead a holy life and yet were in the world could be, at least symbolically, resolved.

The marriage of Anne and Joachim functioned within late medieval texts as an image of the new ideal of godly wedlock. The *Myroure of Our Ladye*—a devotional treatise on divine services[21]—describes the birth of Mary in the Wednesday lesson, identifying, among the laws given to Moses, holy wedlock, symbolized by the marriage of Joachim and Anne. Of such a wedlock is brought forth God's people, the *Myroure* says, and God hallows it by choosing to take from wedlock the mother of his manhood.[22] The story of the birth of Mary, with its concomitant worship of Anne, is to be recounted on the feasts of the Conception and Nativity of Mary and the feast of Anne: "For the holy concepcion, and byrthe of oure lady, wherof ys made mynde in that story, ys great worshyp & praysynge to her mother Anne, of whome she was conceyved and borne in so greate holynesse and clennesse."[23] Saint Bridget of Sweden, in her "Sermo Angelicus," picks up this theme and states that the law of Moses "taught men how God and their neighbor should be loved and how wedlock between man and woman should be kept according to the Law of God and the law of honesty. God . . . to whose sight all things present and to come are clear and manifest, the while he beheld all the righteous and honest wedlocks that were to exist from the making of the first man unto the last day, he yet foresaw none that, in godly charity and honesty, would be like unto the wedlock between Joachim and Anna. Hence it pleased him that the body of his most glorious mother . . . should be begotten in this holy wedlock."[24]

Saint Bridget has a vision of Saint Anne while in Rome getting relics. Anne introduces herself, "I ame Anne, ladi of all weddid folke that were byfor the lawe. Doghtir, wirshepe God of this manere: 'Blissed be thou Jesu Criste, the son of God that chesid the one modir of the weddinge of Joachim and Anne. And, therefor, for the praiers of Anne, have merci of all thame that are in wedeloke or thinkes to be weddid, that thai mai bring furth froite to the wirshipe of Gode.' "[25]

The mechanism by which the figure and myth of Anne mediate

the anxieties about the holiness of the marital state and the validity of remarriage is exemplified in Mirk's *Festial,* a collection of fourteenth-century sermons from England. The sermon for Saint Anne's Day places Anne first within a nominal lineage of Old and New Testament Annas, including Samuel's mother, Raguel's wife, Tobias's wife, and Anna in the temple for the Purification. Through her name, Anne the mother of Mary is typologically connected to a lineage of holy women, mothers, and wives. The sermon also describes Christ's and Mary's descent from David through Joachim, Mary's father and Anne's first husband. Then the second and third marriages of Anne, leading to other daughters and many grandchildren, are outlined. The sermon thus elides, first, the distinction between spiritual relations (based on the nominal identity of the various Annas) and physical relations (based on birth into a family). It also collapses the distinction between Joachim and the lineage of David and Anne's other marriages and the lineages they establish. All are resolved; all somehow conjoin in the figure of Anne. The sermon concludes with a prayer that Saint Anne pray to her holy daughter, Our Lady, who will pray to her son that he grant health in body and soul "and grace to kepe your ordyr of wedlok, and gete such chyldryn that byn plesant and trew servandys to God, and soo com to the blys that Saynt Anne ys yn."[26]

Where Huy uses the maternal as a metaphor for the flesh that bears divinity, N-Town's metaphor is marital, with marriage standing for the mixed life aspired to by the pious members of the lay confraternity.

Digby Candelmas and the Killing of the Children

In their introduction to the edition published by the Early English Text Society, the editors of the Digby manuscript comment that the play of Candelmas and the killing of the children is "not particularly suitable for the Feast of St. Anne."[27] They evaluate two theses about the possible circumstances surrounding the production of this play: first, that it was part of a cycle of plays presented one at a time annually on Saint Anne's Day in a local festival, a thesis argued by Hardin Craig years ago,[28] or, second, that it belonged to a group of plays taken on tour in East Anglia by a professional acting company. The major datum militating against the thesis about a professional acting company is a detail in the Purification scene: the prophetess Anna calls forth her virgins to worship the child, and they are identified in a stage direction as "as many as a man wylle" (line 464). Leaving aside, at least temporarily, the provocative gender issues raised by the line, we can see that, since most touring companies in the fifteenth century had five or six actors, this stage direction for a plenitude of virgins to process supports Craig's theory that this was a village festival play with local girls cast as the bevy of virgins.

It is most likely a play for a large town's celebration of Saint Anne's Day, for which it is highly suitable. What the editors of the Digby manuscript did not perceive was the festive inversion of gender taking place in the episode of the Massacre of the Innocents. In classic festive play with gender definitions, the play shows male acts of violence—comically portrayed in the young soldier Watkyn and seriously portrayed in Herod—tamed by righteous female anger.

Saint Anne is not a dramatized character, but she is important as patron of the occasion for the play. Her festival on July 26 had been officially proclaimed by the church in 1383, most likely in honor of the marriage of Richard II and Anne of Bohemia.[29] Although her feast day does not always have gender associations (see, for example, Roger Crum and David Wilkins's essay, in this volume, on Saint Anne's Day and Florentine republicanism), here it does. The prologue's narrator, called Poeta, announces that the feast is in memory of Saint Anne, mother to Our Lady, and calls on "ye virgines" to "shewe summe sport and plesure" to please the people and worship God. The prologue thus frames the drama as an act of entertainment and worship in which women are symbolically central.

The first and lengthiest section of the play follows Herod's command to kill the children of Israel in revenge for the escape of the three Magi from his kingdom. His messenger, Watkyn, comes forward after four soldiers have been sent to do the bloody task and promises he will fight "manly" and heartlessly ("though thei sharme and crye, I care not a myght, / but with my sharpe sworde ther ribbes I shalle shake, / evyn thurgh the guttes, for anger and despight" lines 142–144). Herod agrees to make the youth a knight if he fights well, so Watkyn goes off vowing to arm himself "manly" and earn the knighthood (line 156). He also confesses that he is somewhat of a coward and dreads "no thyng more thanne a woman with a rokke," that is, a spindle (line 159). He boasts that he will kill the children, but if he sees any wives walking about, he will wait until they are gone and sneak into their houses to find the children. If one of the mothers shows up, he will hide under the bench and lie still until she leaves, at which time "manly I shalle come out and hir children sloon!" (line 189). The four soldiers tease young Watkyn, saying that if he acquits himself well in this great endeavor they will report it to Herod: "If thu quyte the manly amonge the wyves" (who are fierce as lions when they are broken out of their cage toward men), they will recommend better wages for the youth.

Although Mary and Joseph make their escape with the infant Christ, the soldiers, threatening to kill the children, break into houses and are met with resistance by the women, who condemn them as "traitours of cruelle tormentrye" (line 296). The women vow to use all their powers of resistance against the soldiers and are challenged by Watkyn, who claims that "we be bold men and the kyng us ded sende" (line 307), but the mothers call him a coward and offer to dub him knight with their spindles. Watkyn does end up in a fight with the women, who beat him with the symbols of their gender until he is rescued by the other knights. On their return to Herod, Watkyn reports that the men have gone out of the country and that women are crying for vengeance for the slaying of their children. Herod is immediately smitten with madness and dies, as if punished directly by the mothers' curses.

The final scene is set in the temple in Jerusalem, where Symeon, who knows about the Incarnation, asks to see the child before he dies. Anna the prophetess then addresses her virgins and calls them to worship the child in Mary's arms. As Mary and Joseph leave the temple, Joseph's gentleness is contrasted to the bloodthirstiness of Herod and his soldiers. Symeon predicts the Crucifixion, and Anna leads the virgins to worship Jesus, Our Lady, and "Seynt Anne." Poeta then asks the forgiveness of the sovereigns for the rudeness of the dramatic material they have just seen and promises to play the disputation of the doctors next year. The virgins and minstrels conclude the play with a dance and music.

The work of early modern urban historians such as Charles Phythian-Adams and Natalie Zemon Davis suggests the extent to which the social life of the late medieval town ritualized divisions between male and female roles. Phythian-Adams, in his work on Coventry, points out the rigidly defined gender roles in such public rituals as seating at church, marching in the craft guild processions, and attending guild dinners and other ceremonial events, all of which women either did not attend or attended as a gender-based group.

On the other hand, such rituals as that of Purification, which is dramatized in the Digby play, were all-female affairs. Into this ritual context Phythian-Adams places the popular Hock Tuesday play of fifteenth-century Warwickshire, in which it was customary for the men to bind and heave women on Hock Monday and for the women to reciprocate on Hock Tuesday.[30] This is, as he points out, a classic example of ritual role reversal, typically found on festival occasions within societies with significant role differentiations.[31]

The Digby play thus fits rather neatly into this late medieval dynamic of gender distinctions and their ritual overturning or reversals. Within this drama the ritual of Candelmas Day or Purification is associated with Saint Anne's Day: both are female celebrations. The power of the female is parodied by comic elements in the episode on the Massacre of the Innocents, where the young messenger in search of his manhood is overpowered by angry mothers. One might see this play as dramatizing two ways in which women could have power within the late medieval urban structure—either in all-female rituals or in inversions where the women become "manly" and the male is comically unmanned by female symbols. Saint Anne presides as the patron of the games and of the female gender; she is affiliated with the female lineage of Christ and served by a procession of "virgins" who dance and otherwise act as ceremonial punctuation for the whole event.

Gender here functions as a principle of social differentiation. It provides the language of order and disorder for this society. As Natalie Zemon Davis puts it in a chapter entitled "Women on Top," "Sexual symbolism, of course, is always available to make statements about social experience and to reflect (or conceal) contradictions within it. At the end of the Middle Ages and in early modern Europe, the relation of the wife—of the potentially disorderly woman—to her husband was especially useful for expressing the relation of all subordinates to their superiors."[32] Although in Davis's formulation the "woman on top," whose festively inverted behavior does not follow codes of normal female conduct, was regarded as out of control, full of sexual energy, and apt to violate all order, she (the woman on top) was also performing a social function. Through her license, she defended wider standards for the community as a whole and criticized unjust rule.[33] Clearly, in the Digby play, the manly wives avenging their children's death on Watkyn and Herod express a righteous anger at tyranny and presumption through their violent actions. Play with gender definitions thus comments upon political abuses.

Gender here is a metaphor for social differentiation and provides a critique of political power games. What must be pointed out, however, is that the point of view represented in the Digby play is essentially male and civic as well as festive. The image of the female within the framework of town festivity both confirms male social structures and critiques them. Or perhaps it would be more accurate to say that by juxtaposing two images of the female—Saint Anne as ceremonial patroness and the wild mothers—the male power structures define themselves and explore their own limits.[34]

THE REPRESENTATION OF SAINT ANNE in three dramatic texts of the late Middle Ages demonstrates that the task of interpreting such images is far from simple. While the legend of Saint Anne was widely known and her cult was popular among a wide variety of social groups (from peasants in the countryside and nuns in convents to the pious bourgeoisie and learned theologians), these facts alone do not show us how Anne functioned as a cultural symbol.

We need to investigate images as active agents within a series of connected frames—to use the example of Anne, first, as a character within specific scenes, plays, or cycles; second, as a dramatized image performed before a particular kind of audience in a social or festival context; and, third, as activating constellations of signification which play out issues of central concern to a segment of late medieval society. As cultural symbol, Saint Anne is clearly "polyvalent" or "polysemic" or "multivocal" (to use Victor Turner's terms),[35] but we should avoid thinking of Anne's image as *containing* a variety of meanings. Rather, her potency as cultural symbol in the late Middle Ages was a function of her usefulness in *triggering* or activating ideological formations. In particular, we may see her gender as a metaphor with functions that varied according to the social and ideological situation.[36]

The legend of Saint Anne was not so much a story to be believed

in as a symbolic structure that enabled social understandings to be
formed and social dilemmas to be confronted and even, on occasion,
resolved. By studying cultural symbols such as Anne in this complex
way, we can gain at least partial access to the elusive inner worlds
of late medieval people, to the ways in which they made sense out
of their historical situations, and to the forces and commitments that
motivated their actions.

NOTES

1. Cohen, *Mystères et moralités,* 27–38.

2. Block, *Ludus coventriae,* 57–145; see also Meredith, *Mary Play,* on des-
ignating a "Mary Play" within the cycle.

3. Baker, Murphy, and Hall, *Religious Plays,* 96–115.

4. For an introduction to central theories, see de Lauretis, *Alice Doesn't,*
134–56, and Mykyta, "Lacan," 49–57.

5. See, for example, nos. 102 and 112 in Davies's *Medieval English Lyrics.*
An excellent discussion of "the Virgin's gaze in Middle English lyrics of the
Passion," informed by contemporary theory, is offered by Sarah Stanbury.
She comes to the conclusion that "in the attention paid to [the Virgin's] gaze
as a potent feature of the devotional process, it is reductive, surely, to argue
that her gaze is simply defeated or mastered by patriarchal lines of sight.
The power of her gaze over the speaking Christ, the narrator's repeated recognition that her gaze can transform us through our own internalization of
empathy, the speaker's wish, repeated in a number of lyrics, that the Virgin
at the cross look on him (or her?) as she looks on the infant Jesus, attest to the
power of that look in what one reader has labeled the 'holy family romance.' "

6. Bynum, *Holy Feast,* 260–76.

7. Kieckhefer, *Unquiet Souls,* 90.

8. Vauchez, *Sainteté,* 272–80, 427.

9. Petroff, *Consolation,* 34.

10. Klapisch-Zuber, *Women, Family, and Ritual,* 311.

11. Ragusa and Green, *Meditations,* 38, 39.

12. The play was probably written by Katherine Bourlet, whose name is
written on the manuscript and whom Gustave Cohen has shown to have been
a nun of the order between 1478 and 1483.

13. Bynum, *Holy Feast,* 269.

14. Meredith, *Mary Play,* 14–19.

15. Douglas, *Purity and Danger,* 53.

16. My unpublished essay "Kinship, Purity, and Wisdom in N-Town Cycle" provides a full discussion of the "cosmology" of purity in N-Town. Peter Meredith marshals the available evidence of social contexts for this drama in the introduction to his edition of the section of N-Town he calls the Mary Play, (*Mary Play*, 9–12).

17. Kempe, *Book of Margery Kempe*, 84–85. For a good discussion of this and other of Margery's dilemmas, see Atkinson, *Mystic and Pilgrim*.

18. Kempe, *Book of Margery Kempe*, 88.

19. Peter of Vaux, "*Vita* of Colette of Corbie," Sec. 68. The life of Colette originally written in French by Peter of Vaux appears in the *Acta sanctorum* translated into Latin. My quotations are from McNamara's unpublished translation of the Latin. There was social and institutional pressure not to remarry in the late Middle Ages. For example, when the merchant Robert Large (to whom Caxton was apprenticed) died and left a rich widow, Johanna, who had been previously married, she proclaimed at his graveside that she would "avow to God . . . to live in chastity and cleanness of my body from this time forward as long as my life lasteth, never to take other spouse but only Christ Jesu." Within three years, however, she married for a third time, this time to a draper. Stow, in his *Survey of London*, recorded that when they married "they were troubled by the Church, and put to penance, both he and she" (cited in Deacon, *William Caxton*, 43–44).

20. McNamara, "*Vita*," sec. 85.

21. The treatise, together with translations of the office, was used by sisters of the Brigittine monastery of Sion in the fifteenth and sixteenth centuries.

22. Blunt, *Myroure*, 207.

23. Ibid., 277–78.

24. Bridget, *Revelations*, 30–31.

25. Bridget, "*Liber celestis*," 467. I have silently modernized some of the orthography.

26. Erbe, *Mirk's Festial*, 216. I have silently modernized some of the orthography.

27. Baker, Murphy, and Hall, *Religious Plays*, lx. See also Coletti, " 'Wyves and Gossippes, Vergynes and Maides,' " and Baker, "When Is a Text a Play?" 25–29; Baker discusses the manuscript and paleography of the Massacre of the Innocents and notes probable revisions involving the Watkyn character.

28. Craig, *English Religious Drama*, 265–80. David Mills, in "Religious Drama and Civic Ceremonial," 152–66, discusses the Digby Candelmas play within the context of the celebration of the Purification of Mary by a town guild, though he notes that the play is "self-contained" and does not rely "on the context of the specific feast for its meaning." He thus detaches it both from Candelmas, which it ostensibly commemorates, and from Saint Anne's

Day, when it was performed, and instead sees its primary reference point as the life of Christ (163).

29. Pfaff, *New Liturgical Feasts*, 2.

30. Phythian-Adams, *Desolation*, 89–98.

31. See discussion of the relation between festivity and social structure in Handelman, "Reflexivity."

32. Davis, *Society and Culture*, 127.

33. Ibid., 149–50.

34. In Bristol, as David Harris Sacks shows, the boy-bishop in town festivity played a similar symbolic role of criticizing the mayor and councillors for their civic failings ("Celebrating Authority," 201).

35. Turner, *Forest of Symbols*, 50.

36. A review article that comes to this conclusion is Joan W. Scott's "Gender: A Useful Category of Historical Analysis."

BIBLIOGRAPHY

Ashley, Kathleen. "Kinship, Purity, and Wisdom in N-Town Cycle." Unpublished manuscript.

Atkinson, Clarissa. *Mystic and Pilgrim: The Book and the World of Margery Kempe.* Ithaca, N.Y.: Cornell University Press, 1983.

Baker, Donald C. "When Is a Text a Play?" In *Contexts for Early English Drama,* ed. Marianne G. Briscoe and John C. Coldewey, 20–40. Bloomington: Indiana University Press, 1989.

Baker, Donald C., John L. Murphy, and Louis B. Hall, eds. *The Late Medieval Religious Plays of Bodleian MSS. Digby 133 and E. Museo 160.* EETS, o.s., no. 283. Oxford: Oxford University Press, 1982.

Block, K. S., ed. *Ludus coventriae.* EETS, e.s., no. 120. London: Oxford University Press, 1922. Reprint. 1974.

Blunt, John Henry, ed. *The Myroure of Our Ladye.* EETS, e.s., no. 19. London: N. Trübner and Company, 1873. Reprint. Millwood, N.Y.: Kraus Reprint, 1981.

Bridget of Sweden. *"Liber celestis" of St. Bridget of Sweden.* Ed. Roger Ellis. EETS, no. 291. Oxford: Oxford University Press, 1987.

———. *Revelations and Prayers of St. Bridget of Sweden.* Trans. Dom Ernest Graf. London: Burns, Oates, and Washbourne, 1928.

Bynum, Caroline Walker. *Holy Feast and Holy Fast.* Berkeley and Los Angeles: University of California Press, 1987.

Cohen, Gustave, ed. *Mystères et moralités du manuscrit 617 de Chantilly.* Paris: Librairie Edouard Champion, 1920.

Coletti, Theresa. " 'Wyves and Gossippes, Vergynes and Maides': Christian Myth and Female Sexuality in Medieval Drama." Manuscript.

Craig, Hardin. *English Religious Drama of the Middle Ages*. Oxford: Clarendon Press, 1955.

Davies, R. T., ed. *Medieval English Lyrics*. Evanston, Ill.: Northwestern University Press, 1964.

Davis, Natalie Zemon. *Society and Culture in Early Modern France*. Stanford: Stanford University Press, 1975.

Deacon, Richard. *A Biography of William Caxton*. London: Frederick Muller, 1976.

de Lauretis, Teresa. *Alice Doesn't*. Bloomington: Indiana University Press, 1984.

Douglas, Mary. *Purity and Danger*. 1966. Reprint. London: Ark Paperbacks, 1985.

Erbe, Theodor, ed. *Mirk's Festial*. EETS, e.s., no. 96. London: Kegan Paul, Trench, Trübner and Company, 1905. Reprint. Millwood, N.Y.: Kraus Reprint, 1973.

Handelman, Don. "Reflexivity in Festival and Other Cultural Events." In *Essays in the Sociology of Perception*, ed. Mary Douglas, 162–90. London: Routledge and Kegan Paul, 1982.

Kempe, Margery. *The Book of Margery Kempe*. Trans. B. A. Windeatt. London: Penguin, 1985.

Kieckhefer, Richard. *Unquiet Souls: Fourteenth-Century Saints and Their Religious Milieu*. Chicago: University of Chicago Press, 1984.

Klapisch-Zuber, Christiane. *Women, Family, and Ritual in Renaissance Italy*. Chicago: University of Chicago Press, 1985.

McNamara, Jo Ann, trans. "*Vita* of Colette of Corbie." Manuscript.

Meredith, Peter, ed. *The Mary Play*. London: Longman, 1987.

Mills, David. "Religious Drama and Civic Ceremonial." In *The Revels History of Drama in English*, Vol. 1, *Medieval Drama*, ed. A. C. Cawley, Marion Jones, Peter F. McDonald, and David Mills, 152–206. London: Methuen, 1983.

Mykyta, L. "Lacan, Literature, and the Look: Woman in the Eye of Psychoanalysis." *SubStance* 39 (1983): 49–57.

Peter of Vaux. "*Vita* of Colette of Corbie." *Acta sanctorum*, March 6, 539–89.

Petroff, Elizabeth. *The Consolation of the Blessed: Women Saints in Medieval Tuscany*. New York: Alta Gaia, 1980.

Pfaff, R. W. *New Liturgical Feasts in Later Medieval England*. Oxford: Clarendon Press, 1970.

Phythian-Adams, Charles. *Desolation of a City: Coventry and the Urban Crisis of the Late Middle Ages*. Cambridge: Cambridge University Press, 1979.

Ragusa, Isa, and Rosalie B. Green, eds. *Meditations on the Life of Christ*. Princeton: Princeton University Press, 1961.

Sacks, David Harris. "Celebrating Authority in Bristol, 1475–1640." In *Urban Life in the Renaissance,* ed. Susan Zimmerman and Ronald F. E. Weissman, 187–223. Newark: University of Delaware Press, 1989.

Scott, Joan W. "Gender: A Useful Category of Historical Analysis." *American Historical Review* 91 (1986): 1053–75.

Stanbury, Sarah. "Transgression and the Spectator: The Virgin's Gaze in Middle English Lyrics of the Passion." In *Rhetoric and Transgression in Medieval Literature,* ed. Sarah Spence and Katharina Wilson. Forthcoming.

Turner, Victor. *The Forest of Symbols: Aspects of Ndembu Ritual*. Ithaca, N.Y.: Cornell University Press, 1967.

Vauchez, André. *La Sainteté en Occident aux derniers siècles du moyen âge d'après les procès de canonisation et les documents hagiographiques*. Bibliothèque des études française d'Athènes et de Rome 241. Rome: Ecole Française de Rome, 1981.

In the Defense of
Florentine Republicanism

Saint Anne and Florentine Art,
1343–1575

ROGER J. CRUM AND DAVID G. WILKINS

O n Saint Anne's Day, July 26, 1343, the Florentines rose in revolt against Walter VI of Brienne, the so-called duke of Athens.[1] Whether or not the rebels initially invoked the aid of Saint Anne is not known, but after the successful expulsion of Brienne, the Florentines credited the saint with aiding the cause of republicanism and adopted her as a protector of their city. Her feast day was declared a public holiday that, according to the chronicler Giovanni Villani, was as important as Easter.[2] Villani's comparison of Saint Anne's Day with Easter suggests that the resurrection of Florentine liberty under the aegis of the saint was celebrated with as much enthusiasm as was the religious holiday marking Christ's victory over death.

After the expulsion of Brienne, Saint Anne began to figure prominently in Florentine art. From the mid-trecento onward, Florentines employed Saint Anne's name and image to proclaim their liberty and republicanism in the face of internal or external threats of subjugation.[3] This tradition was radically altered in the cinquecento, when the Medici dukes, whose ancestors were held to be among those who had fought to overthrow Brienne, put the image of Saint Anne to their own political advantage.[4] Here we discuss how the Florentines' memory of Brienne and of his expulsion on Saint Anne's Day provided the historical foundation for the representation of the saint in Florentine art. We emphasize, above all, the political content, often ignored, that is inherent in certain Florentine images of the saint.[5]

Before the Medici became dukes of Florence in the sixteenth century, the city had experienced despotism only twice, and on both occasions Brienne was the key player. In May 1325, after having lost Pistoia to Ghibelline forces, Florentine Guelphs petitioned King Robert of Naples to become *signore* of their city for ten years.[6] Robert accepted in favor of his son, Charles of Calabria, who then sent Brienne to Florence as his temporary vicar.[7] Brienne served for only two and one-half months, until Charles arrived in Florence. Although Brienne dismissed the recently elected priors and held new elections, he was generally well received by the Florentines. According to Villani, who was usually critical of despots, Brienne "knew how to exercise authority and was a wise lord of pleasing aspect."[8] Villani's positive assessment is understandable, for Brienne did not disrupt the status quo, allowing the patricians, the class to which Villani belonged, to rule as usual.[9]

It was no doubt Brienne's performance as Charles's vicar that led the Florentines to invite him back in his own right in 1342.[10] In the spring of that year, Florentines approached Brienne at the papal court at Avignon to request that he command their forces against Pisa in the siege of Lucca. Brienne, accepting the commission, arrived in Florence on May 9, "not as a captain," wrote one Florentine chronicler, "but as a friend with a good company."[11] Although Brienne and his forces lost Lucca on July 6, his power increased over the summer as the government granted him civil powers generally not extended to hired generals. Brienne's ascendancy to political dominance in Florence reached its climax on September 8, 1342, when, to the jubilant cries of Florentines assembled in the Piazza della Signoria, he was proclaimed *signore* of the city for life.[12]

Both as a condottiere and as signore of Florence, Brienne was supported by the wealthy, politically dominant patricians. This merchant elite hoped he would preserve their rule—and their fortunes—against the pressures of a disenfranchised working class and a politically emasculated nobility. However, as Brienne secured his rule in Florence, the patricians began to lose their political hold on the city. The nobility implored Brienne to repeal certain prejudicial statutes, such as the ordinances of justice, that had long restricted their political activity; although Brienne allowed the ordinances to fall into abeyance, he did not repeal them and soon lost what little support he had enjoyed among the nobility. Having disillusioned both the patricians and the nobles, Brienne sought to broaden his base of support by cultivating the favor and governmental service of the lesser guildsmen and manual laborers. In the end, however, he failed to please these Florentines as well.

The patricians found Brienne's rigid enforcement of existing tax structures even more onerous than their loss of political control. For purposes of tax assessment, an estimate of personal wealth was required of citizens in early October 1342; on July 15, 1343, the first payment of these taxes fell due. Eleven days later, on the feast day of Saint Anne, disgruntled patricians (including, perhaps, the Medici), nobles, and manual workers stood united as they converged on the Piazza della Signoria in open revolt. According to Villani, who may well have been with the mob, the Florentines cried out, "Death to the duke and his followers and long live the people, the commune, and liberty."[13] After an extended siege of the Palazzo della Signoria, the Florentines expelled Brienne on August 6.[14]

After the successful revolt and expulsion, the desire to celebrate the return to republican government led the Florentine government to embark on commemorations of an exceptional nature. On January 12, 1344, less than a year after the revolt and well before the next Saint Anne's Day, the *signoria* declared the feast of Saint Anne an official holiday. In the declaration, the *signoria* pledged to make offerings at Orsanmichele before an *immagine* of the saint, presumably a painting or statue on an altar. This *immagine,* established to commemorate the successful revolt, was to serve as the locus for a cult dedicated to Saint Anne.[15] To this day, there is an altar to Saint Anne at Orsanmichele located in the bay to the left of Andrea Orcagna's monumental tabernacle. Upon this altar rests a marble *Madonna and Child with Saint Anne* by Francesco da Sangallo that dates to 1526 (fig. 1). It has been suggested that Sangallo's work, which will be discussed later, replaced an earlier cult statue in wood, but no documentary evidence supports this thesis. A statue in wood of Saint Anne with the Madonna and

Fig. 1. Francesco da Sangallo, *Madonna and Child with Saint Anne*. Florence, Orsanmichele. Ca. 1521–26. Photo: Alinari/Art Resource.

Child, now in the Museo Nazionale del Bargello in Florence, has been put forward as a likely candidate, but it seems neither Italian nor as early in date as the 1340s.[16]

The establishment of the *immagine* and cult of Saint Anne at Orsanmichele is of great significance. Financed by public tax monies, Orsanmichele served not only as a church but also as a grain storage and market facility; the exterior of the building was provided with niches assigned to the major trade guilds for sculptural embellishment.[17] Orsanmichele was one of the most important communal buildings in Florence, and the establishment of the Saint Anne *immagine* there clearly indicates the official and civic nature of this veneration.

It would appear that this soon proved inadequate for the cult of Saint Anne. On July 28, 1349, less than a decade after the foundation of the cult at Orsanmichele, the *signoria* ordered that a separate oratory chapel dedicated to the saint be constructed directly opposite Orsanmichele (fig. 2).[18] The chapel, located on the modern Via Calzaiuoli, has received subsequent dedications and innumerable interior renovations; no artistic evidence remains of its original function as the seat of the Saint Anne cult, and documents pertinent to any original decoration have yet to surface. What does remain, however, is the chapel itself, and this is no meager piece of evidence. Its very size, its placement opposite Orsanmichele on the main thoroughfare between the cathedral and the Palazzo della Signoria, and its communal patronage all point to the intensity of civic devotion to Saint Anne in the aftermath of Brienne's expulsion.

The Orsanmichele *immagine* and the oratory across the street are not the only evidence of the new civic devotion to Saint Anne in the 1340s.[19] The revolt against and expulsion of Brienne are recorded as simultaneous events in a fragmentary, detached fresco now in the Palazzo della Signoria (fig. 3).[20] The *Expulsion of the Duke of Athens* was originally painted for the Carceri delle Stinche, the prison in which many were incarcerated during Brienne's rule.[21] Villani, in fact, reports that when the revolt against Brienne broke out, crowds stormed the Stinche and released these prisoners.[22] The artist of the fresco is unknown, but because it shares stylistic affinities with the early works of Andrea Orcagna, a principal Florentine painter of the mid-trecento, it could date from the year of Brienne's expulsion or soon thereafter.[23] It is possible that the fresco was commissioned by the Florentine gov-

Fig. 2. Oratory of Saint Anne (now S. Carlo Borromeo). Begun 1349.
Florence. Photo: Alinari/Art Resource.

Fig. 3. *Expulsion of the Duke of Athens*. Florence, Palazzo Vecchio. 1343 or later. Photo: Alinari/Art Resource.

ernment that came to power after Brienne's expulsion; exactly how this image was meant to function at the Stinche is uncertain.

Saint Anne is shown enthroned at the center of a circular field, next to the Palazzo della Signoria. To her right, the Florentine defenders, dressed in the heraldic white and red colors of the city, carry civic flags. Saint Anne embraces and encourages the Florentine cause as she turns toward the soldiers and grasps the central standard. At the same time, she extends a downturned left hand toward Brienne. Strewn at Brienne's feet, the abused and neglected emblems of justice—broken sword, scales, law book—succinctly indicate the injustice of his rule. A shield with Brienne's coat of arms has been dashed from the palace and lies ignobly at Saint Anne's feet. Inscriptions are evident throughout the fresco, but the surface is so abraded that they are now illegible. Even in the nineteenth century, only the words "ASPRO TIRANNO"—"bitter tyrant"—remained legible.[24]

A winged, bearded figure, most likely the virtue Constancy, drives Brienne from his throne.[25] The figure holds a column in his left hand, and it would appear that in his right he originally raised a spear. Like a soul damned to hell or an Adam expelled from paradise, Brienne looks back over his shoulder toward Constancy—and perhaps also toward his former seat of power, the Palazzo della Signoria. The militant Constancy clearly acts in the service of Saint Anne, whose contrasting gestures of acceptance and rejection relate the *Expulsion of the Duke of Athens* both formally and iconographically to contemporary images of the Last Judgment; Brienne is shown being damned by a judgmental Saint Anne.[26]

Damnation is also suggested by the strange, composite creature held by Brienne as he flees. This creature, which has the deceptive face of a just man joined with a serpentine body and a scorpion's tail, is identifiable as the beast Gerione, "that foul image of fraud," from Dante's *Inferno* (canto 17).[27] As a fraudulent beast in the Inferno, Gerione's function is to sting unsuspecting sinners as it ferries them downward, from the seventh to the eighth circle. In canto 17, Virgil arranges passage for Dante upon the beast's shoulders. The experience is dangerous for Dante, but Virgil averts disaster by sitting between the pilgrim and the beast's venomous tail. Villani, who wrote that Brienne had served Florence in the 1320s as "a wise lord of pleasing aspect," later judged that the expulsion of this man, who had seemed just, was brought about because he betrayed the Florentines.[28] In the Stinche fresco Brienne is identified with Gerione and thus with fraudulence, and this image thus becomes a visual explication of Villani's assessment of the despot's treachery when he was the *signore* of Florence. In other words, the fresco both commemorates Saint Anne's intercessory role in the expulsion and makes evident, through the presence of Gerione, the historical explanation of Brienne's downfall.

This image of Saint Anne, one of the earliest in Florentine art, is unusual in that it shows the saint alone rather than in the company of the Madonna and Child. While in this case there is no question who is the active and significant figure, in most later Florentine images it has been assumed that Anne is present largely as an accessory, an addition to the expected grouping of Madonna and Child. The Stinche fresco, on the other hand, suggests that Florentine works that include Saint Anne should always be reconsidered in light of contemporary political events. The possibility of the primacy of Saint Anne in these images must be raised, especially if there is any evidence that a work might have political significance. In the Stinche fresco, the civic nature of her role is clear, for she encourages the republican forces at the same time that she dismisses Brienne. If the fresco was indeed a civic commission, it may also be significant that it "corrects" history by showing the forces of the commune as an orderly, disciplined group rather than the raging mob reported by Villani. In fact, on Saint Anne's Day there could not have been anything other than the mob reported by Villani, for Brienne had disbanded both the citizen militia and its standard-bearers.[29]

Although clearly intended as a commemorative work, the Stinche fresco may have been part of an official civic campaign aimed at defaming Brienne. In 1344, probably within a year of Brienne's expulsion, a second fresco of similar damning content was commissioned by the *signoria* for the tower of the Bargello, the seat of the Florentine magistrate.[30] Such political effigies of shame, known as *pitture infamanti,* were periodically painted on the exterior of the Bargello by order of the government in power.[31] The *pittura infamante* of 1344, which showed Brienne and six of his associates, was mentioned by Villani but was most thoroughly described by Giorgio Vasari in the sixteenth century: "Around the head of the duke were many rapacious and other sorts of animals signifying his nature and quality; and one of his counselors held the [Palazzo della Signoria] and, like one disloyal and treacherous to the homeland, was offering it to him: and under all the figures were family coats of arms and insignias, and also written passages that today can hardly be read for having been consumed by time."[32] Fortunately, Filippo Baldinucci transcribed the inscriptions from anonymous sources.[33] The inscription that accompanied the image of Brienne expressed the grievances against him with biting economy:

> Avaricious, treacherous, and then cruel
> Lustful, unjust, and false
> Never did he hold his state secure.[34]

The theme of Brienne's *damnatio memoriae* was driven home by the inscriptions that accompanied his condemned counselors, which were written in the first person in such a way that each of the six associates addressed Brienne in an accusatory manner.

In the late 1340s, Villani regarded the Bargello *pittura infamante* as an important, albeit embarrassing, reminder of an ignominious period in the history of his commune.[35] This embarrassment persisted into the last quarter of the century. It was expressed in similar terms by the chronicler Stefani around 1378, and in 1394 the Florentines avoided a different, though equally awkward, embarrassment when the duke of Bari, who was related to Brienne, paid a visit to the city; according to an anonymous diarist, at that time the fresco was temporarily covered so that the visitor "should not see his kinsman painted with all those other unfortunate citizens."[36] In spite of such embarrassment, the survival of the fresco for more than two centuries—throughout a period when other, similar frescoes were painted over or allowed to deteriorate—indicates that the Florentines continued to consider their experience with Brienne a valuable lesson. For later Florentines, as surely as for Villani in the 1340s, the fresco was bitter medicine.

All these commissions—the altar and *immagine* at Orsanmichele, the oratory, and the Stinche and Bargello frescoes—were not only commemorative but politically necessary as well, for after his expulsion the vengeful Brienne conspired to return to Florence and to resume power.[37] After the expulsion of Brienne, however, the Florentines revived their traditional form of republican government and also assumed leadership in an antiimperial and antityrannical union with neighboring states.[38] "God has granted you, citizens," wrote one Florentine soon after the expulsion, and in definite reference to Brienne, "to recover sacred liberty, a gift to be desired above everything else."[39] In December 1344, the Florentine *signoria* offered a reward of ten thousand fiorini in gold for Brienne's capture.[40] In March 1345, they decreed that all acts of his administration be put to flames and, in 1347, ordered that all his coats of arms, even those displayed inside private residences, be destroyed.[41] In their retaliatory content and triumphant expression, the Stinche and Bargello frescoes must be seen as artistic manifestations of the antityrannical atmosphere that developed in Florence after Brienne's expulsion.

While any threat of Brienne's return passed with his death in 1356, Florentines did not forget the lessons learned from his rule. Marvin Becker has noted that "for the rest of the century, whenever an outraged working class pressed its demands upon a tottering signory, [Florentines] conjured the menacing specter of the duke to frighten more generous-minded compatriots."[42] In 1363, when Pandolfo Malatesta, the captain general of the Florentine army, demanded extraordinary judicial powers, Simone di Rinieri Peruzzi cited the example of Brienne to persuade his fellow citizens that Malatesta sought to deprive them of liberty.[43]

That Brienne continued to be an important Florentine example of unwanted tyranny is revealed in evidence of a lost, late-fourteenth-century fresco of the Last Judgment at S. Michele Visdomini in Florence. In this fresco, which is believed to have been painted by Matteo di Rossello (who was active in the last quarter of the fourteenth century), Brienne was shown among the damned.[44]

The Florentine use of Brienne as an example of their resolve to avoid tyranny and exalt republicanism guaranteed the continued importance of Saint Anne, and by the third quarter of the century she had been established as one of the principal protector saints of the city. She appears prominently among Florentine patron and protector saints in a *Coronation of the Virgin* of 1372–73 by Simone di Lapo di Nuccio, Niccolò di Pietro Gerini, and Jacopo di Cione (fig. 4).[45] Begun by the first two painters in 1372 and completed by Cione in 1373, this panel was a joint commission of the Cambio and Calimala guilds for the Florentine mint, the Zecca. Among the saints are Barnabas, Victor, and Anne, all of whom are included because the Florentine

Fig. 4. Simone di Lapo di Nuccio, Niccolò di Pietro Gerini, and Jacopo di Cione, *Coronation of the Virgin*. Florence, Accademia. 1372–73. Photo: Alinari/Art Resource.

republic had won important victories on their feast days.[46] The pre-eminence of Saint Anne in the Zecca picture, however, is clear, for it is she who has been selected to hold and guard the city of Florence (fig. 5).[47] The communal nature of her protection is further suggested by the prominence of the Palazzo della Signoria in the representation of the city. What is perhaps surprising is that this role was given to her rather than to Saint Victor, on whose feast, in 1364, Florence had most recently been victorious—over Pisa at Cascina.[48] The explanation may be that Brienne's expulsion was not a victory over an external, military power but an internal episode in Florentine affairs that brought about the resurrection of republican government. Furthermore, for the administrators of the Zecca, who were members of the patrician class, Saint Anne must have embodied a reminder of how their political and economic power, once seriously compromised by an outsider, had been restored through the intervention of the saint.

In the period between the Stinche fresco of the 1340s and the Zecca panel of 1373, the Florentine attitude toward Saint Anne and Brienne seems to have undergone an important metamorphosis. In the Stinche fresco, Saint Anne is featured as a divine liberator whose will is responsible for the restoration of Florentine liberty. Ultimately, however, the fresco is historically bound, for it specifically addresses the momentous events of July and August 1343. The appearance of Saint Anne in the Zecca panel is in quite a different vein, for there are no overt references to the revolt against or expulsion of Brienne. But because Saint Anne holds the model of Florence, she is awarded "first" position among the grouping of patron and protector saints of Florence, which includes even John the Baptist, traditionally the most important saint for Florence and the one most frequently represented in Florentine art. Saint Anne's prominence indicates that in the Zecca painting the memory of the saint's role in the events of 1343 transcended civic devotion to other saints and was kept alive as an ever-topical lesson.

A discussion of the significance of Saint Anne and Brienne in the late medieval period could easily be brought to a close with the Zecca picture. But what has been discussed so far can also be understood as a foundation for the Florentines' continued remembrance of Brienne's rule and for their sense of protectorship in Saint Anne; a discussion of selected later images of Saint Anne will elucidate our thesis of the con-

Fig. 5. Simone di Lapo di Nuccio, Niccolò di Pietro Gerini, and Jacopo di Cione, *Coronation of the Virgin,* detail. Florence, Accademia. 1372–73.
Photo: Alinari/Art Resource.

tinued significance of Saint Anne in Florentine art. In 1415, Leonardo Bruni, in the sixth book of his *Histories of the Florentine People,* cited Brienne as an important example of a political figure who was hostile to republican institutions: "He was a Frenchman and accustomed to the ways of France, where the plebs have the place of servants. He therefore laughed at the name of the guilds and thought it ridiculous that the city should be ruled by the will of the people."[49] In apology for the considerable space he devotes to Brienne's period as *signore* of Florence, Bruni explains that this "affair is worth setting down in writing either for the admonishment of citizens or the castigation of rulers."[50]

In the early 1420s, only a few years after Bruni's writing, Masaccio and Masolino collaborated on an altarpiece, the *Madonna and Christ Child with Saint Anne,* which in Vasari's day was found in the Florentine church of S. Ambrogio (fig. 6). Eve Borsook has associated the altarpiece with a cult of the Immaculate Conception at that church.[51] Above and beyond the requirements of the cult, however, contemporary political circumstances may also have played a part in establishing the iconography of the altarpiece. In the early 1420s, Florentines faced great uncertainty concerning the future of their independence.[52] The nonaggression pact forged between Florence and Milan in 1420 proved unstable as the Milanese ruler, Filippo Maria Visconti, steadily consolidated his power and holdings in the direction of central Italy. Soon after the pact was established, Visconti absorbed Genoa and Brescia, and in 1423—the date often assigned to Masaccio and Masolino's altarpiece—he seized Forli, on the border of Florentine territory. There ensued a succession of military disasters for the Florentines, including the rout of their forces at Zagonara in July 1424 and the destruction of the whole army at Valdilamone in February 1425. At this point, Florence braced itself for invasion.

There is, admittedly, no evidence in Masaccio and Masolino's altarpiece that relates it to any of these events in either a specific or a general fashion. Yet the manner in which Saint Anne extends her hand over the head of the Christ Child is clearly a protective gesture and, even if its original intent was purely ritualistic and within the context of Immaculate Conception devotions, it could also have been received as a gesture that reminded the viewer of Saint Anne's role as a protector of Florentine civic liberty.

Fig. 6. Masaccio and Masolino, *Saint Anne Altarpiece*. Florence, Uffizi. Ca. 1423–25. Photo: Florence: Soprintendenza.

If fifteenth-century Florentines were to benefit from Bruni's discussion of Brienne, it would appear that the Medici were not among them. After their return from exile in 1434, the Medici steadily insinuated themselves as the de facto rulers of Florence, and, once established, their control was preserved intact until after the death of Lorenzo the Magnificent in 1492.[53] Lorenzo's son, Piero, was unable to hold the family's position secure, and in 1494 the Medici were expelled from Florence. The republican government was then redefined along the Venetian model, and Savonarola, the vitriolic prior of S. Marco, came to the fore as one of the government's most ardent supporters and apologists. As will be seen, Bruni's lesson on Brienne was everywhere in the air.

Enemies of the Medici, and perhaps leaders of the new regime, hastened to expunge certain images of Medici hegemony.[54] At the Bargello, they eradicated the *pitture infamanti* of Medici enemies but, significantly, retained the trecento fresco of Brienne and his associates discussed above. Samuel Edgerton has speculated that the Medici themselves had previously preserved the Brienne fresco as a reminder of former tyranny; the message would have been that the Medici wanted to suggest that they were benevolent rulers in contrast to Brienne.[55] Those who chose to retain the fresco after 1494, on the other hand, may have intended that their contemporaries draw incriminating parallels between the Medici and Brienne. In this regard, it is interesting to note that Bartolomeo Cerretani, in his *Historia fiorentina* of about 1509, drew a parallel between the situation in Florence after Brienne's expulsion and the situation after the more recent Medici ouster.[56]

Some years later, Niccolò Machiavelli, like Leonardo Bruni before him, saw an important historical warning in Brienne's tyranny and disregard for the sanctity of Florentine liberty. For most of Machiavelli's account of Brienne in the *Istorie fiorentine,* he relies heavily on the chronicle of Giovanni Villani. Machiavelli deviates significantly from Villani's text, however, when he writes of what transpired on the night of September 7, 1342. According to Villani, on that night the members of the *signoria* visited Brienne at his quarters to urge him to preserve the traditional liberties of the commune. Villani says nothing more of the conversation, but Machiavelli uses this gap in the narrative as an opportunity to invent what is by far the most extensive speech in direct discourse found in the whole of his history. According to Machiavelli's account, one of the Florentine officials addresses Brienne:

> You are trying to enslave a city which has always been free. . . . Have you considered how important and how strong the name of liberty is in a city like this? No power can overcome it, no period of time can consume it, no other advantage can compensate for it. Think, my Lord, of the troops that are needed to keep such a town in bondage. . . . It is quite certain that time cannot extinguish the desire for liberty. . . . You must believe then that you have either to hold this town, using the maximum force . . . or to be content with the authority we have given you. We . . . remind you that the only lasting government is one based on the people's will.[57]

Unlike Bartolomeo Cerretani, Machiavelli does not draw a specific comparison between Brienne and the Medici. This is not surprising, given that his work was commissioned by the Florentine Studio during a period when Giulio de' Medici was the head. In any case, the manner in which Machiavelli expands upon Villani's model suggests the continuing importance of Brienne in Florentine political rhetoric.

While Florentine writers after the expulsion of the Medici in 1494 drew upon the example of Brienne's tyranny, those responsible for the political imagery of the new regime employed the image of Saint Anne to emphasize the republican nature of the new government. An altarpiece of Saint Anne, for example, was intended to dominate the largely unrealized iconographic program for the Sala del Gran Consiglio in the Palazzo della Signoria. The Sala, constructed between 1495 and 1498 at the urging of Savonarola, was to serve as the political and religious seat of the new republican government.[58]

On May 28, 1498, the Florentine authorities commissioned Filippino Lippi to paint an altarpiece for the Sala del Gran Consiglio.[59] Vasari tells us that Filippino began work on the commission, but by his death in 1504, he had completed only the preparatory drawings.[60] Although it is not mentioned by Vasari, the subject of Filippino's altarpiece was most probably Saint Anne, for on November 26, 1510, when the *signoria* transferred Lippi's commission to Fra Bartolommeo, the latter artist began his *Saint Anne Altarpiece,* now in the Museo di S. Marco, Florence (fig. 7).[61] The civic importance of Fra Bartolommeo's altarpiece was clearly understood by Vasari, who described the

Fig. 7. Fra Bartolommeo, *Saint Anne Altarpiece*. Florence, Museo di
S. Marco. 1510–12. Photo: Alinari/Art Resource.

work as representing "all the protectors of the city and those saints on whose days the city was aided in its victories."[62] The painting is unfinished, and, as some of the figures have no distinctive attributes, it is possible to discern only a few of their identities. Among these, John the Baptist, the major patron saint of Florence, occupies center stage on the lower level. Shown as the youthful proto-Baptist, the Giovannino, he approaches the central group in supplication, as if performing an act of civic tribute. Of those to whom he pays homage, Saint Anne is by far the most important; she is physically detached and emotionally differentiated from the other figures. She alone reacts to the Trinity above and to the book held open by three *putti*. We do not know how the book was to be inscribed, but the ecstatic attention of Saint Anne suggests that the intended message pertained specifically to her. Perhaps it was to bear a biblical passage or a quotation from one of Savonarola's sermons, or it might even have contained a reference, overt or veiled, to Brienne, or the Medici, or both.

Whatever the intended inscription, the evidence of the unfinished altarpiece's history suggests that it transmitted a specifically anti-Medicean message. In 1512, the return of the Medici to Florence precipitated the fall of the republican government, the dismissal of the republican Gran Consiglio, and, it would seem, the cancellation of Fra Bartolommeo's commission. For the greater part of the second and third decades of the century, the altarpiece remained at S. Marco, probably in Fra Bartolommeo's studio, in a state akin to political exile. On March 29, 1529, however, the government of the last Florentine republic (1527–30), which two years earlier had sent the Medici into exile for the last time, ordered that the unfinished altarpiece be brought from S. Marco to the Palazzo della Signoria, where it would have been set up in its originally intended place in the Sala del Gran Consiglio.[63] Assuming the order was fulfilled, for a brief while, the rejuvenated Consiglio would have derived sanction from Saint Anne as she presided over what were to be the final moments of Florentine republicanism. It seems beyond doubt that for the Florentine governments of both 1494–1512 and 1527–30, Fra Bartolommeo's *Saint Anne Altarpiece* embodied a distinctly anti-Medicean message.[64]

Fra Bartolommeo's *Saint Anne Altarpiece* was not the only image of Saint Anne produced in Florence between 1494 and 1512 in the period of renewed republican fervor. Related, though problematically so, must be certain of Leonardo da Vinci's variations on the Saint Anne theme, particularly the lost SS. Annunziata cartoon that the artist produced in Florence.[65] After an absence of about twenty years at the Milanese court of Lodovico Sforza, Leonardo returned to Florence in late 1500 or early 1501 and sometime in 1503 or shortly thereafter produced the SS. Annunziata cartoon. It should be noted that Leonardo was clearly at work on the theme of Saint Anne before his return to Florence. In his study of the Burlington House Cartoon, Jack Wasserman presents strong evidence to suggest that King Louis XII of France commissioned this work from Leonardo in Milan in 1499. Furthermore, Wasserman makes the convincing argument that the King's marriage to Anne of Nantes in January 1499 is the raison d'etre of the commission, its subject, and its iconography.[66] There is ample evidence, however, that Leonardo continued to explore the Saint Anne theme after his return to Florence.

Vasari tells us that upon the artist's return he expressed interest in having the commission for the high altarpiece of the SS. Annunziata. This commission had earlier been awarded to Filippino Lippi, but he relinquished it to Leonardo.[67] Leonardo took up residence at the Annunziata, and, after much procrastination, he "finally made a cartoon containing a Madonna and a St. Anne with a Christ which not only caused all the workers to marvel, but when it was finished, men and women, young and old, went to see it for two days as one is accustomed to go to the solemn holidays."[68] As Jack Wasserman observes, there is no evidence that this cartoon was made in preparation for the Annunziata high altarpiece.[69] Actually, we learn that in 1503, Filippino Lippi began an altarpiece for the high altar with a Deposition on the front and an Assumption of the Virgin on the back; whether these themes followed those stipulated in the original commission is unknown.[70] On the basis of this information, what are we to conclude concerning the origins of Leonardo's lost SS. Annunziata cartoon and the circumstances under which it was produced?

In 1503 the Soderini government commissioned Leonardo to paint the *Battle of Anghiari* for the Sala del Gran Consiglio. This work, intended to commemorate the Florentine victory over Pisa in 1440, joined Michelangelo's *Battle of Cascina* and Fra Bartolommeo's *Saint Anne Altarpiece* as the third civic commission for the Sala del Gran Consiglio.[71] Leonardo, who had earlier left Florence for the patronage of a despotic ruler, must have recognized the commission as a golden opportunity to ingratiate himself with the republicans of Florence. Martin Kemp has suggested that during these years the *Battle of Anghiari* may not have been Leonardo's only work dealing with themes of Florentine liberty, republicanism, and strength. Kemp suggests that two of Leonardo's drawings, a Hercules and a Salvator Mundi, carried strong republican overtones.[72] "In this context," writes Kemp, "Leonardo's St. Anne could be regarded as an attempt to throw his hat into the Republican ring, not perhaps in such a way as to displace Filippino, but certainly as a public contribution to Republican iconography. This would help to explain his otherwise remarkable willingness to display the work or works in cartoon form."[73]

Painted most probably in 1528 or 1529, Pontormo's *Saint Anne Altarpiece* (fig. 8) belongs to the period of the last Florentine republic, when Fra Bartolommeo's altarpiece was at last on display in the Sala di Gran Consiglio.[74] In both its iconography and its patronage, Pontormo's altarpiece is related at once to Fra Bartolommeo's work and to the political circumstances of the last Florentine republic. Vasari tells us that this altarpiece was ordered for the Florentine convent of Saint Anne in Verzaia by the *capitano* and *famiglia* officials who are represented in procession on the feast day of Saint Anne in the tondo at the base of the picture (fig. 9).[75] The tondo thus commemorated the *signoria*'s practice, by now almost two centuries old, of going in solemn procession to the church of Sant' Anna sul Prato every July 26 in commemoration of Saint Anne's role in the revolt against Brienne.[76] It is worth noting, however, that in discussing Pontormo's picture after midcentury—and well after the Medici had become dukes of Florence—Vasari writes of this procession in the imperfect tense, revealing that the ritual no longer occurred in his own day. Like Fra Bartolommeo's *Saint Anne Altarpiece,* Pontormo's painting was probably invested with anti-Medicean sentiment and may well have become politically antiquated with the return of the Medici in 1530.

In iconography and patronage, Pontormo's altarpiece appears to be inextricably tied to the history of Florentine political experience, hagiographic devotions, and historical memory. From the time of the anonymous Stinche fresco, the *Expulsion of the Duke of Athens,* Florentines had employed the image of Saint Anne to underscore their republican resolve. As has been suggested of the Fra Bartolommeo and Pontormo altarpieces, this targeting of Saint Anne imagery may have allowed incriminating parallels to be drawn between the Medici and Brienne.

But in the years after they established themselves as the ducal rulers of Florence, the Medici brought about an important transformation of the tradition of Saint Anne as a protector of civic liberty and republicanism. This is indicated in an altarpiece of 1575 that has been attributed to Giovanni Maria Butteri (fig. 10).[77] As a representation of Saint Anne, the Virgin, and the Christ Child, flanked by various saints, this work appears to present no extraordinary characteristics. A closer examination of the picture, however, reveals that virtually all the saints are identifiable with members of the family of Grand Duke Cosimo I de' Medici. Cosimo (who died in 1574 and is therefore shown posthumously) and his son, Ferdinando, appear at the left as the traditional Medici saints, Cosmas and Damian. The male figures opposite are Cosimo's other son and immediate successor, Francesco, and his son-in-law, Paolo Giordano Orsini, as Saints George and, possibly, Flavian. Orsini was the husband of Cosimo's daughter, Isabella, who may be represented as Saint Catherine, seated at the left. Although Saint Anne and the Madonna are physiognomically less distinctive than the other figures, they may represent, respectively, Cosimo's mother, Maria Salviati, and his wife, Eleanora of Toledo. The Christ Child and the young John the Baptist are difficult to identify as specific individuals.[78]

In all probability, the Medici, the Orsini, or both families were the patrons of the altarpiece; unfortunately, the circumstances of commission and the location for which it was intended are unknown. Despite this paucity of important information, it appears that the commissioning party wished to make evident the importance of the Medici in Florence through references to the city's victory over Brienne and the traditional devotion to Saint Anne. The inclusion of John the Baptist, the patron saint of Florence, gives the same undeniably Florentine emphasis to the altarpiece as it had to Fra Bartolommeo's *Saint Anne Altarpiece*. As in Fra Bartolommeo's work, the presence of Saint Anne calls to mind the revolt against Brienne on July 26, 1343, but it may also embody a reference to the contribution of the Medici family to this Florentine victory. In Fra Bartolommeo's altarpiece, what is celebrated is an ecstasy and perhaps even assumption of Saint Anne in the

Fig. 8. Pontormo, *Saint Anne Altarpiece*. Paris, Louvre. Ca. 1528–29.
Photo: Alinari/Art Resource.

Fig. 9. Pontormo, *Saint Anne Altarpiece*. Paris, Louvre, detail.
Photo: Alinari/Art Resource.

midst of other protector and patron saints of Florence; in Butteri's
work, Saint Anne remains earthbound, as it were, and the focus of
the picture remains undeniably on the members of the Medici family,
whom Saint Anne seems to bless and protect with her outstretched
arms. In his study of the early history of the Medici, Gene Brucker
argues that the political prestige the family enjoyed during the second
half of the trecento was in part attributable to their role in opposing
Brienne.[79] As the possible patrons of Butteri's altarpiece, the Medici
may here have drawn upon the early political history of the family to
justify the painting's extraordinary iconography. In the fifteenth and
sixteenth centuries, the Medici were ever sensitive to republican traditions, even as they transgressed them, and they often appropriated
Florentine political iconography into their own artistic patronage.[80]
With this altarpiece, it appears that the Medici adopted Saint Anne as
a family saint who would, ironically, watch over the past and future
greatness of their own ducal rule.

This Medicean assumption of the republican tradition surrounding
Saint Anne may also inform an interpretation of Francesco da San-

Fig. 10. Giovanni Maria Butteri, *Saint Anne Altarpiece*. Florence, Uffizi. 1575.
Photo: Alinari/Art Resource.

gallo's Saint Anne group for Orsanmichele (see fig. 1).[81] The statue, commissioned from Sangallo on February 12, 1522, by the *capitani* of the Brotherhood of the Holy Virgin, was completed in 1526. As the Medici had returned to Florence in 1512 and were not to be expelled again until 1527, Sangallo's statue falls squarely within a period when the family was politically secure and dominant in Florence. If we are right about the anti-Medicean sentiments of Fra Bartolommeo's and Pontormo's works, it seems improbable that Sangallo's statue could have been created without Medici favor. Whether for aesthetic or for political reasons, Medici sanction was indeed sought, for Sangallo's *modello* for the statue was shown to Giulio de' Medici (the future Pope Clement VII) for approval.[82] We have seen that at the Bargello the quattrocento Medici apparently preserved the trecento *pittura infamante* of the duke of Athens and his associates as a pointed reminder of a time less fortunate than the present. By similar means, the Medici or their sympathizers may have been involved in commissioning Sangallo's statue of the Saint Anne group to serve a similar political objective. This may also explain why, in 1517, Fra Bartolommeo's unfinished altarpiece was temporarily set up on an altar in S. Lorenzo (the Medici church in Florence) and why, many years later, the same picture, which in 1530 had been reclaimed by an anti-Medicean government, was in the possession of Ottaviano de' Medici.[83] While the possibility of any connection in the 1520s between Sangallo's statue and the Medici must remain conjectural, in 1575 Grand Duke Francesco I de' Medici ordered the construction of the present marble altar, presumably to replace an earlier altar, perhaps even the original altar of the fourteenth century.[84] It is perhaps no coincidence that Butteri's altarpiece, in which Francesco appears as Saint Damian, also bears the date 1575.

AS INDICATED EARLIER, there is no way of knowing whether or not the Florentines invoked the aid of Saint Anne when they revolted against Brienne on July 26, 1343. In fact, it may have been only coincidental that the revolt occurred on Saint Anne's Day. To be sure, if the revolt had occurred on another saint's day, the present essay would not have been written, and many of the works of art discussed here would never have been created. Accidental or not, the revolt did occur on July 26, and from that day forward the Florentines celebrated Saint Anne's Day as the anniversary not only of the revolt against Brienne but also, as is clear from the Stinche fresco, of a saintly intervention. Because of the historical circumstances of the expulsion of Brienne on her feast day, Saint Anne was adopted as a protector of Florentine republicanism, and in Florentine life, politics, and art she came to play a role that was essentially unrelated to her legend as the mother of the Virgin Mary and the grandmother of Christ. That she never became a common saint in the Florentine "pantheon" is significant, for new images of Saint Anne seem, in most cases, to have been commissioned in response to specific political needs. When Florence was threatened, from within or without, or when the republic was reestablished after a period of Medicean hegemony, new images of Saint Anne reminded the citizens of Brienne's tyranny and of the saint's will to support their fight for liberty and republicanism. Contrary to the probable political intention, the Medicean appropriation of this tradition in the sixteenth century served to underscore its strength and persistence.

NOTES

1. Based on a suggestion made by David G. Wilkins, this paper was first developed by Roger J. Crum and was presented by him at the Twenty-third International Congress on Medieval Studies at Kalamazoo, Michigan, in May 1988. For good advice and helpful information we would like to thank Marvin J. Eisenberg, Fil Hearn, Dennis Looney, Franklin Toker, and Jack Wasserman.

For a trecento account of the duke of Athens, see G. Villani, *Cronica*, 4:5–37. See also Paoli, *Della signoria;* Becker, "Walter VI of Brienne" and *Florence in Transition,* vol. 1. Walter VI, a French noble and a relative of the *anjou* of Naples, held the title of duke of Athens as a birthright from his father. His father, Walter V, had lost Athens to Catalan forces in 1312, leaving to his son and heir only the duchy of Lecce. Although known as the duke of Athens, Walter VI never recaptured his father's fief. For the house of Brienne, see Sassenay, *Les Brienne.* For convenience' sake, the duke of Athens is referred to simply as Brienne in the present article.

2. G. Villani, *Cronica* 4:37.

3. Trexler, *Public Life,* proposes an additional interpretation of Saint Anne's role in Florentine politics and society. As well as noting that the celebration of Saint Anne's Day marked a victory over Brienne as a foreign power, Trexler believes that the merchant elite also revered Saint Anne as an "anti-plebian" saint and that the celebration of her feast day "was obvi-

ously a backhanded condemnation of the bad lower classes whom Brienne had courted" (222).

4. For the Medicean opposition to Brienne, see Brucker, "Medici," 14. The involvement of the Medici with certain sixteenth-century images of Saint Anne is discussed below.

5. This essay is not presented as a complete catalog of all Florentine images of Saint Anne but rather of those which were, in our opinion, most likely invested with political content. For additional examples, see Kleinschmidt, *Die heilige Anna,* and Riegel, "Die Darstellungen," 109–22. For discussion of Saint Anne imagery in relation to the events of 1343, see Kemp, *Leonardo da Vinci,* 226–27, 234–36.

6. Becker, "Walter VI of Brienne," 26. From 1313 to 1322, Florence had been under the despotism of King Robert of Naples, but this was more in the form of a protectorate. For trecento Florence and despotism, see Rubinstein, "Florence and the Despots," 21–45.

7. For Brienne's activity in Florence in the 1320s, see Becker, "Walter VI of Brienne," 26–31.

8. "[Brienne] seppe reggere saviamente, e fu signore savio e di gentile aspetto" (G. Villani, *Cronica* 2:363).

9. Sassenay, *Les Brienne,* 188.

10. See Becker, "Walter VI of Brienne," 46f. The raison d'être of Brienne's commission is succinctly addressed by Becker: "Among [Brienne's] many other qualifications were his close ties with both the new and old Popes, his kinship with Robert of Naples, and his high military standing as a marshal of the armies of the monarch of France. In a word, Brienne epitomized the ideals of the Guelph alliance system—ties with Naples, France, and the Holy See—and Florence was in dire need of preferential treatment by her old allies" (*Florence in Transition* 1:149).

11. "Non come capitano ma come amico con bella compagnia" (Stefani, as quoted in Becker, "Walter VI of Brienne," 47).

12. Giovanni Villani reports the exclamation of the Florentines: "Sia la signoria del duca a vita, sia il duca nostro signore" (*Cronica* 4:9–10).

13. "Muoia il duca e i suoi seguaci, e viva il popolo e 'l comune e libertà" (Ibid., 4:31).

14. For the revolt and expulsion, see ibid., 4:30–37, and Becker, "Walter VI of Brienne," 122f.

15. Pietro Franceschini quotes but does not provide a reference for the signorial declaration establishing Saint Anne's Day as a civic festival: ". . . a perpetua memoria della grazia conceduta da Dio al Comune e al popolo fiorentino, nel dì della beata Anna, madre della Vergine gloriosa, per la liberazione della città e dei cittadini e per la distruzione del giogo pernicioso e

tirannico, nella ricorrenza della festività di S. Anna, dai Priori, dagli altri Rettori della città e dai Consoli delle Arti, si dovessero offerte davanti alla immagine della detta Santa in San Michele; più, che in tal giorno nessuno potesse esser preso per debito, e che gli uffici e le botteghe dovessero restar chiusi" (*L'oratorio,* 39). For the distribution of the offerings made to Orsanmichele on Saint Anne's Day, see Paoli, *Della signoria,* 51. For the altar and *immagine,* see Franceschini, *L'oratorio,* 39, 40; on the cult, see Paatz and Paatz, *Die Kirchen* 4:502–3.

16. On the wooden statue, see Franceschini, *L'oratorio,* 96 n. 2; von Fabriczy, "Kritisches Verzeichnis," 32; Paatz and Paatz, *Die Kirchen* 4:508.

17. By decree of the *signoria,* construction was begun on the present structure in 1336 after fire had destroyed its predecessor. For Orsanmichele, see Paatz and Paatz, *Die Kirchen* 4:480–558.

18. For the oratory chapel, see Franceschini, *L'oratorio,* 40–42, 63–64; Paatz and Paatz, *Die Kirchen* 1:411–21. The chapel, begun by architects Neri di Fioravanti and Benci di Cione in 1349, was completed in 1404 by Simone Talenti. In 1379, the *signoria* discontinued its patronage and transferred rights to the chapel to the Arte di Por Santa Maria, which changed its dedication to S. Michele Vecchio. In 1616, the Compagnia di Lombardi assumed patronage rights and changed the chapel's dedication to S. Carlo Borromeo, the name by which it is known today. The order of July 28, 1349, is published by Poggi, *Or San Michele,* 56ff.

19. Offner, *Critical and Historical Corpus* 2:76 n. 2, suggests that a midtrecento chapel and fresco cycle dedicated to Saint Anne (Chiostro dei Morti, S. Maria Novella) may have been commissioned in commemoration of the expulsion of Brienne on Saint Anne's Day. According to Offner, "Representations from the legend of St. Anne appear in Florence only after 1343," and this chapel "contains the earliest known Florentine cycle." To the best of our knowledge, the frescoes, which Offner attributes to a follower of Nardo di Cione, contain no portraits of Brienne or any direct references to him or his rule.

20. For the fresco, see Edgerton, *Pictures and Punishment,* 41; Offner, *Critical and Historical Corpus . . . A Legacy of Attributions,* 26; Belting, "New Role of Narrative," 151–68, esp. 157–58.

21. The prison, which was demolished in the nineteenth century, was located on Via Ghibellina not far from the Palazzo del Podestà, now the Museo Nazionale del Bargello. For the prison, see Fraticelli, *Delle antiche carceri,* and Wolfgang, "Florentine Prison." After the demolition of the prison, the fresco formed part of an interior wall of a structure at Via Ghibellina 83. Its original location in the prison and the intended audience are not known.

22. G. Villani, *Cronica* 4:32.

23. Offner, *Critical and Historical Corpus . . . A Legacy of Attributions*, 26, attributes the fresco to the "Statens Nardesque Master."

24. Paoli, *Della signoria*, 3. What appear to be zodiacal symbols line the circumference of the fresco, perhaps suggesting that Brienne's expulsion was astrologically inevitable.

25. Belting, "New Role of Narrative," 157. Offner, *Critical and Historical Corpus . . . A Legacy of Attributions*, 26, identifies the winged figure as Fortitude.

26. For the *Expulsion of the Duke of Athens* and Last Judgment imagery, see Edgerton, *Pictures and Punishment*, 41. It is worth noting that in a late trecento fresco of the Last Judgment at S. Michele Visdomini, which is discussed below, Brienne was apparently included among the damned figures in hell.

27. For Dante's Gerione, see Singleton commentary in Dante, *Divine Comedy: Inferno* 2:294–309.

28. "E cotale fu la fine della signoria del duca d'Atene, che avea con inganno e tradimento usurpata la libertà sopra il comune e popolo di Firenze, per lo suo tirannesco reggiamento mentre che la signoreggiò, e come egli tradi il comune, cosi da' cittadini fu tradito" (G. Villani, *Cronica* 4:37).

29. Baron, "Bruni's *Histories*," 80.

30. For the Bargello fresco, see Edgerton, *Pictures and Punishment*, 78–85. For the document of commission, see Vasari, *Le vite* 1:625 n. 3.

31. For the tradition of *pitture infamanti*, see Edgerton, *Pictures and Punishment*, 59–125, and Ortalli, *La pittura infamante*.

32. "Intorno alla testa del duca erano molti animali rapaci e d'altre sorti, significanti la natura e qualità di lui; ed uno di que' suoi consiglieri aveva in mano il Palagio de' Priori della città, e come disleale e traditore della patria glie lo porgeva: e tutti avevano sotto l'arme e l'insegne delle famiglie loro, ed alcune scritte, che oggi si possono malamente leggere per essere consumate dal tempo" (Vasari, *Le vite* 1:626). The passage is found in Vasari's *vita* of Giottino.

33. Baldinucci, *Notizie* 1:236.

34. "Avaro, traditore, e poi crudele / Lussurioso, ingiusto, e spergiuro, / Giammai non tenne suo stato sicuro" (ibid.).

35. "A cui piacque [the fresco], ma i più de' savi la biasimarono; perocchè fu memoria di difetto e vergogna del nostro comune, che 'l facemmo nostro signore" (G. Villani, *Cronica* 4:62).

36. For Stefani and the anonymous diarist, see Edgerton, *Pictures and Punishment*, 80, 85.

37. Becker, "Walter VI of Brienne," 418f.

38. For Florentine foreign policy in the trecento, and specifically after the expulsion of Brienne, see Brucker, *Florentine Politics*, and Baron, *Crisis*.

39. Rubinstein, "Florence and the Despots," 21.

40. Paoli, *Della signoria,* 47.

41. Ibid., 47, 48. Any who refused to destroy Brienne's coat of arms were to be fined 1000 fiorini in gold.

42. Becker, *Florence in Transition* 1:165. Becker's assessment of Brienne's reputation is compatible with Trexler's designation of Saint Anne as an "anti-plebian" saint.

43. For Peruzzi's speech, see M. Villani, *Cronica* 2:459.

44. For the S. Michele Visdomini fresco, see Richa, *Notizie istoriche* 1:33; Paatz and Paatz, *Die Kirchen* 4:201, 210 n. 59. According to an undocumented Florentine tradition, Brienne is also believed to be represented as Longinus in Andrea Bonaiuti's fresco of the Crucifixion in the Spanish chapel, S. Maria Novella. For Brienne as Longinus, see Offner and Steinweg, *Critical and Historical Corpus,* sect. 4, 6:86 n. 51.

45. Offner and Steinweg, *Critical and Historical Corpus,* sect. 4, 3:88–93. Standing to the sides are Saints John the Baptist and John the Evangelist. Kneeling below John the Evangelist are Saints Barnabas, Zenobius, Reparata, and Anthony Abbot. Opposite this group are Saints Matthew, Victor, Catherine, and Anne.

46. Ibid., sec. 4, 3:88 n. 3.

47. Richard Offner and Klara Steinweg believe that the facade and bell tower of S. Reparata are visible in the model of Florence held by Saint Anne; since the facade of S. Reparata was no longer visible and the bell tower of the church had been destroyed before 1373, they conclude that the Zecca panel may show the city as it appeared in 1343, when Saint Anne became a protector saint of Florence (ibid., sec. 4, 3:88 n. 6). Franklin Toker has told Roger Crum that he questions this conclusion, for he believes that the model lacks sufficient detail to support this interpretation.

48. Ibid., sec. 4, 3:88 n. 3.

49. "Vir enim gallus et galliarum moribus assuetus ubi plebs pene servorum habetur loco, nomina artium artificumque ridebat; multitudinis arbitrio regi civitatem ridiculum existimabat" (Bruni, *Historiae florentini populi* 2:286).

50. "Res enim digna est quae literis annotetur, vel pro admonitu civium, vel pro castigatione regnantium" (ibid., 2:290).

51. Borsook, "Cults and Imagery," 147–202, especially 183. Borsook notes that since no documents are known for Masaccio and Masolino's panel and Vasari states only that the work is "today" in Sant'Ambrogio, doubt must remain as to its original commissioned location.

52. Baron, *Crisis,* 370–87.

53. For the political advancement of the Medici in the fifteenth century, see Rubinstein, *Government of Florence.*

54. Edgerton, *Pictures and Punishment,* 109.

55. Ibid.

56. Gilbert, *Machiavelli and Guicciardini*, 232.

57. Machiavelli, *The History of Florence and Other Selections*, 100–102.

58. Originally known as the Sala del Gran Consiglio, this room became known as the Salone dei Cinquecento when it briefly served as the seat of the Italian parliament in the mid-nineteenth century. It fell into relative disuse after the Medici returned in 1512, only to be revived as the seat of the Gran Consiglio during the short-lived Florentine republic of 1527–30. The present state of the room reflects the renovations begun by Duke Cosimo I de' Medici in the 1540s and continued by his successors throughout the century. For the history of the room prior to the Medici principate, see Wilde, "Hall of the Great Council."

59. Neilson, *Filippino Lippi*, 142–44.

60. "Fece nel palazzo della Signoria . . . un'altra tavola grande, con l'ornamento, per la sala del Consiglio; il qual disegno, morendosi, non cominciò altramente a mettere in opera" (Vasari, *Le vite* 3:474–75).

61. For the document specifying the transfer of the commission, see Scharf, *Filippino Lippi*, 101, doc. 25. For Fra Bartolommeo's *Saint Anne Altarpiece*, see Gabelentz, *Fra Bartolommeo* 1:128, 159–61; Steinberg, *Fra Girolamo Savonarola*, 100–105.

62. "Gli fu da Piero Soderini allogata la tavola della sala del consiglio, che di chiaro oscuro da lui disegnata ridusse in maniera, ch' era per farsi onore grandissimo; la quale è oggi in San Lorenzo alla cappella del magnifico Ottaviano de' Medici onoratamente collocata così imperfetta, nella quale sono tutti i protettori della città di Fiorenza, e que' Santi che nel giorno loro la città ha aute le sue vittorie" (Vasari, *Le vite* 4:198–99).

63. For the government document recalling Fra Bartolommeo's painting, see Roth, *Last Florentine Republic*, 106, 113 n. 127. Jack Wasserman has informed us that the correct date is March 29, 1529.

64. According to J. N. Stephens, these governments were "brave new experiments, newer by far in principle and practice than the 'great estate' of the Medici, whose suppression was their principal *raison d'être*" (*Fall of the Florentine Republic*, 46).

65. See de Tolnay, "Remarques"; Heydenreich, "La Saint Anne de Léonard"; Gould, *Leonardo*, 104–7, 152–62; and Wasserman, "Re-discovered Cartoon" and "Patronage and Dating." For a drawing after Leonardo that may reproduce the composition of the SS. Annunziata cartoon, see Kemp's introduction to Clark's *Leonardo*, 32–34, fig. 5. For the date of the SS. Annunziata cartoon, see Wasserman, "Re-discovered Cartoon," 194–204.

66. Wasserman, "Dating and Patronage," 324.

67. Vasari, *Le vite* 4:38.

68. "Finalmente fece un cartone dentrovi una Nostra Donna ed una Sant' Anna con un Cristo, la quale non pure fece maravigliare tutti gli artefici, ma finita ch' ella fu, nella stanza durarono due giorni d' andare a verderla gli uomini e le donne, i giovanni ed i vecchi, come si va alle feste solenni" (ibid.). In addition to Vasari's account, there exist two letters dated April 3 and 4, 1501, from Fra Pietro da Novellara to Isabella d'Este, which mention Leonardo's work on the Saint Anne theme. For these letters and a discussion of their bearing on Leonardo's work, see Gould, *Leonardo*, 104–7, 152–62.

69. Wasserman, "Re-discovered Cartoon," 201–2.

70. Kemp, *Leonardo*, 221. This work was completed by Perugino after Lippi's death.

71. For the Sala del Gran Consiglio and its intended decoration, see Wilde, "Hall of the Great Council."

72. For the issue of Florentine iconography in Leonardo's works after 1500, see Kemp, *Leonardo da Vinci*, 226; for Hercules and Florence, see Ettlinger, "Hercules Florentinus." Renaissance Florentines regarded Hercules as the legendary founder of their city, and as early as 1281 the mythological hero had appeared on the official seal of Florence. Beginning in the fifteenth century, the Medici used Hercules in their art to promote an image of themselves as virtuous Florentines. In 1494, the Medici were expelled from Florence on the day of Saint Salvatore. It has also been argued that the Salvator Mundi was commissioned by King Louis XII sometime after 1507; see *Leonardo e il leonardismo*, 147–50; Snow-Smith, "Salvator Mundi," 69–81.

73. Kemp, *Leonardo da Vinci*, 226. Certainly related to Leonardo's versions on the Saint Anne theme in iconography, composition, and perhaps even political content are two drawings by Michelangelo that date to the first decade of the sixteenth century. For these drawings, see Hartt, *Michelangelo Drawings*, 34, 65, 66 nn. 9, 57, and Wasserman, "Michelangelo's Virgin," 122–31.

74. Clapp, *Jacopo Carucci da Pontormo*, 167–69; Forster, *Pontormo*, 142–43. In a recent talk on "Nuovi pensieri sul Pontormo—*la Madonna con Bambino e Santa Anna* al Louvre," at the Conference "Giornate di studio sull'arte del Cinquecento in Toscana" (October 24–27, 1989, at the Kunsthistorisches Institut in Florence), Jack Wasserman argued that the dating of Pontormo's *Saint Anne Altarpiece* to the last Florentine Republic is incorrect. He argued that the work should be dated 1524–26.

75. "Il che fece ancora in una tavola che dipinse alle monache di Santa Anna, alla porta a San Friano; nella qual tavola è la Nostra Donna col putto in collo e Sant' Anna dietro, San Piero e San Benedetto con altri Santi: e nella predella è una storietta di figure piccole, che rappresentano la Signoria di Firenze, quando andava a processione con trombetti, pifferi, mazzieri,

comandatori e tavolaccini, e col rimanente della famiglia: e questa fece, perocchè la detta tavola gli fu fatta fare dal capitano e famiglia di Palazzo" (Vasari, *Le vite* 6:272–73). For the convent of Sant' Anna sul Prato, see Paatz and Paatz, *Die Kirchen* 1:57–60, esp. 58.

76. Richa, *Notizie istoriche* 4:222.

77. For a discussion of this picture, with bibliography, see Langedijk, *Portraits of the Medici* 1:118–19, 424.

78. While Langedijk, *Portraits of the Medici* 1:119, notes that this altarpiece is "the only example of any consequence in which members of the family are identified with saints," she takes exception (424) to any attempt to identify Saint Anne or the Madonna with specific individuals.

79. Brucker, "Medici," 14.

80. For the fifteenth century, see Bennett and Wilkins, *Donatello*, 83–90. For the sixteenth-century Medici, see, especially, Cox-Rearick, *Dynasty and Destiny*.

81. For Sangallo's statue in the context of Orsanmichele, see Paatz and Paatz, *Die Kirchen* 4:502–3. See also Heikamp, "Der Werkvertrag," 79–86; Pope-Hennessy, *Italian High Renaissance and Baroque Sculpture*, 356, 456.

82. Heikamp, "Der Werkvertrag," 81.

83. For Fra Bartolommeo's altarpiece in S. Lorenzo, see Paatz and Paatz, *Die Kirchen* 2:511; for the altarpiece and Ottaviano de' Medici, see Vasari, *Le vite* 4:198.

84. Paatz and Paatz, *Die Kirchen* 4:503.

BIBLIOGRAPHY

Baldinucci, Filippo. *Notizie de' professori del disegno.* 6 vols. Turin: Stamperia reale, 1768–1820.

Baron, Hans. "Bruni's *Histories* as an Expression of Modern Thought." In *In Search of Florentine Civic Humanism*, 1:68–93. Princeton: Princeton University Press, 1988.

———. *The Crisis of the Early Italian Renaissance.* 2d ed. Princeton: Princeton University Press, 1966.

Becker, Marvin. *Florence in Transition.* 2 vols. Baltimore: Johns Hopkins University Press, 1967–68.

———. "Walter VI of Brienne to 1343." Ph.D. diss., University of Pennsylvania, 1950.

Béguin, Sylvie. *Leonardo da Vinci au Louvre.* Paris: Ministère de la Culture, 1983.

Belting, Hans. "The New Role of Narrative in Public Painting of the Trecento: *Historia* and Allegory." *Studies in the History of Art* 16 (1985): 151–68.

Bennett, Bonnie A., and David G. Wilkins. *Donatello*. Oxford: Phaidon, 1984.

Borsook, Eve. "Cults and Imagery at Sant' Ambrogio in Florence." *Mitteilungen des Kunsthistorischen Institutes in Florenz* 25 (1981): 147–202.

Brucker, Gene. *Florentine Politics and Society, 1343–1375*. Princeton: Princeton University Press, 1962.

——. "The Medici in the Fourteenth Century." *Speculum* 32 (1957): 1–26.

Bruni, Leonardo. *Historiae florentini populi*. Ed. D. Acciaiuoli. 2 vols. Florence: Felice Le Monnier, 1857.

Clapp, Frederick Mortimer. *Jacopo Carucci da Pontormo*. New Haven: Yale University Press, 1916.

Cox-Rearick, Janet. *Dynasty and Destiny in Medici Art: Pontormo, Leo X, and the Two Cosimos*. Princeton: Princeton University Press, 1984.

Dante. *The Divine Comedy: Inferno*. Trans. and Commentary by Charles S. Singleton. Vol. 2. Princeton: Princeton University Press, 1970.

de Tolnay, Charles. "Remarques sur la Sainte Anne de Léonard." *La Revue des Arts* 6 (1956): 161–66.

Edgerton, Samuel. *Pictures and Punishment: Art and Criminal Prosecution during the Florentine Renaissance*. Ithaca, N.Y.: Cornell University Press, 1985.

Ettlinger, Leopold. "Hercules Florentinus." *Mitteilungen des Kunsthistorischen Institutes in Florenz* 16 (1972): 119–42.

Forster, Kurt W. *Pontormo*. Munich: Bruckmann, 1966.

Franceschini, Pietro. *L'oratorio di San Michele in Orto in Firenze*. Florence: Landi, 1892.

Fraticelli, Pietro J. *Delle antiche carceri di Firenze dinominate le Stinche*. Florence: G. Formigli, 1834.

Freedberg, Sidney. *Painting in Italy, 1500 to 1600*. 2d ed. Harmondsworth: Penguin, 1971.

Gabelentz, Hans. *Fra Bartolommeo*. 2 vols. Leipzig: K. W. Hiersemann, 1922.

Gilbert, Felix. *Machiavelli and Guicciardini: Politics and History in Sixteenth-Century Florence*. Princeton: Princeton University Press, 1965.

Gould, Cecil. *Leonardo: The Artist and the Nonartist*. Boston: New York Graphic Society, 1975.

Hartt, Frederick. *Michelangelo Drawings*. New York: Abrams, n.d.

Heikamp, Detlef. "Der Werkvertrag für die St. Anna Selbdritt des Francesco da Sangallo." In *Kaleidoskop: Eine Festschrift für Fritz Baumgart zum 75. Geburtstag*, ed. F. Mielke, 79–86. Berlin: Mann, 1977.

Heydenreich, Ludwig. "La Saint Anne de Léonard de Vinci." *Gazette des Beaux-Arts* 10 (1933): 207–19.

Kemp, Martin. Introduction to *Leonardo da Vinci*, by Kenneth Clark. New ed. London: Penguin, 1988.

————. *Leonardo da Vinci: The Marvellous Works of Nature and Man*. Cambridge: Harvard University Press, 1981.

Kleinschmidt, Beda. *Die heilige Anna: Ihre Verehrung in Geschichte, Kunst und Volkstum*. Düsseldorf: L. Schwann, 1930.

Langedijk, Karla. *The Portraits of the Medici, Fifteenth–Eighteenth Centuries*. 2 vols. Florence: Studio per Edizioni Scelte, 1981–83.

Leonardo e il Leonardismo a Napoli e Roma. Ed. Alessandro Vezzosi. Florence: Giunti Barbèra, 1983.

Machiavelli. *The History of Florence and Other Selections*. Ed. Myron Gilmore. New York: Washington Square Press, 1970.

Neilson, Katherine. *Filippino Lippi*. Cambridge: Harvard University Press, 1938.

Offner, Richard. *A Critical and Historical Corpus of Florentine Painting*. Sec. 4, vol. 2. New York: Institute of Fine Arts, 1960.

————. *A Critical and Historical Corpus of Florentine Painting: A Legacy of Attributions*. Ed. Hayden Maginnis. New York: Institute of Fine Arts, 1981.

Offner, Richard, and Klara Steinweg. *A Critical and Historical Corpus of Florentine Painting*. Sec. 4, vols. 3 and 6. New York: Institute of Fine Arts, 1965, 1979.

Ortalli, Gherardo. *La pittura infamante nei secoli XIII–XVI*. Rome: Jouvence, 1979.

Paatz, Walter, and Elisabeth Paatz. *Die Kirchen von Florenz*. 6 vols. Frankfurt am Main: V. Klostermann, 1940–54.

Paoli, Cesare. *Della signoria di Gualtieri Duca d'Atene in Firenze*. Florence: Cellini, 1862.

Poggi, Girolamo. *Or San Michele*. Florence: Pellas, 1895.

Pope-Hennessy, John. *Italian High Renaissance and Baroque Sculpture*. Oxford: Phaidon, 1986.

Richa, Giuseppe. *Notizie istoriche delle chiese fiorentine*. 10 vols. Florence: P. G. Viviani, 1754–62.

Riegel, Herman. "Die Darstellungen des heiligen Anna Selbdritt, besonders zu Florenz." In *Beiträge zur Kunstgeschichte Italiens*, 117–18. Dresden, 1898.

Roth, Cecil. *The Last Florentine Republic*. New York: Methuen, 1925.

Rubinstein, Nicolai. "Florence and the Despots: Some Aspects of Florentine Diplomacy in the Fourteenth Century." *Transactions of the Royal Historical Society*, 5th ser., 2 (1952): 21–45.

————. *The Government of Florence under the Medici, 1434–1494*. Oxford: Clarendon, 1966.

Sassenay, Fernand de. *Les Brienne de Lecce et d'Athènes: Histoire d'une des grandes familles de la féodalité française (1200–1356)*. Paris: Hachette, 1869.

Scharf, Alfred. *Filippino Lippi*. Vienna: A. Schroll, 1935.

Snow-Smith, Joanna. "The *Salvator Mundi* of Leonardo da Vinci." *Arte lombarda* 50 (1978): 69–81.

Steinberg, Ronald M. *Fra Girolamo Savonarola, Florentine Art, and Renaissance Historiography*. Athens: Ohio University Press, 1977.

Stephens, J. N. *The Fall of the Florentine Republic, 1512–1530*. Oxford: Clarendon Press, 1983.

Trexler, Richard. *Public Life in Renaissance Florence*. New York: Academic Press, 1980.

Vasari, Giorgio. *Le vite de' più eccellenti pittori scultori ed architettori*. Ed. G. Milanesi. 9 vols. Florence: G. C. Sansoni, 1906.

Villani, Giovanni. *Cronica di Giovanni Villani*. Ed. F. G. Dragomanni. 4 vols. Florence: S. Coen, 1844–45.

Villani, Matteo. *Cronica di Matteo Villani*. Ed. F. G. Dragomanni. 2 vols. Florence: S. Coen, 1846.

von Fabriczy, Cornelius. "Kritisches Verzeichnis Toskanischer Holz- und Tonstatuen bis zum Beginn des Cinquecento." *Jahrbuch der königliche Preussischen Kunstsammlungen* 30 (1909, Supplement): 1–102.

Wasserman, Jack. "The Dating and Patronage of Leonardo's Burlington House Cartoon." *Art Bulletin* 53 (1971): 312–25.

―――. "A Re-discovered Cartoon by Leonardo da Vinci." *Burlington Magazine* 112 (1970): 194–204.

―――. "Michelangelo's Virgin and Child with St. Anne at Oxford." *Burlington Magazine* 111 (1969): 122–31.

Wilde, Johannes. "The Hall of the Great Council of Florence." *Journal of the Warburg and Courtauld Institutes* 7 (1944): 65–81.

Wolfgang, Marvin. "A Florentine Prison: Le Carceri delle Stinche." *Studies in the Renaissance* 7 (1960): 148–66.

Appropriating the Holy Kinship

Gender and Family History

PAMELA SHEINGORN

To people of the late Middle Ages, who focused more on Christ's humanity than on his divinity, it seemed obvious that the incarnate Christ would be, like each of them, a member of a large, multigenerational family. But the structure of such a family, the relative importance of its members and of nuclear units in relation to the whole, and, above all, gender roles and definitions were changing in the course of the fifteenth century and into the sixteenth century. Images of the Holy Kinship served as one of the areas in which such issues could be examined and tested, for its members provided crucial role models in a society so attentive to its saints.

The Holy Kinship developed as a way of reconciling the New Testament language referring to "brothers of Christ" with the belief in the perpetual virginity of Mary. In so doing, the Holy Kinship created familial relationships among various named figures in the New Testament and apocryphal Gospels. With breathtaking economy, it united the available persons into one lineage. Once a genealogical tree had been constructed according to which the three daughters of Anne by her three marriages produced seven remarkably holy children, while Anne's sister Esmeria founded a similarly saintly cadet branch, the Holy Kinship did not change, but the way that the pictorial arts presented the Holy Kinship evolved strikingly over time. I will trace those changes here, not to the end of answering art history's questions as to the development of the Holy Kinship, but rather as a way of reading medieval culture, for at some level these images of Holy Family examine and enact the attempts of medieval people to understand, to structure, and to change both gender roles and human families.

THE EARLIEST REPRESENTATIONS of the Holy Kinship, in the form of genealogical charts, appeared in the history of the Western family at a stage marked by a strong preference for patriarchy. Both the organization and the placement of these charts suggest that they may have appropriated the subject of Holy Kinship as a way of asserting an alternative matriarchal view.

Although in the early Middle Ages there had been a general tendency to trace ancestry through both male and female lines, that is, to take a bilineal approach, from the eleventh century onward western European families began to favor agnatic lineage, or the tracing of kinship through the male line. In David Herlihy's words, "The agnatic lineage . . . [is] a kind of fellowship of males, stretching backwards and forwards over time. . . . Patrilineage is ancestor-focused, in the sense that it traces its descent in the male line back to a known founder."[1] The New Testament provides a genealogy of Christ, but that genealogy was not represented in religious art until the time when patrilineage became important in the kinship patterns of human families. This representation took the form of an image called the Tree of Jesse, an image that arose in the eleventh century and occurred with great frequency by the thirteenth century. The Tree of Jesse was based on exegesis of the first verse of Isaiah 11: "And there shall come forth a rod out of the root of Jesse, and a flower shall rise up out of his root" ("Et egredietur virga de radice Iesse, Et flos de radice eius ascendet"). As early as Tertullian, the rod (*virga*) that comes forth from the root of Jesse was understood to be the Virgin Mary, descended from David (of the house of Jesse), and the flower she produced is Christ.[2] Early representations of this image remained faithful to the exegetical tradition: from the loins of the sleeping Jesse grows a tree that culminates in a large and prominent figure of the Virgin and Child. However, the Tree of Jesse was soon reinterpreted in the light of the genealogy of Christ supplied in the Gospel of Matthew, and a Tree of Jesse was constructed that focused on the male line, especially on Christ's royal ancestors, the kings of Israel. The strength of the new focus was so strong that it obscured the formerly central role of the Virgin. Although a major study of the Tree of Jesse in the pictorial arts attributes this shift to the strength of the genealogical idea,[3] it is important to recognize that it is more than this; Christ's genealogy was deliberately being seen in terms of patriarchy. Choices were made that deemphasized the basic truth that, in order for Christ to have a divine father, his other, human parent had to be a woman. Apparently unwilling to give full recognition to the fact that a female link had been forged into the patriarchal chain at an especially crucial point, most makers of such images in the thirteenth and fourteenth centuries chose instead to trace the lineage of Christ from the male founder, Jesse, through a male line of patriarchs and kings to the male child, Christ.

It is in this context that Holy Kinship diagrams tracing Christ's ancestry to Saint Anne first appear, and it is because of this context that it is tempting to read such diagrams as conscious rebuttals of the patriarchal Tree of Jesse. In a French manuscript of about 1300, the poem "La Généalogie de Nostre Dame," by Gautier de Coincy, is illustrated by a genealogical chart (fig. 1). The text at the top of the page proclaims that what follows has the authority of the four Gospels and the Epistles, and lineage is traced through lines that connect circles within which members of the family are portrayed. Thus the circle at the top enclosing Anne leads down to three circles framing her three daughters at the center of the page, and these in turn connect to three circles for Christ and his six first cousins. Although the six husbands are represented, they appear outside the roundels rather than being paired with their wives.

Two English Psalters—the Imola Psalter and the Queen Mary Psalter—that juxtapose such a clearly female genealogy with the patriarchal Tree of Jesse by placing the two genealogies on consecutive or facing pages seem thereby to issue a particularly clear challenge to the supremacy of the male descent. In his catalog of English manuscripts of the thirteenth century, Nigel Morgan suggests that one of these books may have been made for a nun of Amesbury. It was certainly owned by a community of nuns, for there is an obituary added in a thirteenth-century hand for "Margaret de Quincey, priorissa nostra."[4] This possible association between female patronage and the prominent inclusion of Christ's family through the female line hints at a deliberate focus on matriliny among female religious. The Imola and Queen Mary Psalters, both made in England, may have consciously

Fig. 1. *Holy Kinship*, miniature from French illustrated miscellany that includes "La Généalogie de Nostre Dame en roumans," by Gautier de Coincy. Paris, Arsenal MS. 3517, fol. 7. Ca. 1300.
Photo: Bibliothèque Nationale, Paris.

addressed issues raised in the Salomite controversy. In so doing, they forwarded the view that Christ's earthly family centered on its matriarch, Saint Anne.

The new way of representing the Holy Kinship that flourished in the fifteenth and sixteenth centuries (especially, but not exclusively, in the Mosan-Rhenish region) adds to Anne the matriarch her human role of grandmother. The new composition brings together in one setting Saint Anne as a wise and nurturing grandparent, her three daughters as young, beautiful, and loving mothers, and their children as charming infants and playful toddlers (fig. 2). Thus the genealogy is presented not sequentially but simultaneously. This group of related persons shares not only family ties but also the same time and space, resulting in a new focus on human relationships. It is the kind of grouping envisioned by an English *Life of Saint Anne* describing the female household to which the Virgin returned after the death of Joseph:

> So with Anne and all that progeny
> Dwelled Mary still in that city;
> In Nazareth a great thraw; [while]
> And Jesus was in their company (3085–88).[5]

As in the genealogical charts, here men are relegated to the periphery of the family. They may either be entirely excluded or firmly confined to the space outside the warm, domestic enclosure. Joseph sometimes appears as a shadowy figure, lurking in the background, as if in pictorial acknowledgment of his ambiguous role in the Incarnation. Although a generation of men—Joachim, Cleophas, and Salome —led to a generation of grandsons—Christ and his cousins—these Holy Kinship images deliberately focus on women as progenitors of the sacred. Thus, the genealogical aspect of the image is not eliminated in the new pictorial format but is reinforced by the unified setting. It is telling, for example, that in the painting by the Follower of the Master of Saint Veronica from about 1420, the large halos of Anne and her daughters go a long way toward obscuring their husbands' faces in the background. The setting of an enclosed garden filled with flowers and fruit is surely a deliberate reference to the *hortus conclusus*. A hedge of roses forms its boundaries in the Saint Anne miniature in the *Hours of Etienne Chevalier* of about 1450 (fig. 3).[6] While the lovely roses can be read as metaphors for the beautiful women within the

Fig. 2. Follower of the Master of Saint Veronica, *Holy Kinship*. Cologne,
Wallraf-Richartz-Museum, Inv. Nr. 59. Ca. 1420.
Photo: Rheinisches Bildarchiv, Cologne.

Fig. 3. Jean Fouquet, *Saint Anne and Three Marys* from the *Hours of Etienne Chevalier*. Paris, BN MS. nouv. acq. lat. 1416. Ca. 1450.
Photo: Giraudon/Art Resource.

garden, their thorns, by implication, exclude all intruders, into which category husbands apparently fall.

The center of this large family grouping was often the subject known in German as "Anna Selbdritt" and in Dutch as "Anna te Drieen," but for which there is no equivalent phrase in English. It is made up of Saint Anne with the Virgin and Child, often arranged so that a small figure of the Virgin holding her infant son sits upon the lap of the enthroned Saint Anne. This subject, from which apparently derives the pictorial composition of the Holy Kinship as a group in one setting, emphasizes the female line and its existence in the mind of God from the beginning of time. One frequently used arrangement of these three figures presents Anne and the Virgin seated on a bench or throne and supporting the Christ Child between them, as in a Netherlandish painting of Saint Anne with the Virgin and the Christ Child by the Master of Frankfurt (fig. 4). This composition replicates a popular way of representing the Trinity in which God the Father and God the Son are seated with the dove of the Holy Spirit hovering in the space between them. The painting by the Master of Frankfurt makes the parallel between matriarchal and patriarchal trinities explicit, for the traditional Trinity is actually represented on the vertical axis of the painting. According to John Oliver Hand, "The implication is that the grouping of Anne, Virgin, and Child is equal to and as sanctified as the more traditional triumvirate of Father, Son, and Holy Ghost."[7] When the group of Saint Anne, the Virgin, and Child in this Trinitarian arrangement forms the center of a Holy Kinship grouping, it brings with it this layer of meaning, one that elevates Saint Anne to a position in the group equivalent to the position of God the Father in the traditional Trinity.

The matrilineal Trinity emphasizes, of course, the lineage of Christ's physical body, whereas the traditional Trinity emphasizes the divine origins of his soul. Thus in examining the parentage of Christ, the body is associated with the female progenitor, and the soul with the male. Peter W. Travis observes that, under the influence of incarnational theology, the late Middle Ages found "a sustained and intimate meditation upon the physical details of Christ's body" completely appropriate.[8] Travis cites the work of Leo Steinberg, who finds the ultimate expression of this emphasis upon Christ's body in works of art from about 1400 to 1600 "in which the genitalia of the Christ Child, or of the dead Christ, receive such demonstrable emphasis that one must recognize an *ostentatio genitalium* comparable to the canonic *ostentatio vulnerum,* the showing forth of the wounds."[9]

Two points suggest that the Holy Kinship is a part of this same set of ideas. First, the Incarnation, by providing Christ with mortal kindred, makes him a member of the family of man, or, as Steinberg puts it, "The sexual member exhibited by the Christ Child . . . is an affirmation not of superior power but of condescension to kinship, a sign of the Creator's self-abasement to his creature's condition."[10] Second, the full impact of the Incarnation, of Christ's humanity, can be demonstrated not only through emphasis on his own body but also through representation of those to whom he is physically most unassailably linked. John Bossy refers to this aspect of the Incarnation

Fig. 4. Master of Frankfurt, *Saint Anne with the Virgin and the Christ Child*.
National Gallery of Art, Washington, D.C. Gift of Mr. and Mrs. Sidney K.
Lafoon. 1510–15. Photo: National Gallery of Art.

when he observes, "To show, in the fifteenth century, that Christ was a real man, . . . it was necessary to know that he was someone with human kin."[11] And his human kin were his maternal kin, headed by the matriarch Saint Anne. Thus Steinberg, in explicating an image by Hans Baldung Grien in which Saint Anne touches the penis of the infant Christ (fig. 5), comments, "And because grandmother Anne guarantees Christ's human lineage, it is she who is tasked with the proving."[12] Whereas the cult of saints created a great family of the blessed in heaven, a family centered on the traditional Trinity represented as male, incarnational theology created a family of maternal aunts and cousins, a family centered on a carnal and maternal Trinity.

It has become clear from a number of recent studies that the late medieval interest in incarnational theology, as exemplified by texts such as the play in the Digby manuscript, "The Killing of the Children," corresponds to what Theresa Coletti has called "the late medieval re-thinking of the relationship of woman's sanctity and woman's sexuality."[13] This change in the idea of what behaviors and attitudes appropriately belonged to the female gender allowed for a wider range of possibilities for women. There is a significant rise in the popularity of female saints in the late Middle Ages, a change that has been called "the feminization of sainthood and sanctity."[14] Marriage and motherhood were no bar to sanctity for these women, nor did they discard traditional female behavior in order to pursue the spiritual life. Rather, these female saints carried the behavior of motherhood into the spiritual realm, as, for example, when they acted as mother to a band of spiritual children.[15] After citing a number of examples, David Herlihy concludes that this emphasis on the maternal behavior of saints suggests that "the mother played a far more active role, and enjoyed higher prestige and stature, than we have hitherto recognized."[16]

The Holy Kinship, as represented in the pictorial arts, emphasizes these aspects of women's behavior in the late Middle Ages. Christ owed his physical body, the Incarnation itself, to his maternal ancestors, and a glorification of his body implied a glorification of all aspects of maternal parenting. Thus, as Coletti observes, "The later Middle Ages sought to validate the ordinary, privileging in religious terms what centuries of tradition had associated with the female: corporeal creation, the material world, the flesh."[17] Speaking of the fully developed version of the Holy Kinship in the pictorial arts, Siegfried

Fig. 5. Hans Baldung Grien, *The Holy Family*. P. 62,
Kupferstichkabinett, SMPK, Berlin. 1511.
Photo: Jörg P. Anders.

Gohr reminds us that it is "Anne the family mother, who stands at the head of a numerous kindred, a highly matriarchal concept of the family. Think of the attention that Dürer gave to his mother during his life and to which we owe one of the best portraits in German art, and think also of the fact that Dürer composed a family chronicle." [18]

Saint Anne's appearances in visions to two female saints give further evidence that an important aspect of late medieval society was its assertion of the positive value of marriage and motherhood. In Bridget's vision, Anne pronounced herself "ladi of all weddid folke" and offered herself as intercessor on behalf of fruitful marriages. Anne's own example asserted the availability of the spiritual life for married women and set aside the emphasis on virginity that had dominated earlier Christian teaching. But the cult of Anne was not confined to "weddid folke." Rather, Anne's appearance to the virgin saint Colette of Corbie and Colette's subsequent devotion to Anne indicate that the role of married female merited respect even from those who chose the convent. Colette's vision of the Holy Kinship challenged her negative view of marriage and especially of remarriage, even though in this view she reflected a venerable and continuing Christian tradition, for canonists of this period, according to James Brundage, "deplored remarriage on the grounds that it displayed an unseemly desire for continued sex after the death of a prior spouse." [19] The miniature of Colette's vision illustrates a manuscript of the life of Saint Colette made in about 1474–76 and commissioned by Charles the Bold, duke of Burgundy, and his wife, Margaret of York. [20] In fact, the patrons are shown as observers of this scene, in which they surely had a deep personal interest, for the marriage of Charles the Bold and Margaret of York was the duke's third. [21]

Images of the Holy Kinship could, however, emphasize other aspects of their complex subject and, in so doing, forward other ideologies. For example, representing the Virgin Mary in Holy Kinship images as the Virgin of the Immaculate Conception served to remove her from the congenial world of female affairs and to place her instead in the intellectual world of theology. In a painting of the Holy Kinship now in the Walters Art Gallery (fig. 6), not only does the Immaculate Conception become a major subject of the central panel, but, as if a necessary consequence, Anne's two other daughters shrink to a very

Fig. 6. Master of the Magdalene Legend (attributed), *Holy Kinship*. Walters
Art Gallery, Baltimore, 37.290. 1480–90. Photo: Walters Art Gallery.

small scale.[22] They are simply background figures, necessary links in
the process whose goal was the production of male saints. Thus the
large figures of John the Baptist and Saint Servatius on the side panels
of the altarpiece not only occupy dominant positions but also direct
their gazes at the Christ Child in the central panel rather than at Anne
and Mary. Even in works of art that focus on Anne and her daughters,
there can be a tension between their prominence and the far more important roles of their male children in salvation history, a tension that
is heightened when these children display the attributes of their adult
roles as apostles: James with his scallop shell and pilgrim's wallet, Jude
with his boat, and John writing in a little book. In this same period,
the great rise in the cult of Saint Monica, mother of Saint Augustine,
similarly presents a mother who is important not in her own right but
because she is the mother of a major figure in the church.[23]

Further, the appeal of the Holy Kinship to married laypersons had its negative as well as its positive side. From its beginnings, the church had established a clear hierarchy of values in sexual behavior, ranking celibacy far above marriage, which was left for those who lacked the gift of continence. Some of the loudest and most persistent attacks on the church in the late medieval period had as their targets the many monks and nuns who failed to live up to the ideal of chastity while still, hypocritically, holding themselves superior to the married laity. It is in this context that altarpieces and stained-glass windows in late medieval churches, especially parish churches, can be read as a contribution to the debate on celibacy versus marriage. Traditionally reserved for figures of the saints, most of them virgins and martyrs, in the fifteenth century these highly visible locations often displayed the Holy Kinship, and did so in a new format. In the windows of about 1470 at Holy Trinity, Goodramgate, York, for example, there is a separate panel for each individual family within the Holy Kinship (fig. 7), so that the Holy Kinship becomes a juxtaposed series of nuclear families. Even more striking is the altarpiece of the Holy Kinship painted in 1505 by Bernhard Strigel.[24] Contrary to the usual arrangement for altarpieces, the central panel does not represent one large scene; rather, it is divided into smaller units, each one devoted to one family of the Holy Kinship. In other representations of the Holy Kinship, even when all members of the family are gathered in one space, there is a tendency to group them according to nuclear units. Such works of art were certainly meant to champion marriage and the family and to implicitly challenge the superiority of celibacy and the convent. But they do more than that: they also challenge both matriarchal organization and the notion of the extended family.

Thus the presentation of the Holy Kinship as a series of individual families represents much more than a criticism of the late medieval church. It suggests, at least at some levels of society, a shift in emphasis from the extended to the nuclear family. Lawrence Stone observes, "In the late middle ages the nuclear family of the landed elite was no more than a loose core at the centre of a dense network of lineage and kin relationships."[25] He might have been describing a painting of the grouped Holy Kinship. Later in his book Stone points to "the decline of kinship and clientage as the main organizing principles of landed society" which took place in England between 1500 and 1700.[26] Instead, the nuclear family became increasingly important, just as it did

Fig. 7. *Saint Mary Cleophas, Alpheus, and Children*, detail from east window of
Holy Trinity Church, Goodramgate, York. Fifteenth century.
Photo: Royal Commission on the Historical Monuments of England.

in the Holy Kinship. And both in the historical family and in the Holy Kinship, authority rested in the father.

It would be an oversimplification to suggest that the transformation of the Holy Kinship image took place in a series of steps that moved univocally through time from appropriation by females to appropriation by males, from a matriarchal to a patriarchal image, just as it is an oversimplification to describe the Reformation in terms of a linear process. As we have just suggested, the Holy Kinship image was never completely univalent. One can point to various elements introduced into Holy Kinship images that create a different set of power relationships within the family and decisively redefine gender roles. Although such changes predate the Reformation, their cumulative import was consciously articulated as part of Reformation ideology.

Sacred fathers come into their own in the late Middle Ages, and at the expense of holy mothers. Theological attention to Joseph in the course of the fifteenth century resulted in a new understanding of him as both husband of Mary and protector of her virginity. Late medieval vernacular plays treating the subject of Joseph's doubts about Mary's pregnancy dramatized the process through which Joseph came to understand that God had entrusted him with an important role. Thus in the Annunciation play of the English Towneley cycle, an angel explains God's plan to Joseph, who responds joyfully:

> Ah, Lord, I love thee all alone,
> That vouchsafes that I be one
> To tent that child so young. (338–40)

Works of art began to appear in which Joseph takes an active role in tending the Christ Child; an example is a German engraving in which Joseph teaches him to walk (fig. 8). The cult of Joseph, whose feast was first included in the Roman breviary in 1487, centered on his role as father.

Joachim similarly came to prominence in the late fifteenth century, though his cult lagged behind that of Joseph. His feast appears in a Venetian breviary of 1522, where it is described as having been established by Pope Julius II. It is, of course, his fatherhood of Mary that makes him an important figure.

In images of the Holy Kinship, first these two saintly fathers and

Fig. 8. Anonymous German artist, *Joseph and Christ Child*.
National Gallery of Art, Washington, D.C., Rosenwald
Collection. Fifteenth century. Photo: National
Gallery of Art.

then the others increasingly breach the barrier of the *hortus conclusus* until, no longer having a function, it disappears completely. Husbands take their places next to their wives. Attention shifts away from Anne, whose three husbands form, in the best of circumstances, a rather awkward clump, and toward individual family units. In some less-accomplished works, the result is a crowded group portrait with little indication of the relative importance of its members (fig. 9). In this setting, Christ's earthly family seems just like any other family; in fact, they are oddly reminiscent of the lined-up figures, with faces like variations on a theme, captured in amateur snapshots taken in grand-mother's backyard on a Sunday afternoon. If one message here is that everyone should belong to a family, that message certainly correlates with the Reformation hostility toward celibacy and emphasis on uni-versal marriage and family life. In 1523 Heinrich of Kettenbach, "a Franciscan convert to the Reformation and a Lutheran pamphleteer," [27] wrote, "I believe that God has so established marriage that a pious married person, even one who has been married three times, is more esteemed by God than a monk or nun who has been chaste for thirty years." [28] Surely this former Franciscan was thinking of Saint Anne's three marriages and their positive example.

As we have seen, the representation of the Holy Kinship in separate

Fig. 9. *Holy Kinship*, probably from a church near Weimar. Thüringer Museum Eisenach. Ca. 1510. Photo: Thüringer Museum.

panels also preceded the Reformation, though inherent in these images was an attitude critical of the celibate life. In Reformation ideology, such images idealized the family unit and the embedding of women within it. Protestant hostility toward the convent resulted in the destruction of female communities, just as the breaking down of the *hortus conclusus* in the Holy Kinship destroyed its lushly female atmosphere. As Steven Ozment comments, "The first generation of Protestant reformers died believing they had released women into the world by establishing them firmly at the center of the home and family life, no longer to suffer the withdrawn, culturally circumscribed, sexually repressed, male-regulated life of a cloister."[29] A Catholic commentator might well have reversed the terms, viewing the cloister as providing opportunities for the development of individual spirituality and female culture and the home as culturally circumscribed, sexually oppressive, and male regulated. A description of the home by a historian of the Reformation makes it clear that the man held much of the power: "A further consequence of the extinction of monasticism was the elevation of the home as the area where the gospel precepts can most readily be exemplified. . . . In the home . . . the father exercises authority and is comparable to a magistrate. . . . The pious household, where the father was priest as well as magistrate, where family prayers and the recital of the catechism were daily exercises—this picture marked for centuries the Lutheran household."[30]

Another way in which the Holy Kinship was appropriated by males was in the introduction of male portraits. It was not unusual in the fifteenth and sixteenth centuries for artists to portray sacred figures with the features of living contemporaries, especially when the two shared the same name. In the case of Saint Anne, as Myra Orth shows in her essay in this volume, a miniature in which the familiar scene of Saint Anne teaching the Virgin to read can also be interpreted—and the added layer of meaning is intentional—as Anne of Brittany teaching her daughter, Renée. Such an identification allows the French royal family to share in Saint Anne's renown but does not disturb the traditional interpretation of the familiar iconography. A disturbance does take place, however, when the husbands in the Holy Kinship become portraits of living persons. In 1509 Lucas Cranach the Elder painted an altarpiece of the Holy Kinship commissioned by Frederick the Wise, elector of Saxony (fig. 10). At first glance the center panel seems to

Fig. 10. Lucas Cranach the Elder, *Holy Kinship,* center panel of *Saint Anne or Torgau Altarpiece.* Frankfurt, Städelisches Kunstinstitut. Ca. 1509. Photo: Städelisches Kunstinstitut, Frankfurt.

present a traditional version of the Holy Kinship, with the families of the Virgin's two sisters relegated to the side panels and Anne's three husbands confined to a balcony in the background. However, a closer look reveals that, for the first time, "the Holy Kinship serves as pretext for a group of portraits. The Elector Frederick [as Alpheus] and Duke John [Frederick's son, as Zebedee] appear as members of the Holy Family on the inner side panels, along with the emperor, whose portrait is incorporated in a similar way in the center panel, where he is shown sitting in the balcony with his court chaplain, Wolfgang von Maen. The painter gave his own features to Joachim."[31] James Snyder suggests that it is "perhaps due to Frederick's sympathies for Luther and his pride in humble family ties, [that] the elector of Saxony chose to cast his ancestry in the guise of the Holy Kinship."[32] In appropriating this subject as a way of flattering the males of his own family, Frederick the Wise certainly diminishes the importance of mothers and the matriarchal line.

Nor is this an isolated example. A painting presumably commissioned in 1515 by Emperor Maximilian portrayed members of his family. Represented were Maximilian, his first wife, Mary of Burgundy, their son-in-law, Ludwig II, their son, Philip (king of Castile), and his two sons, Karl and Ferdinand. The three young men, virtually boys, wear marriage wreaths, for the purpose of the painting was to celebrate their marriages. These formed part of Maximilian's foreign policy: "By means of his clever politics of marriage three of his grandchildren were supposed to play an important role in European history."[33] After Maximilian's death, this painting, which does not survive, was apparently copied by Bernhard Strigel as part of a larger commission given him by Johannes Cuspinian, who had Strigel transform the painting into a Holy Kinship by adding the appropriate inscriptions.[34] Presumably following Cuspinian's instructions, Strigel created a diptych by adding a panel showing Cuspinian himself as Zebedee, his second wife as Salome, and their two sons as James the Less and John the Evangelist. A painting of the actual Holy Kinship was added on the back, paired with a long inscription.[35]

In newer versions of the Holy Kinship, not only do fathers move into the central space, but they also take over some of the responsibilities formerly reserved for mothers, particularly that of education. In many representations of the Holy Kinship, Saint Anne holds or reads a book, and in some images she teaches Christ to read while her daughters instruct their sons. But in a woodcut by Lucas Cranach the Elder and dated about 1510, these roles are beginning to shift (fig. 11). Saint Anne retains responsibility for educating the rather inattentive Christ Child (who is distracted by his father, Joseph), but it is Alpheus (in the lower left), brandishing the schoolmaster's rod in his hand, who teaches his children to read, and it is Zebedee who sends his son off to school.[36] The mothers' role here is restricted to the nurturing of infants, as it also is in a wing of an altarpiece from Lower Saxony made about 1520 (fig. 12). Literacy belongs to the males, who form a protective circle around the nursing female.[37] Even more destructive to the cult of the Holy Kinship is the reuse of Cranach's woodcut in the direct service of Reformation ideology.[38] After 1518 it was reissued twice with a poem added at the bottom written by the Reformation scholar and close associate of Luther, Philip Melancthon. The title indicates that the verse is actually a song with which the children of Wittemberg were conducted to school on the first day, Saint Gregory's Day. No reference is made to Saint Anne or the Holy Kinship; rather, the song informs the children that learning to read and write are necessary preconditions to the Christian life.

These images capture societal changes later described in such popular German literature as the writings of George Wickram, described by Miriam Usher Chrisman as "the central figure in the development of a popular literature that addressed itself to the interests of the ordinary citizen."[39] In 1555 Wickram published a book considered to be one of the first German novels, *Der Jungen Knaben Spiegel*. There he "reflects a new concern with the family and explores the relationships between parents and children."[40] One of the major characters in the story, Willibald, "is shown to be careful with his own children, never permitting them to be idle, teaching them to work according to their God-given talents. The daughters learn from their mother to spin, sew, embroider, knit, and weave. . . . The boys are sent to school to receive a thorough education."[41] Such sentiments were apparently quite popular, for Wickram published a series of books with similar themes in the 1550s, among them *Der Irr Reitend Pilger*, in which he "develops the themes of the close relationship of father and son, the obedience of the son to the father, and the responsibility of father for the son."[42]

CARMEN QVO SOLENT PVERVLI AD STVDIVM LITERARVM
IN SCHOLAM EVOCARI, DIE GREGORII, CIRCA AEQVI-
NOCTIVM VERNVM.

Vos ad se pueri primis inuitat ab annis,   Vos igitur læti properate occurrere Chrifto,   Hoc illi gratum officium eft, hoc gaudet honore,
Atqi fua Chriftus uoce uenire iubet,   Prima fit hæc Chriftum nofcere cura ducem,   Infantum fieri notior ore cupit,
Præmiaqi oftendit uobis uenientibus ampla,   Sed tamen ut dominum pofsis agnofcere Chriftum,   Quare nobifcum ftudium ad commune uenite,
Sic uos ô pueri curat amatqi Deus.   Ingenuas artes difcito parue puer.   Ad Chriftum monftrat nam Schola noftra uiam.

Fig. 11. Lucas Cranach the Elder, *Holy Kinship*. B. 5 Kupferstichkabinett,
Staatliche Museen Preussischer Kulturbesitz, Kupferstichkabinett, Berlin.
Ca. 1510; reissued with added text after 1518. Photo: Jörg P. Anders.

Fig. 12. *Mary Cleophas and Family,* right wing of *Holy Kinship Altarpiece.*
Münster, Westfälischer Kunstverein. Ca. 1520. Photo: Westfälisches
Landesmuseum für Kunst und Kulturgeschichte, Münster.

In a fascinating essay, Ton Brandenbarg suggests that this shift to the patriarchal nuclear family replaced images of the Holy Kinship with the new subject of the nuclear Holy Family: "A powerful grandmother was perhaps no longer suited to a middle class ideal, in which all attention was directed at the male. . . . The concept of an old woman wanting to get married was regarded as unfitting. . . . Instead of the picture of the extended Holy Family with Anne as the radiant centre, attention became placed completely on the Holy Family of Mary, Joseph and the Child Jesus (or Anne, Joachim and Mary). This image corresponded particularly well with the attitudes concerning the ideal family model held by the urban upper class in this period." [43]

The Holy Family may have been particularly well suited to replace the Holy Kinship, which was centered on the matriarchal Trinity, because the Holy Family was increasingly presented as an earthly Trinity. Although one medieval view of Joseph saw him as a tired old man, the more positive view that came to prevail by the sixteenth century held him to be "the hard-working foster-father of Christ, the worthy companion and helpmate to Mary, and the strong, capable head of his household." [44] According to Cynthia Hahn, this positive view of Joseph combined with a typological pairing based on a metaphor of Ambrose in which Joseph the artisan figures God the Father as artisan of the soul. This allowed for the visual presentation of the Holy Family as an earthly Trinity. Moreover, "the new iconography of the Earthly Trinity and Holy Family serve as a model for the new notion of the nuclear family led by the *pater familias*." [45] Thus the matriarchal earthly Trinity of Anne, Mary, and Christ, in which Anne was typologically paired with God, gives way to a patriarchal earthly Trinity featuring Joseph. As John Bossy observes, the new conception of the Holy Family "made a great deal of difference to the history of the human Christ, and probably to the history of the European family as well." [46]

THE HOLY KINSHIP, a subject whose roots lie both in the cult of the Virgin and in the incarnational theology of the late Middle Ages, effectively promoted ideas about human kinship, that is, attitudes toward the family and the roles of men and women in relation to the family, in the late Middle Ages and Reformation. Beginning in the twelfth century as an image through which Christ's matrilineal ancestry could be asserted, by 1400 the Holy Kinship focused on motherhood and on positive relationships among women, though never obscuring the importance of their sacred progeny. But the meaning of the Holy Kinship underwent a virtual reversal as kinship patterns and religious structures changed, until eventually it championed fatherhood and the isolation of women in nuclear families. This powerful image has offered "an excellent opportunity to watch the birth, growth, decay, and transformation of ideologies."[47]

NOTES

1. Herlihy, *Medieval Households*, 82.
2. Watson, *Early Iconography*, 3.
3. Ibid., 46.
4. Morgan, *Early Gothic Manuscripts* 1:74.
5. MS. University of Minnesota Z. 822, N. 81. For the edition from which this quotation is taken, see Parker, *Middle English Stanzaic Versions;* quotation is on page 80.
6. This miniature from the *Hours of Etienne Chevalier* is in Paris (BN nouv. acq. lat. 1416). For illustration and discussion of the miniatures, most of which are in the Musée Condé, Chantilly, see Fouquet, *Hours.*
7. Hand, "Saint Anne," 49.
8. Travis, "Social Body," 19.
9. Steinberg, *Sexuality of Christ*, 1.
10. Ibid., 47–48.
11. Bossy, *Christianity in the West*, 8.
12. Steinberg, *Sexuality of Christ*, 8.
13. Coletti, " 'Wyves and Gossippes,' " 37.
14. Herlihy, *Medieval Households*, 129.
15. Ibid., 122.
16. Ibid., 124; see also Glasser, "Marriage."
17. Coletti, " 'Wyves and Gossippes,' " 40.
18. Gohr, "Anna Selbdritt," 1:254 (my translation).
19. Brundage, *Law, Sex, and Christian Society*, 514.
20. *Vita Coletae*, Ghent, Poor Clares, MS. 8, fol. 40v. For color illustration, see Corstanje, *Vita Sancta Coletae*, plate 2. For Delaisse's suggestion that the manuscript was made in Brussels, see Kren, *Renaissance Painting*, 15.
21. For a more extensive discussion of the points made in the first sections of this essay, see Sheingorn, "Holy Kinship."
22. On this painting, see Bailey, "A *Holy Kinship*."

23. See Atkinson, "'Your Servant, My Mother.'"

24. See Baum, "Der Mindelheimer Altar," and Otto, *Bernhard Strigel.*

25. Stone, *Family, Sex, and Marriage,* 85.

26. Ibid., 93. Barbara A. Hanawalt (*Ties That Bound*) has shown that Stone's conclusions do not hold true for the household unit of the peasants, which showed a strong preference for nuclear families. Ralph A. Houlbrooke (*English Family*), arguing that the nuclear family was, in general, the dominant form in England by the fifteenth century and remained so through the eighteenth (253), does not want to see the changes noted by Stone. Mary Beth Rose's comment in *The Expense of Spirit* is useful here: "Though some of Stone's conclusions have been hotly debated, many of his arguments have withstood controversy, and I have relied on some of them in my account. For example, he demonstrates that in the conduct of marriage and the formation of the family during the sixteenth and seventeenth centuries there was a gradual shift from the predominant emphasis on arranged marriages as property-based alliances between kin groups to a contrasting emphasis on the conjugal couple and the isolated nuclear family" (2).

27. Ozment, *When Fathers Ruled,* 6.

28. Quoted in ibid., 31, from a pamphlet by Heinrich von Kettenbach.

29. Ibid., 49.

30. Bainton, *Reformation,* 256.

31. Schade, *Cranach,* 28, 29.

32. Snyder, *Northern Renaissance Art,* 375.

33. *Martin Luther,* 189 (my translation).

34. For discussions of this work, see Otto, *Bernhard Strigel,* 2, 65, 101–2, and Thümmel, "Bernard Strigel's Diptychon."

35. It should be noted, however, that the representation of sacred figures as portraits of specific living persons seems to be a characteristic of early-sixteenth-century German art. For example, an altar representing the Adoration of the Magi by the Master of Frankfurt and his workshop shows the Magi as Maximilian, Frederick III, and possibly the patron of the altarpiece. Another example confirms the attempt in these works of art to match the roles of the subject with those of the person portrayed: in a painting of Jerome in his study, Cranach gives Jerome the features of Cardinal Albrecht of Brandenburg. For illustrations and discussions of these paintings, see *Martin Luther,* catalog entry 56, p. 56, and entry 164, p. 142 (illustrated in color on p. 78).

36. Kleinschmidt, *Die heilige Anna,* 275.

37. Pieper, *Die deutschen,* 450.

38. See Andersson, "Religiöse Bilder," for a discussion of this and other works by Cranach as they were interpreted to further Reformation ideology.

39. Chrisman, *Lay Culture,* 209.

40. Ibid., 210.
41. Ibid., 212.
42. Ibid., 213. Similar shifts toward patriarchal power within the nuclear family can be seen in the family portraits from Stuart England, which are discussed in Goldberg, "Fatherly Authority."
43. Brandenbarg, "St Anne and Her Family," 124.
44. Hahn, " 'Joseph Will Perfect,' " 55.
45. Ibid., 65.
46. Bossy, *Christianity in the West*, 10–11.
47. Atkinson, " 'Your Servant, My Mother,' " 164.

BIBLIOGRAPHY

Andersson, Christiane D. "Religiöse Bilder Cranachs im Dienste der Reformation." In *Humanismus und Reformation als kulturelle Kräfte in der deutschen Geschichte*, ed. L. W. Spitz, 43–79. Veroffentlichen der Historischen Kommission zu Berlin 51. Berlin: Walter de Gruyter, 1981.

Atkinson, Clarissa W. " 'Your Servant, My Mother': The Figure of Saint Monica in the Ideology of Christian Motherhood." In *Immaculate and Powerful: The Female in Sacred Image and Social Reality*, ed. Clarissa W. Atkinson, Constance H. Buchanan, and Margaret R. Miles, 139–72. Boston: Beacon Press, 1985.

Bailey, Stephen M. "A *Holy Kinship* Attributed to the Master of the Magdalen Legend." *Journal of the Walters Art Gallery* 41 (1983): 7–16.

Bainton, Roland H. *The Reformation of the Sixteenth Century*. Boston: Beacon Press, 1952.

Baum, Julius. "Der Mindelheimer Altar des Bernhard Strigel." *Jahrbuch der koenigliche preussischen Kunstsammlungen* 35 (1914): 9–21.

Bossy, John. *Christianity in the West, 1400–1700*. Oxford: Oxford University Press, 1985.

Brandenbarg, Ton. "St Anne and Her Family: The Veneration of St Anne in Connection with Concepts of Marriage and the Family in the Early Modern Period." In *Saints and She-Devils: Images of Women in the Fifteenth and Sixteenth Centuries*, ed. Lène Dresen-Coenders, 101–27. London: Rubicon Press, 1987.

Brundage, James A. *Law, Sex, and Christian Society in Medieval Europe*. Chicago: University of Chicago Press, 1987.

Bynum, Caroline Walker. *Holy Feast and Holy Fast: The Religious Significance of Food to Medieval Women*. Berkeley and Los Angeles: University of California Press, 1986.

Chrisman, Miriam Usher. *Lay Culture, Learned Culture: Books and Social Change in Strasbourg, 1480–1599.* New Haven: Yale University Press, 1982.

Coletti, Theresa. "'Wyves and Gossippes, Vergynes and Maides': Christian Myth and Female Sexuality in Medieval Drama." Manuscript.

Corstanje, Charles van, Yves Cazaux, John Decavele, and Albert Derolez. *Vita Sancta Coletae (1381–1447).* Leiden: Brill, 1982.

Cranach the Elder, Lucas. *1472–1553 Lucas Cranach d. Ä. Das gesamte graphische Werk.* Munich: Rogner and Bernhard, 1972.

Fouquet, Jean. *The Hours of Etienne Chevalier.* New York: Braziller, 1971.

Glasser, Mark. "Marriage in Medieval Hagiography." *Studies in Medieval and Renaissance History* 4 (o.s. 14) (1981): 3–34.

Gohr, Siegfried. "Anna Selbdritt." In *Die Gottesmutter: Marienbild in Rheinland und in Westfalen,* ed. Leonhard Küppers, 1:243–54. Recklinghausen: Aurel Bongers Recklinghausen, 1974.

Goldberg, Jonathan. "Fatherly Authority: The Politics of Stuart Family Images." In *Rewriting the Renaissance: The Discourses of Sexual Difference in Early Modern Europe,* ed. Margaret W. Ferguson, Maureen Quilligan, and Nancy J. Vickers, 3–32. Chicago: University of Chicago Press, 1986.

Hahn, Cynthia. "'Joseph Will Perfect, Mary Enlighten, and Jesus Save Thee': The Holy Family as Marriage Model in the Mérode Triptych." *Art Bulletin* 68 (1986): 54–66.

Hanawalt, Barbara A. *The Ties That Bound: Peasant Families in Medieval England.* New York: Oxford University Press, 1986.

Hand, John Oliver. "*Saint Anne with the Virgin and the Christ Child* by the Master of Frankfurt." *Studies in the History of Art* 12 (1982): 43–52.

Herlihy, David. *Medieval Households.* Cambridge: Harvard University Press, 1985.

Houlbrooke, Ralph A. *The English Family, 1450–1700.* London: Longman, 1984.

Kleinschmidt, Beda. *Die heilige Anna: Ihre Verehrung in Geschichte, Kunst, und Volkstum.* Düsseldorf: Schwann, 1930.

Kren, Thomas, ed. *Renaissance Painting in Manuscripts: Treasures from the British Library.* New York: Hudson Hills, 1983.

Martin Luther und die Reformation in Deutschland. Ausstellung zum 500. Geburtstag Martin Luthers veranstaltet vom Germanischen Nationalmuseum Nürnberg in Zusammenarbeit mit dem Verein für Reformationsgeschichte. Frankfurt am Main: Insel, 1983.

Morgan, Nigel J. *Early Gothic Manuscripts, 1190–1250.* Vol. 4 of *A Survey of Manuscripts Illuminated in the British Isles.* 2 vols. London: Harvey Miller, 1982.

Otto, Gertrud. *Bernhard Strigel.* Munich: Deutscher Kunstverlag, 1964.

Ozment, Steven. *When Fathers Ruled: Family Life in Reformation Europe.* Cambridge: Harvard University Press, 1983.

Parker, Roscoe E., ed. *The Middle English Stanzaic Versions of the Life of Saint Anne.* 1928. Reprint. Millwood, N.Y.: Kraus, 1987.

Pieper, Paul. *Die deutschen, niederländischen, und italienischen Tafelbilder bis um 1530.* Aschendorff: Münster, 1986.

Rose, Mary Beth. *The Expense of Spirit: Love and Sexuality in English Renaissance Drama.* Ithaca, N.Y.: Cornell University Press, 1988.

Sandler, Lucy Freeman. *Gothic Manuscripts, 1285–1385.* Vol. 5 of *A Survey of Manuscripts Illuminated in the British Isles.* London: Harvey Miller, 1986.

Schabacker, Peter H. "The Holy Kinship in a Church: Geertgen and the Westphalian Master of 1473." *Oud Holland* 89 (1975): 225–42.

Schade, Werner. *Cranach: A Family of Master Painters.* New York: Putnam, 1980.

Sheingorn, Pamela. "The Holy Kinship: The Ascendancy of Matriliny in Sacred Genealogy of the Fifteenth Century." *Thought* 64, no. 254 (Sept. 1989): 268–86.

Snyder, James. *Northern Renaissance Art: Painting, Sculpture, the Graphic Arts from 1350 to 1575.* New York: Abrams, 1985.

Steinberg, Leo. *The Sexuality of Christ in Renaissance Art and in Modern Oblivion.* New York: Pantheon, 1983.

Stone, Lawrence. *The Family, Sex, and Marriage in England, 1500–1800.* New York: Harper and Row, 1977.

Thümmel, H. G. "Bernhard Strigel's Diptychon für Cuspinian." *Jahrbuch der Kunsthistorische Sammlungen Wien* 76 (1980): 97–110.

The Towneley Plays. Ed. George England and Alfred W. Pollard. 1897. Reprint. Millwood, N.Y.: Kraus, 1975.

Travis, Peter W. "The Social Body of the Dramatic Christ in Medieval England." *Acta* 8 (1985): 16–36.

Watson, Arthur. *The Early Iconography of the Tree of Jesse.* London: Oxford University Press, 1934.

"Madame Sainte Anne"
The Holy Kinship, the Royal Trinity, and Louise of Savoy

MYRA D. ORTH

D evotion to Saint Anne in the opening decades of the sixteenth century in France is of particular interest in the context of the royal court. Family and motherhood were the essential meta-phors of devotion to Saint Anne wherever she was popular, but at this court, maternal piety developed unexpected political overtones when the devotion itself was redefined. This moment in French history—between the Italian military victories of the new king François I in 1515, his alliance with the Medici pope in 1516, and his failure, in June 1519, to be elected emperor—was one of political confidence and intel-lectual openness. Biblical humanism, personified in France by Jacques Lefèvre d'Etaples, whose interests initially paralleled those of Eras-mus, thrived. Lefèvre's treatises on the Magdalene (1517) and on Saint Anne (1518) created heated controversy in their time; in this essay I will discuss how the royal family came to be involved in the dispute over Saint Anne that was part of the gathering crisis of the Refor-mation in France.[1] The popular late medieval devotion to Saint Anne and her extended family, the Holy Kinship, fell victim to Lefèvre's learned biblical humanism, which reduced the family to four persons and established that the Virgin Mary was the only daughter of Saint Anne.[2] The royal family was drawn into the affair by a manuscript of 1518–19 known as the *Petit Livret faict à l'honneur de Madame Sainte Anne,* written specifically for Louise of Savoy, mother of the king.[3]

The presentation miniature from the *Petit Livret* (fig. 1) serves
to show, somewhat schematically, those principally involved in the
making and receiving of the manuscript: Lefèvre is shown kneeling
before Louise of Savoy, presented by the Franciscan author of the
manuscript, François Du Moulin (or Desmoulins),[4] former tutor to
the king. Through him, Lefèvre was seeking patronage and protection from the furor caused by his critical analysis of the Holy Kinship. Du Moulin's strategies of pious flattery, identifying Saint Anne
with Louise to solicit support for Lefèvre, were promoted through the
medium of a unique, confidential, decorated manuscript in which Du
Moulin's polemic and very personal interpretation of Lefèvre's learned
Latin thesis could be read in the familiar vernacular and treasured in
the safe shelter of royal protection.

Before focusing on the *Petit Livret,* I need to summarize the background of devotion to Saint Anne at the French court before 1518 and
investigate the historical circumstances behind Louise of Savoy's sudden and unexpected interest in the saint. I will also pose questions
raised by paintings of the Italian High Renaissance that arrived at the
French court in 1517–18, exactly those years when the controversy
over Saint Anne was the focus of attention with the royal family:
Does the predominance of the Holy Family as the subject of these
paintings represent choice or coincidence? How would the court have
interpreted them?

Throughout Europe in around 1500 the popular devotion to the
seventeen to twenty-three persons of the Holy Kinship—or Christ's
maternal family tree, if you will—was influential principally on the
visual arts of Germany and the Netherlands.[5] Italian art focused on
the Trinitarian group of Saint Anne, the Virgin, and Christ, often
with the addition of the infant Saint John or his symbol, the lamb,
as in Leonardo da Vinci's painting in the Louvre, about which more
will be said later. Devotion to the Holy Kinship in France appeared
with some frequency in the visual arts of the fifteenth and sixteenth
centuries, notably in sculpture, stained glass, and manuscripts, but
the focus was principally on Saint Anne alone. Only after 1511 did
printed treatises devoted to the Kinship appear, and they followed
earlier German prototypes.[6] To judge from the visual evidence, devotion to Saint Anne was widespread in France but did not necessarily

Fig. 1. *Dedication of the Petit Livret to Louise of Savoy,* miniature on paper from the *Petit Livret faict à l'honneur de Madame Sainte Anne.* Paris, Bibliothèque de l'Arsenal, MS. 4009, fol. 1. 1518–19. Photo: Arsenal.

Fig. 2. Jean II Pénicaud, *Holy Kinship,* enamel triptych. New York, The
Frick Collection. 1540s. Photo: The Frick Collection.

focus on the Holy Kinship, nor did it enjoy the kind of popularity
evident in Germany and the Netherlands.

Although this essay deals primarily with an episode that involved
the denial of the existence of the Holy Kinship, it would be useful to
review what the Holy Kinship was believed to be. The Kinship shown
here in a French enamel triptych from the 1540s serves to illustrate
the grouping (fig. 2). According to the *Golden Legend,* Saint Anne
first married Joachim. The Virgin Mary was their daughter. Then,
after Joachim's death, Anne married Cleophas, with whom she had
a second daughter, Mary Cleophas. Widowed a second time, Anne
wed Salome and gave birth to a third Mary, Mary Salome. These
two Marys married, respectively, Alpheus and Zebedeus and in their

turn produced an apostolic and saintly brood. Mary Cleophas was the mother of James the Less, Joseph the Just, Simon, and Jude. Mary Salome was the mother of James the Greater and John the Evangelist. From the early fifteenth century onward, artists often added the parents of Anne, her sister, and the Virgin's cousin, Elizabeth, with John the Baptist. The twenty-third member was Saint Servatius, supposed to be a distant relative. The enamel, which lacks the full complement of family members, has substituted David (as an ancestor of the Virgin) for Zebedeus and has omitted James the Less and Jude.

Not only were family and motherhood powerful metaphors at court; they also obviously determined the biological fate of the ruling class. Louise of Savoy was widowed in 1496; her husband, Charles of Angoulême, was a first cousin of Louis XII (1498–1515), making the young François d'Angoulême next in line for the throne in the event that King Louis and Queen Anne of Brittany could not produce a son. In the very early years of the century, Louise and her children, François and Marguerite, were brought to live at the royal court at Amboise, where Louise militantly and successfully supervised their education and assiduously promoted her son as dauphin. Claude, the older daughter of Queen Anne and King Louis, was betrothed to François during that time; they married in May 1514, and François became king in January 1515.[7] Queen Anne of Brittany was the most politically important Anne in that period,[8] following Anne of Beaujeu, the daughter of Louis XI, who served as regent for Charles VIII, to whom Anne of Brittany was first married; at his death in 1498 she married his successor, Louis XII. The duchy of Brittany, which Anne brought to these two royal marriages, was considered a vital addition to the kingdom of France and was passed to her daughter Claude at Anne's death in January 1514.

Not surprisingly, Anne of Brittany claimed Saint Anne. In the magnificent book of hours painted for her by Jean Bourdichon,[9] the *Grandes Heures* of 1508, the matron saint stands behind the queen, along with Ursula and Helen, closely echoing the right wing of the triptych by the Master of Moulins, where Anne of Beaujeu is similarly presented.[10] In both cases the representation is straightforward; there is nothing unusual, no reference to the Holy Kinship. In spite of there being two powerful Annes at the French court, there was no proliferation of devotion to Saint Anne to match that in the Germanic countries.

More interesting iconographically, although less notable in artistic quality when compared to the work of either Bourdichon or the Master of Moulins, is the manuscript *Primer* for Queen Anne's daughter, Claude.[11] At the very beginning of the book is the image of the kneeling princess Claude, who is being presented to her own patron saint by Saint Anne (fig. 3). The other young girl is ostensibly the Virgin Mary, identifiable by her halo, but she can also be understood as Claude's younger sister, Renée, and, of course, Anne of Brittany is Saint Anne. The arms of Brittany, the ermine, and the fleur-de-lis of France appear in the lower margin. Claude's book is closed on the prie-dieu. The *Primer* is a book in Latin and French to teach the young girl to read her prayers. The closing miniature (fig. 4), traced almost directly on the other, shows the still-kneeling Claude with an open book, attentively adoring Saint Anne, who is herself teaching the Virgin (or Renée) to read. This image of nurturing and education, which had been for some time common in books of hours in France and Flanders, is worth observing even though it is not directly relevant to the critical fortunes of the Holy Kinship.

Pious as the teaching image is in its generic sense, at court it assumed new valences in the early Renaissance. As any twentieth-century child realizes at some point, literacy is power. Not only was Anne of Brittany teaching her daughter her prayers, but Louise of Savoy was, with even more success, making her two children not just mildly literate but educated.[12] It would be an exaggeration to pretend that the royal family had reached the level of literacy possessed by humanist scholars. The royal family knew little Latin, and listening to reading aloud at court was still widely enjoyed. However, the lively proliferation of unique vernacular texts written by Du Moulin and others for Louise and her children proves their interest in and their use of books as purveyors of both information and moral instruction. These manuscripts, including the *Petit Livret,* have until recently been rarely scrutinized in studies of the period, but they are essential components of the wider intellectual and political picture.[13]

If Louise of Savoy identified with any one saint, it was usually Saint Louis. What won her over to Saint Anne after almost two decades of flinching at the very mention of the name because of its association with Anne of Brittany? Her counselor, the Franciscan abbot Du Moulin, lured her into it for reasons that were more political than

Fig. 3. *Claude of France Presented to Saint Claude by Saint Anne,*
miniature on vellum from the *Primer of Claude of France.*
Cambridge, Fitzwilliam Museum, MS. 159, p. 1. Ca. 1505.
Photo: Fitzwilliam Museum, University of Cambridge.

Fig. 4. *Claude of France Presented to Saint Anne by Saint Claude*,
miniature on vellum from the *Primer of Claude of France*.
Cambridge, Fitzwilliam Museum, MS. 159, p. 14. Ca. 1505.
Photo: Fitzwilliam Museum, University of Cambridge.

devotional. It is a surprising fact that Du Moulin was closely involved with biblical humanism and the court's invitation to Erasmus in 1517; in the *Petit Livret* Du Moulin claimed proudly that he was the disciple of Lefèvre d'Etaples.[14] A close reading of any of Du Moulin's several tracts for the royal family reveals a biting anticlerical and satirical tone and a readiness to question customary church practices while sincerely promoting personal piety.[15]

Lefèvre's revisionist scholarship (published in Latin) weighed popular beliefs against their origins in the Bible and the writings of the church fathers. Where there was no gospel core left after peeling away accumulated legend, Lefèvre and like-minded humanists discarded the crowd-pleasing devotion. He had already debunked the Magdalene legend and separated that popular saint into three separate persons, an inquiry unwittingly prompted by Louise's devout request that Du Moulin write a life of the Magdalene after a royal pilgrimage to her Provençal shrine of La Sainte-Baume in 1516.[16] Lefèvre's *De Maria Magdalena,*[17] dedicated to Du Moulin and published in Paris in November 1517, was received with outrage by the faculty of theology of the University of Paris (the Sorbonne), which, with the parlement, was the powerful body of censure and the bastion of orthodoxy whose troubles with French reformers were just beginning. In the early 1520s the evangelical group of Meaux, led by Bishop Guillaume Briçonnet and Lefèvre, among others, pushed critical, bookish humanism into an active, preaching, vernacular tool for spiritual reform, along with a campaign of publication of Lefèvre's translations of the Psalms and the Bible.[18]

Du Moulin's manuscript on the life of the Magdalene predated Lefèvre's first controversial publication. To charm his royal patron, Du Moulin directed the illuminator, Godefroy le Batave, in illustrating the popularly accepted events of the Magdalene's life in seventy tiny roundels while narrating her story in a text full of lively asides that cast grave doubt on the veracity of the legend. For example, the reliquary skull of the Magdalene, revered by both Anne of Brittany and Louise of Savoy, was depicted in the manuscript with the spot on the forehead piously called the "Noli me tangere," where Christ supposedly touched the Magdalene after the Resurrection (fig. 5). Within the manuscript, the roundel provided a fitting and pious memento mori as the last of the series of illuminations, but careful reading of the

Fig. 5. Godefroy le Batave, *Reliquary Skull of the Magdalene,*
miniature on vellum from the *Vie de la Magdalene.* Paris,
Bibliothèque Nationale, MS. fr. 24.955, fol. 72. 1517.
Photo: Bibliothèque Nationale.

accompanying text reveals that Du Moulin called the spot the "Noli
me credere," reflecting Lefèvre's own doubts.[19]

Lefèvre's second edition of *De Maria Magdalena,* also dedicated to
Du Moulin, appeared in the summer of 1518.[20] He added an essay that
reduced the twenty-three persons in the Holy Kinship to a nuclear
family of four, maintaining that Saint Anne had been married only
once and had borne only one child, the Virgin Mary. This time, the
analysis of the Saint Anne question may have been prompted not by
Louise but by the king, who asked Du Moulin in church about the
genealogy of Mary during the singing of the lineage of Joseph.[21] Unlike the Magdalene manuscript, the *Petit Livret* was written in some
haste after the publication of Lefèvre's tract and possesses none of the
visual finesse and charm of the Magdalene manuscript. It was copied
on paper in an upright hand very different from the minuscule Roman
of the Magdalene. The illuminations are in a heavy, opaque grisaille,
yet here and there traces of more delicate drawing appear under the
paint (see figs. 1, 6, 7, 8). The architectural frames around the miniatures are delineated in a nervous, delicate pen line shaded with trans-
parent wash. It is possible that Godefroy provided the preliminary

sketches and left the execution to a less adept artist since he was then working on a more elaborate project.[22]

Grisaille miniatures were popular with the royal family and their Franciscan authors in those years. Godefroy's are the finest examples, but the anonymous painter of the complex narrative miniatures that accompany a work by Du Moulin's Franciscan colleague, Jean Thenaud's *Triumphe des vertuz,* cannot be ignored.[23] The artist of the *Petit Livret* is neither of these, yet he, like Godefroy, worked under the close supervision of Du Moulin. Like the Magdalene manuscript, the *Petit Livret* seems a pious, conventional account until one pays attention to the text: the quadripartite illustration of the life of Anne takes us from the Annunciation to Joachim to the Birth of the Virgin (fig. 6); the miniature of the family of Mary Cleophas gives no hint that Du Moulin is carefully explaining that she is not related to the Virgin (fig. 7).

The opening pages convey a unique flavor, one very different from Lefèvre's sober exposition of the problem (see fig. 1).

> I would gladly have presented to the king this little book made in honor of Madame Saint Anne . . . but for good reason my opinion changed in consideration that to you MADAME everything I can do should first of all be reserved. As the king and you and Madame the Duchess [Marguerite] share everything and what is good for the one is sufficient for the other as much as your wills are perfectly united . . . and if there is an invisible, impalpable, and imperceptible similarity that makes you three so similar then I can operate on you as the wise Lefèvre has done for the Magdalene. For of one of your persons I make three. And then of those three I make one as Lefèvre has done for the three Marys whom he has reduced to one daughter of Saint Anne, mother of our savior, as you will see.[24]

Du Moulin's sleight of pen, this shell game of saints, conveniently obfuscated the issue for Louise. She could not easily read the Latin of either of Lefèvre d'Etaples's treatises; she probably did not care what corrections had been wrought as long as she could continue her slightly rearranged devotions to these saints, which were made the more content because Du Moulin had explained the issues in personally charged terms. The real reason for this little French treatise was to plead with Louise for royal protection for Lefèvre, whom Du Moulin represented as carrying out a pious task of interpretation prompted

Fig. 6. *Life of Saint Anne,* miniature on paper from the *Petit Livret faict à l'honneur de Madame Sainte Anne.* Paris, Bibliothèque de l'Arsenal, MS. 4009, fol. C1. 1518–19. Photo: Arsenal.

Fig. 7. *The Family of Mary Cleophas,* miniature on paper from the *Petit Livret faict à l'honneur de Madame Sainte Anne.* Paris, Bibliothèque de l'Arsenal, MS. 4009, fol. E5v. 1518–19. Photo: Arsenal.

in the first place by royal requests. Only royal prerogative joined to the king's new allegiance to the pope could protect Lefèvre from the Sorbonne. Toward the end of the manuscript an unusual miniature—Lefèvre struggling with the snake of calumny (fig. 8)—accompanies Du Moulin's plea, which has already been made in other parts of the text: "They are saying bad things about Lefèvre and I humbly pray you Madame please to tell the king what a fine man he is. . . . You must not imagine that Lefèvre offended God in his book on the Magdalene or in his book on St. Anne. He, and I as his disciple, submit ourselves to the benediction of the Holy Father and the judgment of the Catholic and Universal Church which we in no way mean to contradict." [25]

In the opening pages, Du Moulin charted the Old Testament ancestors of the Virgin and followed this schema with a similar genealogical sketch of the Holy Kinship. Both the Latin inscription alongside the genealogy and the accompanying text bring us to the crux of the argument: "This image is apocryphal and false although the Theologians of Paris have long approved of it. And speaking in reverence to you, MADAME, those who said so lied. For Saint Anne, good and chaste widow, was satisfied with one husband—that is Joachim who was father only of the Virgin Mary." [26] And here Du Moulin directly appealed to Louise, who was widowed in 1496 and who never remarried. Virtuous widowhood was upheld as an example of moral conduct (we remember that Anne of Brittany had remarried after her first husband died): "Such women, when they are virtuous and content with only one husband can have no better example than Saint Anne. . . . Other widows of the past could not have been more constant and firm in their chaste love as the mother of the Mother of Christ. And the Apostle says that true and good widows are those who have only ever wanted one husband. Would it not be great folly to think that Saint Anne was not also perfectly perfect in her widowhood?" [27]

It was common practice at the French court to consider the terrestrial ruler as a reflection of the divine, the royal family as the Holy Family. François I, Marguerite, and Louise of Savoy were consistently called the "royal trinity." Thus to identify Louise doubly with Saint Anne and the Virgin Mary was more ingenious than shocking. And that is exactly what Du Moulin did in the Petit Livret. When comparisons to Anne failed, Du Moulin predictably turned to the Virgin (not always with biographical accuracy, as has recently been pointed out):

Fig. 8. *Lefèvre d'Etaples Struggles with the Snake of Calumny*, miniature on paper from the *Petit Livret faict à l'honneur de Madame Sainte Anne*. Paris, Bibliothèque de l'Arsenal, MS. 4009, fol. G8v. 1518–19. Photo: Arsenal.

"As the virgin was 15 years old when she conceived by the Holy Spirit the Prince of Life. So you were MADAME when by your late husband you conceived the King of France."[28] (In fact, it was Marguerite, not François, who was conceived when Louise was fifteen years old.)

The plea made through the book was a success, and Lefèvre continued to be protected by the royal family to the time of his death in 1536 at Marguerite de Navarre's castle of Nérac.

The *Petit Livret* was not the only instance of the royal family's interest in Saint Anne, but it is unique in its involvement with Lefèvre's theories. A Mass for Saint Anne, copied and decorated for Marguerite of Angoulême, contrasts, by its conventional text, with Lefèvre's radical, reductionist approach. This codex (but not necessarily the main body of the text) cannot be earlier than 1517 because of its dedication to Marguerite as duchess of Berry. The Holy Kinship is described in traditional terms, indicating that the manuscript's presentation epistle predates the *Petit Livret;* of the three members of the "royal trinity," Marguerite was the most attracted to the intellectual currents of the French reform. That Lefèvre's interpretation did not fire the more popular imagination of the publishing trade even after 1518 can be observed in a Lyons edition of Marian poems of 1523: it is clearly dedicated to Marguerite with, as frontispiece, the Holy Kinship woodcut that first appeared in the Lyons edition of the life of the three Marys of 1511 and that served as a model for the 1529 French tract that polemically reasserted the existence of the Holy Kinship.[29]

If we turn to very different public and monumental testaments to the devotion to Saint Anne at the French court, we find not a conveniently corroborating text but images that are their own statements. The artists would not have intended the pictures to assert Lefèvre's interpretation of the Holy Kinship, but the fact that these major Italian paintings arrived at court in precisely the same years that the Three Marys controversy raged makes us wonder at the way the royal family perceived these works.

The symbolism of the Holy Family and Saint Anne as manifested in Leonardo da Vinci's *Virgin and Child with Saint Anne* (Louvre) would not have been lost on Louise, Marguerite, Claude, or François (fig. 9). In 1517 the painting, or at least a similar composition, as well as Leonardo himself were in residence at Amboise, where Louise also spent a significant amount of time. Leonardo began to work on the group-

Fig. 9. Leonardo da Vinci, *The Virgin and Child with Saint Anne*, Paris, Musée National du Louvre. Ca. 1510. Photo: Alinari/Art Resource.

ing of the Virgin and Saint Anne in Milan and Florence in 1498–1500, leading some scholars to think that Louis XII may have known of such compositions in Milan in 1499.[30] The groupings in both the *Burlington House Cartoon* (London, National Gallery) and the *Virgin and Child with Saint Anne* express such forceful consolidation of the two adult women that it becomes impossible to imagine how they might be separated. The political meaning of Saint Anne for the Florentine republic[31] was irrelevant in a French context, and the artist's search for a formal resolution to the metaphor of maternal union was probably lost on his Amboise audience. Nevertheless, the fame of the elderly artist and the sheer size of the image cannot but have impressed Louise and her family; when she was told, then, that Anne had but one daughter, no tiny image in a manuscript could have made the point as well as Leonardo's composition did, nor could the royal family/Holy Family have been more succinctly represented.

A pyramidal figural massing similar to Leonardo's is evident in Andrea del Sarto's *Charity* (Louvre). That this work also uses a specific kind of configuration as a symbol of the indissoluble family is no coincidence: the painting was intended for the royal family and was done at court in the second half of 1518, while the artist was in residence.[32] Finally, different in composition but not in reverberations of parenthood is the impressive Raphael–Giulio Romano *Holy Family of François I* (Louvre), sent in 1518 as a Medici gift to Queen Claude on the occasion of the betrothal of Lorenzo di Pierfrancesco de' Medici to Madeleine de la Tour d'Auvergne (fig. 10).[33] (They became the parents of Catherine de' Medici, queen mother extraordinaire.) This painting was identified from the time of its arrival in France as an expression of monarchic family power as well as an icon of the Italian Renaissance. When it was restored in 1537–40 by Primaticcio,[34] Raphael's painting was called simply *Saint Anne*, as it doubtless had been since 1518. Andrea del Sarto's *Holy Family with Angels* (Louvre),[35] also at court then, was probably also understood as a "Saint Anne," even if today we identify both as depicting the Holy Family with Saint Elizabeth. The open question posed by these Italian paintings is this: Was it coincidence that all these Holy Families appeared in the years 1517–18? The artists could have known nothing about Lefèvre's thesis. They were, after all, following mainstream Italian iconography. However, it is more than possible that the predeliction for general metaphors of

Fig. 10. Raphael and Giulio Romano, *Holy Family of François I*. Paris, Museé National du Louvre. 1518. Photo: Giraudon/Art Resource.

family and motherhood at court was known to Raphael's agents; del Sarto was working at the French court; Leonardo's contribution was coincidence.

Monumental painting of this kind could only be imported. The indigenous French arts that have come down to us are often small in scale but speak no less loudly if one knows how to listen. Some time ago I published a brief note on a round portrait enamel in the Walters Art Gallery.[36] I identified it as probably depicting Louise of Savoy because of the reverse (fig. 11), a copy after Marc Antonio Raimondi's engraving of the Holy Family with Saint Anne. What has been said about family imagery in this paper explains its double symbolism: the fleur-de-lis added over the head of the Child resonates with the Holy Family/royal family similes in the Petit Livret, and, most importantly, the inscription, "AVE MATER MATRIS DEI," echoes phrases used by Du Moulin. The way the inscription is placed, with Anne's head dividing it into two parts, allows two readings. The image fully combines the textual metaphors of Holy Family/royal family expressed by Du Moulin and the paintings of the Italian High Renaissance already known to the court.

The evangelical purism of Lefèvre d'Etaples suffered an eclipse around 1530, when in France the Reformation became politically undesirable. Again, a book, a printed one this time, documents the victory of the forces of conservatism. Jean Bertaud's Encomium trium Mariarum of 1529, the only illustrated book published by the humanist press of Josse Bade in Paris,[37] adapted both the woodcuts and the texts of the earlier publications on the Holy Kinship and upheld the existence of this devotion with prayers, music, and numerous vivid polemics.

Judging from the paucity of visual evidence, the devotion to Saint Anne in France lost popularity in the following decades. Only in French enamels of the 1540s can we trace a small group of examples showing the entire Kinship. Two using Marc Antonio's engraving are known. In the one illustrated here, now in the Frick Collection, the Holy Kinship has been superimposed on the iconic central group, vitiating the protective, encompassing gesture of Saint Anne (see fig. 2).[38] (Earlier in this article I noted that the customary personages are slightly altered.) Another example is in the Louvre, as well as a third, in which the Italian engraving was not the model.[39] The Italian prototype was used with no thought of its meaning; its style blended

Fig. 11. Jean II Pénicaud (attributed), *The Holy Family,*
enamel, after Marc Antonio Raimondi. Baltimore, Walters
Art Gallery. Ca. 1530. Photo: Walters Art Gallery.

imperceptibly with the mature French Renaissance forms. If the Italian monumental paintings of the Holy Family had made any impression at court, their iconographical meaning was lost on the enamelers. The Holy Kinship, revived in a climate of return to religious orthodoxy in France, was once again banished—by the Counter-Reformation.

This Renaissance and Reformation coda to the story of the devotion to Saint Anne has offered a few surprises. The royal family's perception of Saint Anne was traced through the intimate medium of the manuscript, where metaphors of family and dynasty, holy and secular, were manipulated. The public showpieces of Italian painting at court in 1518–19 must surely have gained unexpected power and meaning in the eyes of the royal family, who would have seen in them messages that only awareness of the insistently personal dimension of their devotion could have produced.

NOTES

1. See Rice, *Prefatory Epistles,* 399–400, 561. On Lefèvre generally, see Hughes, *Lefèvre,* esp. 118–28. For a brief historical summary of the early reform period, including a lengthy bibliography, see Greengrass, *French Reformation,* 14–18. For political history and the Sorbonne, see Knecht, *Francis I,* 141–45.

2. Lefèvre d'Etaples, *De Maria Magdalena, triduo Christi, et ex tribus una Maria* (1518).

3. Du Moulin, *Petit Livret.* This manuscript on paper has seventy-two leaves (152 × 110 mm) and is foliated as an octavo printed book (A-I7; A1 = fol. 2). The six grisaille miniatures are framed by lightly drawn Italianate architecture. From the royal children's birth and death dates mentioned in the text (fols. I6v–I7), one can date the codex to between October 1518 and late March 1519. See Orth, "Progressive Tendencies," 98–100. The place of this manuscript with others written for the royal family is analyzed in Lecoq, *François I,* 89–90, 394–95. The text of the *Petit Livret* is cited and discussed at length in Holban, "François Du Moulin," esp. 155–65. The specific place of the *Petit Livret* in the debate appears in Porrer, "Three Maries." I am indebted to her and to D. P. Walker for their discussing with me a number of important points during the writing of my dissertation.

4. On Du Moulin and these manuscripts, see Orth, "Progressive Tendencies," chaps. 2, 4; Lecoq, *François I,* esp. 77–80; Holban, "François Du Moulin," and below, n. 14.

5. Kleinschmidt, *Die heilige Anna,* 263 ff. and 281. For more recent accounts, see Wirth, "Sainte Anne est une sorcière," and Brandenbarg, "St Anne and Her Family."

6. For the French, the most influential were the woodcuts in the 1501 Strasbourg publication, *Legenda de Sancta Anna.* See esp. Bertaud, *Encomium trium Mariarum,* and Leroy, *La Vie des trois Maries de leur mere de leurs enfans et de leurs maris* (Lyon: C. Nourry, 1511), described in Baudrier, *Bibliographie lyonnaise* 12:109–10, illustrated. For an account of the Netherlandish and German editions and their authors, see Brandenbarg, "St. Anne and Her Family," 105, 111–12.

7. For the early years of the Angoulême children, see Jourda, *Marguerite d'Angoulême* 1:8–30. An example of Louise's fanatic concern that François succeed to the throne can be seen in her elation that Anne of Brittany's male child of 1511 was stillborn: see Lecoq, *François I,* 131, and Jourda, *Marguerite d'Angoulême* 1:37.

8. For Anne of Brittany, see, most recently, the entire issue of *Mémoires de la Société d'histoire et d'archéologie de Bretagne* 55 (1978).

9. Delisle, *Les Grandes Heures,* pl. 1, and Harthan, *Books of Hours,* 127, illustrated.

10. Sterling, "Jean Hey, le maître de Moulins."

11. Cambridge, Fitzwilliam Museum, MS. 159, 10 vellum folios (two of which are blank) measuring 260 × 175 mm. The Latin and French text pages are framed with illuminated vignettes. The full-page illuminations discussed occur on p. 1 (the codex is paginated recto and verso; page 1=fol. 2v) and p. 14. See also Harthan, *Books of Hours,* 136–37. I think that the same artist illuminated a book of hours now at the Mount Angel Abbey, Saint Benedict, Oregon, included in an exhibition catalog: see Parshall, *Illuminated Manuscripts from Portland Area Collections,* 19.

12. Jourda, *Marguerite d'Angoulême* 1:19–28.

13. See Lecoq, *François I,* 77–80.

14. On the French invitation to Erasmus in which Du Moulin was involved, see *Correspondence of Erasmus* 4:203. See text citation below, n. 25, for Du Moulin's statement of his discipleship.

15. See Lecoq, *François I,* 86, 90, 135, and above, n. 4.

16. Du Moulin reminded Louise of her request in the *Petit Livret:* "Le livre de la magdalene vous doyt estre dedié et mys en votre protection. Aussi faict celuy de sainct Anne. Car vous MADAME estez cause de ce que en a esté faict. Ne vous souvient il MADAME que vous me commandastez à paris de rediger briefvement en figure toute l'histoire de la magdalene je croy que en avez souvenance aussi bonne comme j'ay heue de vous obeyr et soliciter mons. fabri de lire et estudier jusquez à ce que la verité feust trouvée" (fols. A2–

A2v). On the illuminations in the Magdalene manuscript (Paris, BN, MS. fr. 24.955), see Orth, "Magdalen Shrine."

17. Lefèvre d'Etaples, *De Maria Magdalena* (1517); Rice, *Prefatory Epistles,* 399–400, 561. On the dating of the edition to November 1517, see also Porrer, "Three Maries," 156–58, and Tootill's review of Rice, *Prefatory Epistles.*

18. See above, n. 1. Recently, Screech, "Histoire des idées et histoire du livre," 554–56, has shed new light on the perilous history of the censorship of Lefèvre's translations of Scripture.

19. *Vie de la Magdalene,* Paris, BN, MS. fr. 24.955, fol. 71v. The Greek inscription (literally, "Death, hatred, breath, and beauty") is echoed by the Latin in the upper corner. Both point to the disfiguring power of death over the Magdalene's beauty. The gold cover of the reliquary head depicted her face. (It was shown closed on the preceding verso in the manuscript.) As far as we know, the Greek inscription did not appear on the actual reliquary. Each miniature in the manuscript is surrounded by an inscription in one of several languages; while these merit further investigation, they are not relevant to this study. For more information on the reliquary, destroyed at the Revolution, see Orth, "Magdalen Shrine," 209 and nn. 40, 41.

20. See above, n. 2.

21. "Pource que le roy de sa grace m'en a aultreffois tenu propos quant on chantoit en l'eglise la genealogie de Joseph" (Arsenal MS. 4009, fol. A4).

22. Work had begun on the *Commentaires de la Guerre Gallique,* a three-volume work originally meant to flatter François I's ambitions to be elected emperor. See Orth, entry no. 24 in *Renaissance Painting in Manuscripts,* 181–86, and Lecoq, *François I,* 229–44, both illustrated.

23. On Thenaud and his *Triumphe,* see Lecoq, *François I,* 101–14, 282–301 (illustrated).

24. "J'eusse voluntiers prins deliberation arrestée de luy presenter ce petit livret faict a l'honneur de madame saincte Anne . . . maiz à bonne cause mon opinion se changea. Par consideration que à vous MADAME premierement tout ce que je puis faire doit estre reservé. Aussi que le roy et vous et madame la duchesse n'aves rien parti ensemble. Et ce qui est bon pour l'ung est bien faict pour l'autre d'autant que vostre volunté est unie parfaictement. Et combien qu'elle soyt dilatée et aulcunement divisée par personnez apparentes et sensiblez si y a il quelque similitude invisible inpalpable et insensible qui vous rend si veritablement semblablez que aulcunefoiz je foyz de vous comme le sage FABRI a faict de la magdalene. Car d'une de voz personnes j'en foyz troys. Et puys de rechief de troys j'en foyz une comme FABRI a faict des troys mariez lesquellez il a reduytez a une fille de saincte Anne. Et mere de noustre sauveur comme voyrrez cy apres" (Arsenal MS. 4009, fols. A1–A1v). This, and all subsequent, translations are my own.

25. "Et ne fault imaginer que monsieur Fabri ayt offencé dieu en son livre de la magdalene ou en son livre de saincte Anne. . . . . Davantage luy comme mon precepteur et moi comme son disciple nous soubmetons à la benediction de nostre sainct pere et au jugement de l'eglise catholique et universelle à laquelle en aulcune fasson ne vouldrions contrarier" (ibid., fols. H1–H2v).

26. "Comme contient la figure qui s'ensuyt. Laquelle est apocriphe et mensongere combien que les theologians de Paris l'ayent par long temps approuée. En parlant en reverance de vous MADAME ceulx qui l'ont dyt ont menti. Car Saincte Anne bonne et pudicque vefue fut contante d'ung seul mari savoir est de Joachim pere seulement de la vierge marie" (ibid., fols. A7–A8). And, alongside the genealogy: "Apocripha eiusdem virginis genealogia, non in omnibus veritati consona, eo quod ex nullius aucthoritatis sartoribus sit excepta" (ibid., fol. A7v).

27. "Lesquelles femmez quant ellez sont vertueusez et contantez d'ung seul mari ne sauroient avoir meilleur exemple que saincte Anne. . . . Car il n'est licite de pancer que les aultrez vefuez du temps passé ayent esté plus constantez et fermez en leur amour pudique que celle qui a esté mere de la mere de Ieuschrist. Et puys que l'apoustre dyt queles vrayez et bonnez vefuez ce sont cellez qui n'ont iamais voulu auoir qu'un mari ne seroit ce pas grand follie de pancer que saincte Anne n'euste estre parfaictement parfaicte en sa viduité" (ibid., fols. C3v–C4v).

28. "Combien que la vierge mere de dieu estoit de l'aage de xv ans quant elle conceut du sainct esprit le prince de vie. Comme vous estiez MADAME quant de feu monsieur vous conceustez le roy de france" (ibid., fol. E3v). Lecoq, *François I*, 336, points out that Louise conceived Marguerite, not François, when she was fifteen. See Lecoq, *François I*, 333 (on the Virgin and Louise), 393 (on the Trinity).

29. *Messe de Sainte Anne*, Paris, BN, MS. fr. 1035, sixteen folios, 237 × 173 mm, original blue silk binding. Marguerite became duchess of Berry in 1517 (Académie des Sciences Morales et Politiques, *Ordonnances* 2:172, no. 139, dated October 11, 1517). The Holy Kinship is described in conventional terms (fol. 2); the remarkable dedication (fols. 3v–5v) needs further analysis. Holban, "Le Vrai Jean Thenaud," 193–205, attributes it in passing to Thenaud (p. 194) and dates the text back to the time of Anne of Brittany (1510–12). Lecoq, *François I*, does not mention it. The dedication miniature is reproduced in Couderc, *Album des portraits,* pl. 148. The 1523 printed book dedicated to Marguerite, illustrated with her arms, and ending with her name in an anagram is *Le Parthenice Mariane* by Baptista Mantuanus, listed by Ader, Picard, Tajan (Paris) in their auction of September 16, 1988, lot 100, illustrated. The Holy Kinship woodcut is repeated from the Nourry edition of 1511.

30. The Louvre painting is on panel, h. 168 × w. 130 cm (Béguin, *Léonard*

de Vinci au Louvre, 77–79). Louis XII very much admired Leonardo's work in 1499 in Milan and may also have seen a version of the Saint Anne: see Wassermann, "Leonardo's Burlington House Cartoon." See also Cox-Rearick, *La Collection de François I,* 21. Leonardo was in France at least by early 1517, probably as a result of negotiations with his former Medici patrons. He died at Amboise in 1519.

In "Note sur le Sainte Anne," D. Arasse concentrates on the formal aspects of Leonardo's Louvre painting and gives some insight into the composition in an Italian context.

31. See the essay by Crum and Wilkins in this volume. Given the close connections between the Medici and the French royal family in 1518, the Florentine republican connotations of Saint Anne would have been wholly unsuitable.

32. On canvas, h. 185 × w. 137 cm, signed and dated. See Béguin, *Le XVIe siècle florentin,* 23–24; in early 1988 Sylvie Béguin generously discussed with me her research in progress on the del Sarto *Charity* where she focuses on the family connotations in the work (to be published in *Paragone*). See also Cox-Rearick, *La Collection de François I,* 27. The painting is signed and dated 1518; del Sarto arrived in France in May–June 1518 and left before October 1519.

33. Panel transferred to canvas, h. 207 × w. 140 cm, signed and dated. Recent cleaning has brought to light more of Raphael's own work in this painting. See Béguin, *Raphael dans les collections françaises,* 93–95. See also Cox-Rearick, *La Collection de François I,* 31–32.

34. "Le Saint Michel, la Sainte Marguerite, et Sainte Anne et le portrait de la Vice Reyne de Naples" (Laborde, *Les Comptes du bâtiments du roi* 1:136).

35. On panel, h. 141 × w. 106 cm. See Béguin, *Le XVIe siècle florentin,* 21, and Cox-Rearick, *La Collection de François I,* 26. The painting dates from 1516 and may have been sent in advance of del Sarto's residence at the French court.

36. The oval enamel, 80 × 72 mm, is in its original silver mount; the Holy Family is in gold *camaïeu.* See Verdier, *Catalogue of the Painted Enamels,* no. 51, pp. 104–5, where it is attributed to Jean II Pénicaud (active 1534–51) and dated to the second third of the sixteenth century. This seems unnecessarily late for the portrait on the obverse, but Verdier makes a good case for Pénicaud's repeated use of the Marc Antonio engraving in his enamels, including the Frick and Louvre examples cited below, nn. 38, 39. See Orth, "Portrait Enamel"; on the engraving (Bartsch XIV. 63), see also Béguin, *Raphael,* 349.

37. Bertaud, *Encomium trium Mariarum;* Harvard College Library *French Sixteenth-Century Books* 1:73–75, illustrated.

38. *The Frick Collection VII,* no. 12, p. 19. The triptych of Saint Anne measures 293 × 191 mm, and it is attributed to Jean II Pénicaud.

39. Also by Jean II Pénicaud, an enamel plaque (Louvre, ORF 496) shows Saint Anne, again blessing with both hands, standing behind the Three Marys, who are seated with four children surrounding them. The Virgin has a half-moon on her head. This enamel is mentioned in passing by Verdier, *Catalogue of Painted Enamels,* 104, along with another Kinship plaque in a private collection. One by Colin Nouailher (Louvre M. L. 140) is illustrated in Baratte, "Département des objets d'art." P. 101, fig. 8.

BIBLIOGRAPHY

Académie des Sciences Morales et Politiques. *Ordonnances des rois de France: Règne de François I.* Paris, 1916.

Arasse, Daniel. "Note sur le Sainte Anne." In *Symboles de la Renaissance* 2:73–87. Paris: Ecole Normale Supérieure, 1982.

Baptista Mantuanus. *La Parthenice Mariane.* Trans. Jacques de Mortières. Lyons: Nourry and Besson, 1523.

Baratte, Sophie. "Département des objets d'art: Nouvelles acquisitions d'émaux peints." *Revue du Louvre* 2 (1988): 97–102.

Baudrier, Henri. *Bibliographie lyonnaise.* 13 vols. Paris: De Nobele, 1895–1921.

Béguin, Sylvie. *Léonard de Vinci au Louvre.* Paris: Réunion des Musées Nationaux, 1983.

———. "A propos des peintures de Andrea del Sarto au Louvre." *Paragone.* In press.

———. *Le XVIe siècle florentin au Louvre.* Les Dossiers du Département des Peintures, no. 25. Paris: Réunion des Musées Nationaux, 1982.

———. *Raphael dans les collections françaises.* Paris: Réunion des Musées Nationaux, 1983.

Bertaud, Jean. *Encomium trium Mariarum.* Paris: Bade, 1529.

Brandenbarg, Ton. "St Anne and Her Family: The Veneration of St Anne in Connection with Concepts of Marriage and the Family in the Early Modern Period." Ed. Lène Dresen-Coenders. Trans. C. Sion. *Saints and She-Devils: Images of Women in the Fifteenth and Sixteenth Centuries,* 101–27. London: Rubicon Press, 1987.

Couderc, Camille. *Album des portraits d'après la collection du Département de manuscrits de la Bibliothèque nationale.* Paris: Bertaud, 1910.

Cox-Rearick, Janet. *La Collection de François I.* Les Dossiers du Département des peintures, no. 5. Paris: Réunion des Musées Nationaux, 1972.

Delisle, Léopold. *Les Grandes Heures de la Reine Anne de Bretagne et l'atelier de Jean Bourdichon.* Paris: Morgand, 1913.

Du Moulin, François. *Petit Livret faict à l'honneur de Madame Saincte Anne.* Paris, Bibliothèque de l'Arsenal, MS 4009.

Erasmus. *The Correspondence of Erasmus*. Trans. R. A. B. Mynors and D. F. S. Thomson. Annotated by Wallace K. Ferguson. *Collected Works of Erasmus*. 22 vols. Toronto: University of Toronto, 1974–.

The Frick Collection VII: Limoges Enamels. New York: Frick Museum, 1955.

Greengrass, Mark. *The French Reformation*. Oxford: Basil Blackwell, 1987.

Harthan, John. *Books of Hours and Their Owners*. London: Thames and Hudson, 1977.

Harvard College Library, Department of Printing and Graphic Arts. *Catalogue of Books and Manuscripts*. Part 1, *French Sixteenth-Century Books*, Comp. R. Mortimer. 2 vols. Cambridge: Harvard University Press, Belknap Press, 1964.

Holban, Marie. "François Du Moulin de Rochefort et la querelle de la Madeleine." *Humanisme et Renaissance* 2 (1935): 26–43, 147–71.

———. "Le Vrai Jean Thenaud." In *L'Humanisme français au début de la Renaissance*, 193–205. Colloque de Tours, no. 14. Paris: Vrin, 1973.

Hughes, Philip E. *Lefèvre: Pioneer of Ecclesiastical Renewal in France*. Grand Rapids, Mich.: Eerdmans, 1984.

Jourda, Pierre. *Marguerite d'Angoulême: Duchesse de Alençon, reine de Navarre (1492–1549)*. 2 vols. Paris: Champion, 1930.

Kleinschmidt, Beda. *Die heilige Anna: Ihre Verehrung in Geschichte, Kunst, und Volkstum*. Düsseldorf: Schwann, 1930.

Knecht, R. J. *Francis I*. Cambridge: Cambridge University Press, 1982.

Laborde, Léon de. *Les Comptes du bâtiments du roi, 1528–1571*. 2 vols. Paris: Baur, 1877.

Lecoq, Anne-Marie. *François I imaginaire: Symbolique et politique à l'aube de la Renaissance française*. Paris: Macula, 1987.

Lefèvre d'Etaples, Jacques. *De Maria Magdalena et triduo Christi disceptatio, ad Clarissimum virum D. Franciscum Molineum, Christianissimi Francorum Regis Francisci Primi Magistrum*. Paris: H. Estienne, 1517.

———. *De Maria Magdalena, Triduo Christi, et ex tribus una Maria, disceptatio, ad Clarissimum virum D. Franciscum Molinum, Christianissimi Francorum Regis Francisci Primi Magistrum*. 2d ed. Paris: H. Estienne, 1518.

Legenda de Sancta Anna et de universa eius progenie. Strasbourg: B. Kistler, 1501.

Orth, Myra D. "The Magdalen Shrine of La Sainte-Baume in 1516: A Series of Miniatures by Godefroy le Batave." *Gazette des Beaux-Arts* 98 (1981): 201–14.

———. "A Portrait Enamel of the French Renaissance." *Walters Art Gallery Bulletin* 31, no. 7 (April 1979): 2–3.

———. "Progressive Tendencies in French Manuscript Illumination, 1515–1530: Godefroy le Batave and the 1520s Hours Workshop." Ph.D. diss., Institute of Fine Arts, New York University, 1976.

Parshall, Peter. *Illuminated Manuscripts from Portland Area Collections*. Portland, Oreg.: Portland Art Museum, 1978.

Porrer, Shiela. "The Three Maries: A Study of the Debate about Maria Magdalena and the Daughters of St. Anne, Which Began in Paris in 1517." Ph.D. diss., London University, 1972.

Renaissance Painting in Manuscripts. Treasures from the British Library. Ed. Thomas Kren. New York: Hudson Hills Press, 1983.

Rice, Eugene F., Jr. *The Prefatory Epistles of Jacques Lefèvre d'Etaples and Related Texts*. New York: Columbia University Press, 1972.

Screech, Michael A. "Histoire des idées et histoire du livre: Une optique personelle et une profession de foi." In *Le Livre dans l'Europe de la Renaissance*, 553–66. Actes du XXVIIIe international d'études humanistes de Tours. Paris: Promodis, 1988.

Sterling, Charles. "Jean Hey, le maître de Moulins." *Revue de l'art* 1 (1968): 27–33.

Tootill, Gwyneth. Review of *The Prefatory Epistles of Jacques Lefèvre d'Etaples and Related Texts,* by Eugene F. Rice, Jr. *Renaissance Quarterly* 27 (1974): 75.

Verdier, Phillippe. *Catalogue of the Painted Enamels of the Renaissance*. Baltimore: Trustees of the Walters Art Gallery, 1967.

Wassermann, Jack. "The Dating and Patronage of Leonardo's Burlington House Cartoon." *Art Bulletin* 53 (1971): 312–25.

Wirth, Jean. "Sainte Anne est une sorcière." *Bibliothèque d'humanisme et Renaissance* 40 (1978): 449–80.

Notes on Contributors

KATHLEEN M. ASHLEY is a professor of English at the University of Southern Maine. She has edited *Victor Turner and the Construction of Cultural Criticism: Between Literature and Anthropology* (Indiana University Press, 1990) and has written numerous articles on medieval literature and culture.

ROGER J. CRUM has been an Andrew W. Mellon Pre-Doctoral Fellow at the University of Pittsburgh, where he is completing his dissertation "Medici Palace: Private Patronage and Political Ascendancy." He has published "Cosmos, the World of Cosimo: The Iconography of the Uffizi Facade" in a recent *Art Bulletin*. During 1989–90 he was a Samuel H. Kress Foundation Fellow at the Kunsthistorisches Institut, Florence.

GAIL MCMURRAY GIBSON is an associate professor of English and humanities at Davidson College. She is the author of *The Theater of Devotion: East Anglian Drama and Society in the Late Middle Ages* (University of Chicago Press, 1989). She has also written articles on Chaucer and on medieval drama, iconography, and spirituality.

MYRA D. ORTH is Head of Reference for the Photo Archive at the Getty Center. She has taught Italian and Northern Renaissance and Baroque art history at the American College in Paris. Her publications include many articles on French Renaissance manuscripts and printed books. She also publishes on Netherlandish art.

FRANCESCA SAUTMAN is an associate professor of French at Hunter College, CUNY, and the CUNY Graduate Center. She has published numerous articles on folklore and popular culture of the Middle Ages and Renaissance.

PAMELA SHEINGORN is a professor of art at Baruch College, CUNY, and a member of the medieval studies faculty at the CUNY Graduate Center. She is the author of *The Easter Sepulchre in England* (Kalamazoo: Medieval Institute, 1987) and numerous articles treating the roles of art in medieval culture.

DAVID G. WILKINS is a professor and chair in the Henry Clay Frick Fine Arts Department at the University of Pittsburgh as well as director of the University Art Gallery. Garland published his dissertation *Maso di Banco: A Florentine Artist of the Early Trecento* in its series "Outstanding Dissertations in the Fine Arts." He has also published a book, *Donatello* (Oxford: Phaidon, 1984), with Bonnie A. Bennett and has written many articles on Italian Renaissance art and on American art.

Index

References to pages with illustrations are in boldface type.

Abraham, 54, 70–71
Acle poem, 99–101
Adultery, 117
Advent, 80
Albrecht (cardinal of Brandenburg),
    195 (n. 35)
Alpheus, 12, 14, 189, 190, 202–3
Ambrose, Saint, 193
Anderson, Bonnie, 1
Annalatrie, 25
Anna Perenna, 91 (n. 74)
Anna Selbdritt, 25, 84, 175
"Anna te Drieen," 175
Anna the prophetess, 70, 122, 123
Anne, Saint, 1, 2, 6–7, 90 (n. 50); as
    saint of childbirth, 2, 43, 49, 84–85,
    96, 107, 113; cult of, 3, 10, 13, 21,
    43, 48, 49–51, 52–53, 82–84, 85, 98–
    99; in folklore, 4–5, 69–70, 71–72,
    73–74, 75, 80; conception of Mary,
    7–9, 12–13, 48–49, 54, 55, 56, 72, 86
    (n. 9); as mother, 11, 91 (n. 74), 96;
    trinubium controversy, 12, 13–17, 21–
    25, 27, 43, 75–76, 88–89 (n. 31), 116,
    118, 119; in literature, 17–18, 27,
    100, 104, 107; relics of, 18–21, 27,
    82, 84; Carmelites and, 21, 27–30,
52; and Holy Kinship, 25, 100–101,
    169, 171, 173–76, 178–80, 185, 187–
    90, 193; artistic depictions of,
    30–35, 50–51, 108–9 (n. 20), 181;
    miracles of, 43, 48–49; appearance
    in visions, 43, 75–76, 120, 180;
    Reformation and, 47–48; as patron
    of woodworkers, 49, 52, 74, 76–77,
    80; bourgeoisie and, 50–51, 52, 53,
    101, 158–59 (n. 3); dramatic
    representations of, 52, 111, 112–13,
    114, 115, 116, 118, 119, 120–21, 124,
    125–26; as patron of seamstresses,
    80–81; in Florentine art, 131–32,
    135, 138, 139, 141–45, 148, 150, 151,
    152–57, 158, 160 (n. 19); French
    royalty and, 199, 200–202, 203,
    204, 214, 216, 218, 220, 224 (n. 31);
    Holy Kinship, biblical humanists
    and, 199, 208, 209, 212, 214, 225
    (n. 39). *See also* Saint Anne's Day
Anne of Beaujeu, 203
Anne of Bohemia (queen of England),
    21, 98, 122
Anne of Brittany (queen of France),
    51, 187, 203, 204, 207, 212, 221
    (n. 7)

Anne of Burgundy, 51
Anne of Nantes (queen of France), 151
Annunciation, 7, 21, **24**
Anselm, Saint, 108 (n. 5)
Anselm (abbot of Bury Saint
  Edmunds), 12, 98
Antony, Saint, 95
Anu, 91 (n. 74)
Apt Cathedral, 18, 77
Ardener, Edwin, 3
Ardener, Shirley, 3
Arena Chapel (Padua), 18
Art: women in, 1–2, 5; representations
  of Anne, 11, 30–43, 50; Holy
  Kinship in, 43–47, 108–9 (n. 20),
  169–71, 178–80, 184, 200–202, 214;
  Luther and, 47; German, 84, 195
  (n. 35), 200–202; Florentine, 131–32,
  139, 141, 143–45, 157–58, 160
  (n. 19); Italian, 200, 214;
  Renaissance, 200, 216–18
Ashley, Kathleen, ix, 52
Asmodeus, 30
Athens, 158 (n. 1)
Athens, Duke of. See Brienne,
  Walter VI of
Augustine, Saint, 181

Bade, Josse, 218
Baker, Derek, 1
Baldinucci, Filippo, 140
Bari, Duke of, 140
Barnabas, Saint, 141–43
Bartolommeo, Fra, 148–50, 151,
  152–55, 157
Battle of Anghiari (Leonardo), 151–52
Battle of Cascina (Michelangelo), 151
Becker, Marvin, 141
Becoming Visible: Women in European
  History (Bridenthal), 1

Bedford, John of Lancaster, duke
  of, 51
Bedford Hours, 51
Bell, Susan Groag, 6
Bernard, Saint, 13
Bertaud, Jean, 218
Bertram, Master, 18
Blois, Count of, 18, 82
Boccaccio, Giovanni, 72–73
Bokenham, Osbern, 101–2, 103,
  104, 107
Bollandists, 77
Bonaiuti, Andrea, 162 (n. 44)
Borsook, Eve, 145, 162 (n. 51)
Bossy, John, 17, 176–78, 193
Bourchier, Lady Isabel, 102
Bourdichon, Jean, 203
Bourgeoisie, 50–51, 52, 53, 101
Bourlet, Katherine, 126 (n. 12)
Bourque, Susan C., 2
Brandenbarg, Ton, 52, 193
Briçonnet, Guillaume (bishop of
  Meaux), 207
Bridenthal, Renate, 1
Bridget of Sweden, Saint, 43, 120, 180
Brienne, Walter V of, 158 (n. 1)
Brienne, Walter VI of: Florentine
  revolt against, 50, 131–33, 140–41,
  145, 157–58, 158 (n. 1), 159 (n. 10);
  artistic depictions of, 135, 138–40,
  141, 143, 147, 148, 150, 152–53, 155,
  160 (n. 19), 161 (nn. 24, 26), 162
  (n. 44)
Brotherhoods, 51–52
Broughton, Anne, 109 (n. 28)
Broughton, Sir John, 104
Brucker, Gene, 155
Brundage, James, 180
Bruni, Leonardo, 145, 147
Burgh, Betrice, 102
Burgh, Thomas, 102, 103

Burgundy, Charles the Bold, duke
   of, 180
Burlington House Cartoon (Leonardo),
   151, 216
Bury Saint Edmunds abbey, 98
Butteri, Giovanni Maria, 153, 155, 157
Buxtehude Altar, 18, **20**
Bynum, Caroline Walker, 115
Byzantine church, 9
Byzantine Empire, 11

Caesarius of Arles, 75
Candelmas Day, 124, 127–28 (n. 28)
Canicula, 73, 80
Carmelites, 25, 27–30, 35, 51–52
Carnival, 73
Carthusians, 25
Catherine, Saint, 153
Caxton, William, 127 (n. 19)
Celibacy, 182, 185
Celtic folklore, 69, 72
Cerretani, Bartolomeo, 147
Chamberleyn, Sir William, 108 (n. 8)
Champagne, Henry the Liberal, count
   of, 14
Charity (del Sarto), 216
Charland, Abbé, 70
Charles VIII (king of France), 203
Charles of Angoulême, 203
Charles of Calabria, 132
Charles the Bold. *See* Burgundy,
   Charles the Bold, duke of
Chartres breviary, 75
Chartres Cathedral, 18, 75
Chastity, 118, 119, 182
Chaucier, Elizabeth, 98
Chevain, 81
Childbirth: Anne as saint of, 2, 43,
   49, 84–85, 96, 107, 113
Chrisman, Miriam Usher, 190
Christopher, Saint, 73–74

Church of Saint Nicholas (Denston),
   106
Cione, Benci di, 160 (n. 18)
Cione, Jacopo di, 141
Cione, Nardo di, 160 (n. 19)
Claude, Saint, 205, 206
Claude (queen of France), 203,
   204, 216
Clement VII, 157
Cleophas, 12, 75, 100, 173, 202
Clopton, Elizabeth, 104
Clopton, Fraunces, 104
Clopton, John, 98–99, 100, 101, 103–4
Clopton, William, 104, 109 (n. 28)
Cohen, Gustave, 126 (n. 12)
Colette of Corbie, Saint, 35, 75–76,
   119, 127 (n. 19), 180
Coletti, Theresa, 178
Comestor, Peter, 14–16
Compagnons, 77–78, 80
Compostella, 74
Conception of Anne. *See* Feast of the
   Conception
Conception of Our Lady, 74
Conway, Jill K., 2
Coronation of the Virgin (Cione),
   141–43, **142, 144**
Corpus Christi, 98
Cosmas, Saint, 153
Council of Basel (1438), 25
Council of 754, 11
Council of Trent (1545–63), 43–47
Counter-Reformation, 220
Craig, Hardin, 121, 122
Cranach, Lucas, the Elder, 18–21, 187,
   190, 195 (n. 35)
Crum, Roger, 50
Crusades, 18
Cuspinian, Johannes, 189

Damasus, 9

Damian, Saint, 153, 157
Damnation, 138
D'Ancona, Mirella Levi, 13
Dante Alighieri, 91 (n. 74), 138
d'Auvergne, Madeleine de la Tour, 216
David (king of Israel), 17, 113, 121,
    170, 203
Davis, Natalie Zemon, 123–25
Death: Anne as comforter in, 50
Defensorium beatae Annae (Jean de
    Fribourg), 16
de Gaiffier, Baudouin, 59 (nn. 33, 34)
Delooz, Pierre, 6
del Sarto, Andrea, 216, 218
Denemarken, Jan van, 27, 48
Denston, Anne, 104–7
Denston, John, 104, 109 (n. 28)
Denston, Katherine Clopton, 101,
    103, 104–7, 109 (n. 28)
Deschamps, Eustache, 91 (n. 74)
Desmoulins. See Du Moulin, François
de Vere, Elizabeth Howard, 102, 103
Digby Candelmas and Killing of the
    Children, 52, 98, 103, 111–12,
    121–25, 127–28 (n. 28), 178
Dominicans, 18, 25
Dorlant, Peter, 27
Douglas, Mary, 116–17
Drama: representations of Anne, 52,
    111–13, 114, 115–16, 118, 119, 120–
    21, 124, 125–26; Saint Anne's Day
    presentations, 96–98, 111–12, 121–
    22, 124, 127–28 (n. 28); Mary in,
    111, 112–13, 115–16, 117, 123, 126
    (n. 5), 184
"Driu liet von der maget" (Wernher),
    18, 19
Drury, Margery, 104
Du Moulin, François, 200, 204–8,
    209–14, 218, 221–22 (n. 16)

Durandus, William, 75, 88–89 (n. 31)
Dürer, Albrecht, 180

Eadmer, 13, 59 (n. 37)
Early English Text Society, 102, 121
East Anglia, 111, 117, 121; devotion to
    Anne in, 49, 52, 98
Easter, 131
Eck, Johannes, 43
Edgerton, Samuel, 147
Education, 189–90, 204
Education of the Virgin, 21
Eleanora of Toledo, 153
Elias, 27–30
Elijah, Vision of, 35
Elisha, 43
Eliud, 14, 27
Elizabeth, Saint: in paintings, 11, 27,
    216; genealogy of, 14, 17, 48,
    116, 203
Elizabeth of Hungary, Saint, 102
Emerentiana, 27–30, 52
Emiu, 27
Encomium trium Mariarum (Ber-
    taud), 218
England, 108 (n. 5); cult of Anne in,
    12–13, 21, 59 (n. 37), 98; family in,
    182–84, 195 (n. 26), 196 (n. 42)
English Family, The, 1450–1700
    (Houlbrooke), 195 (n. 26)
Epiphanus, 86 (n. 9)
Erasmus, Desiderius, 199, 207
Esmeria, 14, 16, 30, 169
"Esplumoir," 73
Euthine, 54
Evesham, Chronicles of, 21
Expense of Spirit, The (Rose), 195
    (n. 26)
Expulsion of the Duke of Athens, 135–39,
    137, 152

Family: Anne and, 2, 53, 100, 112–13, 117–18, 199; Holy Kinship and, 49, 170, 178, 185, 187, 193; in England, 104, 182–84, 195 (n. 26), 196 (n. 42); in French court, 203, 216–18

Fanuel, Saint, 70, 71, 72, 74, 75, 80

Feast of the Conception, 9, 12–13, 58 (n. 18), 59 (n. 37), 120

Feminism, 2–4, 57 (n. 5), 113

Ferdinand of Castile, 189

Fertility, 48–49, 53, 85

Festial (Mirk), 120–21

Fioravanti, Neri di, 160 (n. 18)

Flavian, Saint, 153

Flight into Egypt, 78

Florence, 150, 159 (n. 6), 164 (n. 72); republicanism, 5, 131, 133, 140–43, 145, 147, 148, 150, 152–53, 155–57, 158, 216, 224 (n. 31); expulsion of Walter of Brienne, 50, 131–32, 140–41, 157–58; art, 131–32, 139, 141, 143–45, 157–58, 160 (n. 19); and Milan, 145

Folk culture, 4–5, 69, 72–73, 82

Follower of the Master of Saint Veronica, 173

Forgeais, A., 76

Förster, Max, 25

Foulques (bishop of Paris), 88–89 (n. 31)

Fouquet, Jean, 175

France, 145, 159 (n. 10); devotion to Anne in, 12, 50, 70, 73–74, 76–77, 80, 82–83, 204; royal devotion to Anne, 51, 199, 200–202, 203, 212, 214, 216, 224 (n. 31); cult of the Three Marys in, 75–76; Reformation in, 218

Franceschini, Pietro, 159–60 (n. 15)

Francis, Margery, 104

Franciscan Book of Hours and Missal, 83

Franciscans, 18, 25, 113

Francis of Assisi, Saint, 95, 100

François I (king of France), 199, 203, 208, 212, 214, 221 (n. 7), 222 (n. 22)

Frederick III (emperor of the Germans), 195 (n. 35)

Frederick the Wise (elector of Saxony), 18, 187, 189

Fulbert of Chartres, 12

Fursy, Saint, 72

Gaignebet, Claude, 73, 89 (n. 43)

Galatians, Epistle of Paul to, 13–14, 16

Galpern, A. N., 51

Gautier de Coincy, 171

Gelasius, 9

Gender symbolism, 3–4, 52, 111, 122, 124–25

"Généalogie de Nostre Dame" (Gautier de Coincy), 171, **172**

George, Saint, 153

Gerini, Niccolò di Pietro, 141

Gerione, 138, 139

German art, 84, 195 (n. 35), 200–202

Gerson, Jean, 21–25

Gervaise of Tilbury, 88–89 (n. 31)

Gibson, Gail McMurray, 49

Gijsel, Jan, 10, 16, 58 (n. 26)

"Ginevra" (Boccaccio), 72–73

Giotto, 18

Giulio Romano, 216

God, 70–71

Godefroy le Batave, 207, 208–9

Gohr, Siegfried, 178–80

Golden Legend, 16, 17–18, 101, 116, 202

Gospels, 7, 17; Matthew, 10, 16, 17, 95, 170; Mark, 14; Luke, 17, 70

Grandes Heures (Bourdichon), 203

"Grapes of Saint Anne," 77

Gregory of Tours, 95
Grien, Hans Baldung, 178
Guelphs, 132, 159 (n. 10)
Gui, Bernard, 82
Gypsies, 76

Hagiography, 95
Hahn, Cynthia, 193
Hanawalt, Barbara A., 195 (n. 26)
Hand, John Oliver, 176
Hannah, 6–7
Harling, Anne, 98, 108 (n. 8)
Harris, Ann Sutherland, 1–2
Haymo of Auxerre, 11, 13, 59 (n. 34)
Haymo of Halberstadt, 59 (n. 34)
Hebrew Bible, 14, 27
Heinrich of Kettenbach, 185
Helen, Saint, 203
Henry the Liberal. See Champagne,
    Henry the Liberal, count of
Herbert of Bosham, 14
Hercules, 164 (n. 72)
Herlihy, David, 170, 178
Herod, 122, 123, 125
Heures à l'usage d'Angers (Vostre), 79
Historia fiorentina (Cerretani), 147
Historia nativitatis laudabilisque
    conversationis intactae Dei genitricis
    quam scriptam reperi sub nomine Sancti
    Jacobi fratris domini (Hrosthwitha), 10
Historia perpulchra de Anna sanctissima
    (Dorlant), 27
Histories of the Florentine People
    (Bruni), 145
Historie van Sint-Anna, Die
    (Denemarken), 48
History: women in, 1
History of Their Own: Women in
    Europe from Prehistory to the Present
    (Anderson and Zinsser), 1
Hock Tuesday, 124

Hodegetria with Life of Mary, 7, **8,** 9–10
Holiness, 117
Holy Family, The (Pénicaud), 218, **219,**
    224 (nn. 36, 38)
Holy Family of François I (Raphael and
    Giulio Romano), 216, **217,** 224
    (n. 33)
Holy Family with Angels (del Sarto),
    216, 224 (n. 35)
Holy Kinship, 12, 21, 48, 49, 52, 169–
    70, 171–73; in artistic depictions, ix,
    3, 12, 25, 35, 43–47, 178–80, 180–
    94, 214; in the Golden Legend, 17;
    biblical humanism and, 199, 200–
    203, 208, 212, 214, 218–20, 223
    (n. 29)
Holy Kinship (Follower of the Master
    of Saint Veronica), **174**
Holy Kinship (Gautier de Coincy), **172**
Holy Kinship (Lucas Cranach the
    Elder), 187–89, **188, 191**
Holy Kinship (Master of the Magdalene
    Legend), **181**
Holy Kinship (Pénicaud), **202**
Holy Kinship Altarpiece (at Münster),
    26, 190, **192**
Holy Trinity, 176, 178
Holy Trinity Church
    (Goodramgate), 182
Holy Trinity Church (Long Melford),
    96, **97,** 98–99, 103–4, **105,** 108
    (n. 9), 109 (n. 28)
"Homilia in nativitatem Beatae
    Mariae Virginis" (John Dama-
    scene), 77
Hortus conclusus, 25, 173, 184–85, 187
Houlbrooke, Ralph A., 195 (n. 26)
Hours of Etienne Chevalier (Fouquet),
    173–75, **175**
Hours of Simon Vostre, 84
Hrosthwitha, 10

Hugh of Lincoln, 76
Humanism, 43, 51, 204; biblical,
    199, 207
Huy *Nativity,* 52, 111, 112–15, 116,
    119–20, 121

Iconoclasts, 11
Immaculate Conception: relation of
    Anne to, 4–5, 48, 116, 119, 145,
    180–81; proclaimed as doctrine, 9,
    25; *trinubium* of Anne and, 12–13, 14,
    18, 25; Thomas Aquinas and, 16;
    feast of, 35, 108 (n. 5); Council of
    Trent and, 47
Immaculists, 18
Imola Psalter, 14, **15,** 171–73
Incarnation, 173, 176–78
Incest, 117
Inferno (Dante), 138
Innocent I, 9
Irr Reitend Pilger, Der (Wickram), 190
Isaac, 54
Isachar, 27
Isaiah, Book of, 170
Isakar, 116
Istorie fiorentine (Machiavelli), 147–48
Italy: Anne in, 80–81; art of, 200, 214.
    See also Florence

Jacobus de Voragine, 17
James, Book of. See *Protevangelium*
    of James
James (brother of Jesus), 13–14, 181
James the Great, Saint, 12, 73–74,
    75, 203
James the Less, Saint, 12, 75, 189, 203
Jean de Fribourg, 16
Jean de Venette, 76
Jeffrey, David, 95
Jerome, Saint, 195 (n. 35); and

Protevangelium, 9, 10, 11, 16, 58
    (n. 25)
Jesus, 6, 53, 158, 181; genealogy of, 3,
    7, 17, 49, 75, 118, 121, 124, 171–73,
    175–78, 184, 189–90, 193–94;
    brothers of, 9, 11–12, 13–16, 169; in
    folklore, 71, 75, 78, 81, 84; in
    drama, 112, 113–15, 118, 121, 123,
    124; in Florentine art, 145, 151, 153;
    in Italian art, 200
Jewish law, 12
Joachim, Saint, 25, 50–51, 54; artistic
    depictions of, 7, 18, 30, 35, 75, 86
    (n. 9), 189, 193, 209; and descent of
    Jesus, 12, 55, 56–57, 100, 121, 173,
    202, 212; marriage to Anne, 30, 120;
    bourgeoisie and, 50–51, 53, 101,
    107; feast of, 61 (n. 65), 184; in
    folklore, 70, 71, 72, 77, 81; in
    drama, 116, 117
John VII, 11
John Damascene, Saint, 77
John the Baptist, Saint, 181; genealogy
    of, 14, 17, 27, 200, 203; in Floren-
    tine art, 143, 150, 153
John the Evangelist, Saint, 16, 181;
    genealogy of, 12, 75, 189, 203
Joseph, Saint: artistic depictions of, 7,
    21, 96, 173, 184, 185, 190; and
    descent of Jesus, 9, 14, 17, 49, 173,
    193; cult of, 76, 80, 184; dramatic
    representations of, 113, 116, 117,
    123, 184
Joseph and Christ Child, **185**
Joseph the Just, 12, 203
Judah, 17
Jude, Saint, 14, 75, 181, 203
Judith, 54
Julius II, 61 (n. 65), 184
Jungen Knaben Spiegel, Der
    (Wickram), 190

Justinian I (emperor of Byzantium), 9

Karl of Castile, 189
Kelly, Joan Gadol, 3
Kemp, Martin, 152
Kempe, Margery, 118
Kentwell Manor, 99
Kieckhefer, Richard, 114
Kirshner, Julius, 1
Klapisch-Zuber, Christiane, 114
Koonz, Claudia, 1

Langedijk, Karla, 165 (n. 78)
Large, Johanna, 127 (n. 19)
Large, Robert, 127 (n. 19)
Last Judgment, 141
Lefèvre d'Etaples, Jacques, 43, 199,
    200, 207–8, 209–12, 214, 216, 218
Legenda aurea. See Golden Legend
Legendys of Hooly Wummen
    (Bokenham), 102
Leonardo da Vinci, 150–52, 164
    (nn. 68, 73), 200, 214–16, 218,
    223–24 (n. 30)
Liège, 80
Life of Saint Anne, 173
"Life of Saint Mary Magdalene"
    (Bokenham), 102, 103
Lippi, Filippino, 148, 151, 152
Literacy, 27, 204
Literature: women in, 1; Anne in,
    27, 100
Lombard, Peter, 13–14, 75
Lon, Gert van, 26
Long Melford church. See Holy
    Trinity Church
Long Melford Nativity, 96, 97, 107
Louis, Saint (Louis IX, king of
    France), 204
Louis XI (king of France), 203

Louis XII (king of France), 151, 164
    (n. 72), 203, 214–16, 223–24 (n. 30)
Louis de Béaumond (bishop of Paris),
    88–89 (n. 31)
Louise of Savoy, 199, 200, 203, 221
    (nn. 7, 16); devotion to Anne,
    204–7, 209, 212, 214, 216, 218
Louvre, 218
Ludolph the Carthusian, 88–89
    (n. 31), 114
Ludwig II, 189
Luke, Gospel of, 17, 70
Luther, Martin, 25, 43, 47–48, 189
Lutherans, 187
Lydgate, John, 100, 101

Machiavelli, Niccolò, 147–48
Madeleine, La, Church of, 88–89
    (n. 31)
Madonna and Child with Saint Anne
    (Francesco da Sangallo), 133, **134**
Madonna and Christ Child with Saint
    Anne (Masaccio and Masolino), 145
Maen, Wolfgang von, 189
Magi, 96, 113, 122, 195 (n. 35)
"Maiden without Hands," 72
Malatesta, Pandolfo, 141
"Mannekinne," 72
Margaret, Saint, 103
Margaret de Quincey, 171
Margaret of Anjou, 102–3
Margaret of York (duchess of
    Burgundy), 180
Marguerite de Navarre, 214
Marguerite of Angoulême (duchess of
    Berry), 203, 212, 214, 223 (n. 29)
Maria Magdalena, De (Lefèvre), 207–8
Mark, Gospel of, 14
Marriage: Anne as ideal of, 30, 48, 53,
    119, 120–21, 180; medieval view of,

118, 119–20, 127 (n. 19), 178, 180;
Catholic church and, 182;
Reformation and, 185, 189
Mary, 6, 25–27, 53, 81, 84, 88–89
(n. 31), 158; perpetual virginity, 5,
9, 11, 169; Immaculate Conception,
7–9, 12–13, 16, 47, 48, 58 (n. 18),
72, 119; as a mother, 10–11, 49;
genealogy of, 12, 17, 75, 170, 173,
175–76, 180, 193, 202; artistic
depictions of, 18, 21, 35, 78, 96,
151, 153, 181, 200, 225 (n. 39); birth
of, 35, 56, 57, 59 (n. 37), 100, 120;
Luther and, 47; dramatic depictions
of, 111, 112–13, 115–16, 117, 123, 126
(n. 5), 184; biblical humanism and,
199, 208, 209, 212–14; French royal
family and, 204
Mary Cleophas, 12, 14, 202–3, 209
Mary Cleophas and Family, **192**
Mary Jacobus, 75, 88–89 (n. 31), 113
Mary Magdalene, Saint, 102; in
trinubium controversy, 11, 75–76, 88–
89 (n. 31); Reformation and, 199,
207–8, 222 (n. 19)
Mary of Burgundy (empress of the
Germans), 189
Mary Salome, 12, 14, 16, 75, 88–89
(n. 31), 113, 202–3
Masaccio, 145, 162 (n. 51)
Masolino, 145, 162 (n. 51)
Massacre of the Innocents, 122, 124
Master of Frankfurt, 175–76, 195
(n. 35)
Master of Moulins, 203
Master of the Magdalene Legend, 181
Matriarchy, 170, 182, 189
Matthew, Gospel of, 10, 16, 17,
95, 170
Maurice (prior of Kirkham), 59 (n. 43)

Maximilian (emperor of the
Germans), 189, 195 (n. 35)
Medici, Catherine de', 216
Medici, Cosimo I de', 153, 163 (n. 58)
Medici, Ferdinando de', 153
Medici, Francesco I de', 153, 157
Medici, Giulio de' (Clement VII),
148, 157
Medici, Lorenzo de' (the Magnifi-
cent), 147
Medici, Lorenzo di Pierfrancesco
de', 216
Medici, Ottaviano de', 157
Medici, Piero de', 147
Medici dukes, 133, 224 (n. 31);
political appropriation of Anne, 131,
152–53, 155–57, 158; rule of
Florence, 132, 147, 148, 150, 163
(n. 64), 164 (n. 72)
Medieval Women (Baker), 1
"Medieval Women Book Owners:
Arbiters of Lay Piety and
Ambassadors of Culture" (Bell), 6
Medieval Women's Visionary Literature
(Petroff), 1
Medieval Women Writers (Wilson), 1
Meditations on the Life of Christ, 114, 115
Melancthon, Philip, 190
Men, 2–3, 4, 5; and Holy Kinship, 17,
171–73, 187–90; as fathers, 184, 187,
189–90
Meredith, Peter, 117
Merlin, 72, 73
Michelangelo Buonarotti, 151, 164
(n. 73)
Milan, 145
Miles, Margaret, 5–6
Milky Way, 73, 74
Miracles: of Jesus, 16; of Anne, 43,
48–49

Mirk's *Festial,* 120–21
Molinet, Jean, 77–78, 80
Monasticism, 11, 187
Monica, Saint, 181
Morgan, Nigel, 171
Moses, law of, 30, 120
Motherhood, 124, 203, 216–18; Anne
    as ideal of, 5, 10–11, 112–13, 114–15,
    180, 199; Anne as intercessor for,
    48, 49, 84–85, 107; Holy Kinship
    and, 178–80, 189, 190, 193–94
Motif Index of Folk Literature
    (Thompson), 86–87 (n. 10)
Muslim conquests, 10
Myroure of Our Ladye, 120
Mysticism, 114

Nagel, Carl, 60 (n. 64)
Nantes, Bishop of, 75
Naples, 159 (n. 10)
Nativity and Adoration of Magi, 96, **97**
Nativity of Mary, 78; feast of, 9, 10,
    80, 84, 120; in the *Golden Legend,* 17;
    artistic depictions of, 21, 82, **83,** 96,
    97
Nebuchadnezzar, 73, 87 (nn. 17, 18)
Netherlands: art of, 200–202
Neuschel, Kristin B., 3
New Testament, 6, 9, 11–12, 13, 16,
    169, 170
Newton, Judith, 57 (n. 5)
Nochlin, Linda, 1–2
Norfolk, 100
Norman Conquest, 12
Normandy, 80
Notre-Dame-de-la-Mer chapel, 75,
    88–89 (n. 31)
N-Town Mary play, 52, 98, 100, 101,
    111, 112, 115–21
Nuccio, Simone di Lapo di, 141
Nuns, 2, 114–15

Oedipus, 72–73
Offner, Richard, 160 (n. 19), 162
    (n. 47)
Old Testament, 6, 30
Oratory of Saint Anne (Florence), **136**
Orcagna, Andrea, 133, 135
Original Sin, 13, 59 (n. 37)
Orsanmichele (Florence), 50, 133, 135,
    140, 155–57
Orsini, Isabella Medici, 153
Orsini, Paolo Giordano, 153
Orth, Myra D., 51, 187
Osbert of Clare, 98
*Our Hidden Heritage: Five Centuries of
    Women Artists* (Tufts), 1–2
Ozment, Steven, 187

Palazzo della Signoria (Florence), 135,
    143, 148, 150
Pallas Athena, 101–2
Paris, 73, 80
Paris, University of (Sorbonne),
    207, 212
Patriarchy, 49, 170, 171, 193
Patronage, 6
Paul, Saint, 14
Paul I, 11
Pénicaud, Jean II, 202, 219, 224
    (nn. 36, 38), 225 (n. 39)
Perrault, Charles, 72–73
Peruzzi, Simone di Rinieri, 141
Pestblätter, 81
Peter, Saint, 78
Peter of Nantes, 88–89 (n. 31)
Peter of Vaux, 127 (n. 19)
*Petit Livret faict à l'honneur de Madame
    Sainte Anne* (Du Moulin), 199–200,
    201, 204, 207, 208–14, **210, 211, 213,**
    218, 220 (n. 3), 221–22 (n. 16)
Petroff, Elizabeth A., 1
Phanuel, 70

Philip (king of Castile), 189
Phythian-Adams, Charles, 123–24
Plague, 49
Plato, 73
Playfair Hours, 21, **24**
Poetry, 77
Pontormo, Jacopo da, 152–53, 157, 164
   (n. 74)
Poverty, 118
Prayer, 114
Presentation of Mary in the Temple,
   7, 9, 21
Primaticcio, Francesco, 216
Primer of Claude of France, 204, **205, 206**
Procopius, 9, 43
Protestantism, 48, 187
Protevangelium of James, 7–9, 10, 14, 18,
   30, 53–57, 58 (nn. 18, 25), 72, 75, 85
Provence, 75, 76
Pseudo-Matthew, 10, 16–17, 18, 30,
   35, 58 (n. 26)
Purification of Mary, 124, 127–28
   (n. 28)

Queen Mary Psalter, 171–73

Raimondi, Marc Antonio, 218, 224
   (n. 36)
Raphael, 216–18, 224 (n. 33)
Raphael the angel, 30
Réau, Louis, 18
Reformation, 96, 184; and Holy
   Kinship, 43, 47–48, 185–87, 190,
   193–94; in France, 199, 218, 220
Relics: of Anne, 18–21, **22**, 27, 82, 84;
   of Mary Magdalene, 207, **208**
Relics of Saint Anne (Lucas Cranach the
   Elder), 18–21, **22**
Reliquary Skull of the Magdalen (Gode-
   froy le Batave), 207–8, **208**
Renaissance, 48, 200, 204, 216, 218–20

René (king of Provence), 75, 76
Renée (princess of France), 187, 204
Republicanism, Florentine, 131, 133,
   140–43, 145, 147, 148, 150, 152–53,
   155–57, 158
Reubel, 53–54, 56
*Rewriting the Renaissance: The Discourses
   of Sexual Difference in Early Modern
   Europe* (Ferguson), 4
Reynes, Robert, 99–101, 108
   (n. 14), 117
Richard II (king of England), 98, 122
"Road of Saint James," 74
Robert (king of Naples), 132, 159
   (nn. 6, 10)
Robles, Juan de, 48–49
Roman Catholic church: Immaculate
   Conception doctrine, 9; and cult of
   Anne, 43, 98, 122, 212; and sexual
   morality, 182
*Romanz de Saint Fanuel et de Sainte Anne
   et de Nostre Dame et de Nostre Seigneur
   et de ses Apostres,* 70, 74
Rose, Mary Beth, 195 (n. 26)
Rossello, Matteo di, 141

Sacks, David Harris, 128 (n. 34)
Saint Anne (Raphael and Giulio
   Romano), 216
Saint Anne Altarpiece (at Frankfurt),
   27–43, **28, 29, 31, 32, 33, 34, 36, 37,
   38, 39, 40, 41, 42, 44, 45, 46,** 51–52
Saint Anne Altarpiece (Butteri), 153–55,
   156, 165 (n. 78)
Saint Anne Altarpiece (Fra
   Bartolommeo), 148–50, **149,** 151,
   152–55
Saint Anne Altarpiece (Masaccio and
   Masolino), 145, **146**
Saint Anne Altarpiece (Pontormo),
   152–53, **154, 155,** 164 (n. 74)

St.-Anne-de-Bois day, 80
Saint Anne or Torgau Altarpiece (Lucas
 Cranach the Elder), **188**
Saint Anne's Day: feast of, 9, 12–13,
 21, 25–27, 50, 77, 80; dramatic
 presentations, 96–98, 111–12, 120,
 121, 122, 124, 127–28 (n. 28); in
 Florence, 131, 133, 152, 157–58,
 158–59 (n. 3), 159–60 (n. 15)
Saint Anne Trinitarian (Vostre), **79**
Saint Anne, Virgin, and Child (Grien),
 179
Saint Anne with the Virgin and the
 Christ Child (Master of Frankfurt),
 175–76, **177**
Saint Mary Cleophas, Alpheus, and
 Children, 183
Saints, 48, 49, 51, 69, 95–96, 178. See
 also names of individual saints
Saints Christopher, George, Anne and the
 Virgin, and Mary Magdalene, **23**
Salome, 12, 14, 16, 96, 100, 173,
 189, 202
Salomites, 14, 171–73
Salviati, Maria, 153
Samuel, 6
Sangallo, Francesco da, 133, 155–57
Santa Maria Antiqua church (Rome),
 10–11
Sara, Saint, 76
Sarah, 30, 54
Sautman, Francesca, 49, 52
Savonarola, Girolamo, 147, 148, 150
Schiferl, Ellen, ix
Scott, Joan W., 2
Selbdritt, 25, 84, 175
Sergeantson, Mary, 102
"Sermo Angelicus" (Bridget of
 Sweden), 120
Servatius, Saint, 14, 27, 75, 181, 203
Sewing and embroidery, 80–81, 85

Sex, 180, 182
Sexual morality, 117, 118
Sforza, Lodovico, 151
Sheingorn, Pamela, ix, 49
Showalter, Elaine, 3–4
Simon, Saint, 14, 75, 203
Sirius, 73–74
Sixtus, Saint, 77
Sixtus IV, 25, 47
"Sleeping Beauty" (Perrault), 72–73
Snyder, James, 189
Soderini, 151
Sorbonne, 207, 212
Spain, 25, 48–49, 50
Spelman, Elizabeth V., 4
Stafford, Ann, countess of, 102
Stanbury, Sarah, 126 (n. 5)
Stefani, 140
Steinberg, Leo, 176, 178
Steinweg, Klara, 162 (n. 47)
Stephens, J. N., 163 (n. 64)
Stollanus, 27, 30
Stone, Lawrence, 182, 195 (n. 26)
Strigel, Bernhard, 182, 189
Stuard, Susan, 1
Susanna, 27
Symeon, 123

Talenti, Simone, 160 (n. 18)
Tertullian, 170
Thenaud, Jean, 209
Thomas Aquinas, Saint, 16
Ties That Bound, The (Hanawalt), 195
 (n. 26)
Time, 69, 73, 78–80, 85
Tischendorf, Constantin, 16–17, 58
 (n. 26)
Tobias, 30
Tobit, 30
Toker, Franklin, 162 (n. 47)
Towneley cycle, 184

Tractatus de laudibus sanctissimae Matris Annae (Johannes Trithemius), 27
Transfiguration, feast of, 77
Travis, Peter W., 176
Tree of Esmeria, 27
Tree of Jesse, 14, 27, 49, 85, 170–71
Tree of Life, 70
Trexler, Richard, 50, 158–59 (n. 3)
Trial by Water, 7
Trinubium, 12, 13–17, 59 (n. 33), 74, 116, 118; defenses of, 21–25, 27, 75; attacked by humanists, 43–47, 51
Trithemius, Johannes (Tritheim), 27, 43, 81
Triumphe des vertuz (Thenaud), 209
Tufts, Eleanor, 1–2
Turner, Victor, 5, 125

Urban VI, 98
Ursula, Saint, 203

Vasari, Giorgio, 139–40, 148–50, 151, 152, 162 (n. 51)
Vauchez, André, 114
Verdier, Phillippe, 224 (n. 36)
Vetula, 91 (n. 74)
Victor, Saint, 141–43
Vie de la Magdalene (Du Moulin), 207–8, **208**
Villani, Giovanni, 131, 132, 133, 135, 138–39, 140, 147, 159 (n. 12)
Villedieu-les-Poêles, 80
Virgin and Child with Saint Anne (Leonardo), 214, **215,** 216, 223–24 (n. 30)
Virginity, 5, 118, 119
Visconti, Filippo Maria, 145
Visions, 114; appearance of Anne in, 35, 43, 75–76, 120, 180

Vita Jesu Christi (Ludolph the Carthusian), 114
"Vita Sanctae Annae matris Sanctae Mariae" (Bokenham), 101–2, 107
Vostre, Simon, 79, 84

Wace, 74
Wars of the Roses, 103
Wasserman, Jack, 151, 164 (n. 74)
Water, 76, 81–84, 85
Watkyn, 122–23, 125
Weisbrod, Carol, ix
Wemple, Suzanne, 1
Wernher, 18
Weybridge Priory, 100
Whooping cough, 81
Wickram, George, 190
Widowhood, 212
Wilkins, David, 50
Wilmart, André, 13
Wilson, Katharina M., 1
Wilson, Stephen, 48
Women, 1, 2–4, 53, 80, 91 (n. 74), 113; in childbirth, 2, 43, 84–85, 96; saints, 103, 178; mysticism, 114; Holy Kinship and, 115, 178, 187, 193–94; in Digby play, 121, 122, 123, 124–25, 178
Women Artists, 1550–1950 (Nochlin and Harris), 1–2
Women in the Middle Ages and the Renaissance (Rose), 4
Women of the Medieval World (Kirshner and Wemple), 1
Woodworkers: Anne as saint of, 2, 49, 52, 74, 76, 77, 78–80
Woolf, Rosemary, 101

Zebedee, 12, 189, 190, 202–3
Zinsser, Judith, 1